STRAIGHT SHOOTER

MATTHEW LLOYD
STRAIGHT SHOOTER

MATTHEW LLOYD
WITH ANDREW CLARKE

EBURY
PRESS

An Ebury Press book
Published by Random House Australia Pty Ltd
Level 3, 100 Pacific Highway, North Sydney NSW 2060
www.randomhouse.com.au

First published by Ebury Press in 2011

Copyright © Matthew Lloyd 2011

The moral right of the author has been asserted.

All rights reserved. No part of this book may be reproduced or transmitted by any person or entity, including internet search engines or retailers, in any form or by any means, electronic or mechanical, including photocopying (except under the statutory exceptions provisions of the Australian *Copyright Act 1968*), recording, scanning or by any information storage and retrieval system without the prior written permission of Random House Australia.

Addresses for companies within the Random House Group can be found at
www.randomhouse.com.au/offices

National Library of Australia
Cataloguing-in-Publication Entry

Lloyd, Matthew.
Straight shooter/Matthew Lloyd & Andrew Clarke.

ISBN 978 1 86471 293 3 (hbk.)

Lloyd, Matthew.
Australian football players – Biography.

Other Authors/Contributors:
Clarke, Andrew.

796.336092

Internal design by Post Pre-Press Group
Typeset in 12.5/17 pt Minion by Post Pre-Press Group
Printed in Australia by Griffin Press, an accredited ISO AS/NZS 14001:2004 Environmental Management System printer

10 9 8 7 6 5 4 3 2 1

The paper this book is printed on is certified against the Forest Stewardship Council® Standards. Griffin Press holds FSC chain of custody certification SGS-COC-005088. FSC promotes environmentally responsible, socially beneficial and economically viable management of the world's forests.

For Lisa, Jaeda, Kira and my wonderful family. Thank you for your constant love and support.

Matthew Lloyd

For Byron and Gabi – this doesn't mean you can barrack for Essendon.

Andrew Clarke

Contents

Foreword
by Lisa Lloyd — xi

Foreword
by Scott Lucas — xv

Introduction — 1

Chapter 1
Sleeping with Footballs — 10

Chapter 2
More than Blood — 19

Chapter 3
A Junior Jet — 25

Chapter 4
The Schoolboy Footballer — 35

Chapter 5
Sweet Pea Lines Up — 44

Chapter 6
Backwards and Forwards — 52

Chapter 7
Building Bulk . . . Slowly — 60

Chapter 8
Looking at a Future 66

Chapter 9
Self versus Team 75

Chapter 10
Part of the Team 85

Chapter 11
Our Most Painful Loss 99

Chapter 12
On a Mission 109

Chapter 13
Premiership Glory 119

Chapter 14
Back-to-Back Is Harder than It Sounds 132

Chapter 15
If It Bleeds . . . 144

Chapter 16
The Time Had Come 149

Chapter 17
Cultural Shift 152

Chapter 18
The Prodigal Sons' Return 163

Chapter 19
Losing Quality 171

Chapter 20
Back in Touch 178

Chapter 21
Reality Check 189

Chapter 22
Captain in Training 203

Chapter 23
Head   212

Chapter 24
The Spartans   222

Chapter 25
Fighting Back from the Brink   236

Chapter 26
New Era . . . New Opportunities   251

Chapter 27
Jekyll & Hyde Football   259

Chapter 28
Finding My Feet . . . Again   270

Chapter 29
Confidence Lost   282

Chapter 30
Lost Love   290

Chapter 31
Killing Bambi   304

Chapter 32
My New Game Plan   319

Chapter 33
Friends and Foes   329

Chapter 34
Other People's Thoughts   339

Epilogue
by Andrew Clarke   363

Acknowledgements   367

Statistics   370

Foreword

by Lisa Lloyd

To the outside world and the football public, Matthew Lloyd is and will always be remembered as the champion Essendon full-forward who threw grass in the air before kicking one of his many goals. A rare talent who always kept his eyes on the ball, and a great role model on and off the field. Some may argue that his long and tedious goalkicking routine was annoying, but his professionalism, determination and motivation to succeed made him unbeatable on match day.

To me, he is all of the above and so much more. He is my husband, soul-mate and the father of my children. He is my partner in life, and he fills our home with love and laughter. He has such an uncontrollable laugh that he often ends up in tears. Matt is a dedicated and hands-on father to our two girls, Jaeda and Kira, and they absolutely adore him.

I am his biggest fan, and together we have experienced many highs and lows throughout his fifteen-year career. We met while in Year 12 in 1995. He was a shy seventeen-year-old and the nicest boy I had ever met. We instantly shared a connection and have been together ever since.

I wasn't a football fan when we met so I didn't realise there were such big raps regarding Matt's football ability. But I soon cottoned on and went to almost every match he played, sitting with his parents, John and Bev, and my mother, Mary, to cheer him on from the grandstand. I was constantly anxious, always hoping he would play well, as I knew he went above and beyond in his preparation.

In the days leading up to a match Matt was always very focused and intense. He is very much a creature of habit: the night before he kicked thirteen goals against the Sydney Swans in 1999, he had eaten tuna pasta and so this became his pre-match meal on most occasions. The menu only changed if he had played badly the week before – then we would alter the pasta sauce but still stick to the same routine.

He prepared for every match like it was his first, and was just as nervous every week throughout his entire career. I don't think he realised how talented or invincible he was on the field. He has never had the ego or arrogance of most people who are at the top of their profession, which is particularly true in sport, and I believe this is what makes him a unique individual. I will never forget some of his amazing games. It was a privilege to witness so many of his unbelievable marks and goals and, due to our close bond, to share in his joy and excitement.

Matt hasn't changed since the day we met. He is still the same down-to-earth, grounded person who always appreciates his family and friends, and I have no doubt that this is because of his parents, John and Bev, and the wonderful upbringing he had with his brothers, Simon and Brad, and sister, Kylie. I have watched him grow and become a champion of his sport, and he is now relishing his media and coaching roles.

The times leading up to Matt's decision to retire were the most challenging and difficult of his career, apart from when he ripped his hamstring off the bone against the Western Bulldogs in 2006. That injury required such a long recovery process. Matt couldn't sit comfortably for months without the wound from the surgery bleeding, which made his rehabilitation even more challenging. But his determination is definitely one of his greatest attributes. I was so proud of his comeback to football, particularly when the media were already pre-empting his retirement due to the nature of the injury.

In 2008 Matt was out of form and under intense media scrutiny. I know him better than anyone, and I had never seen him so stressed and withdrawn. But his drive to get back to his best was amazing.

When Matt made the decision to retire in 2009, I took it pretty hard and felt it was premature. I had just given birth to our second daughter, Kira, so it was a very emotional time in any case, but in the end I understood that he wasn't enjoying playing football anymore. There was no talking him out of it, as I had done in 2008.

I am so proud of Matt. I am honoured to be his wife and the mother of his children. He is an inspiration and one of the best people you will ever meet. I hope our children inherit his ambition and motivation to succeed in life. I am extremely proud of his burgeoning media career, and I know that he is approaching this work with the same dedication and professionalism that he showed in his playing days. I love him and our two girls so much, and I am greatly looking forward to this new chapter in our lives.

Foreword

by Scott Lucas

MATTHEW LLOYD IS ONE of the true greats of the Essendon Football Club and the AFL. This is a view universally acknowledged by those who have watched any amount of football, and by the numerous opponents whom Lloydy terrorised over the years. I had the best seat in the house to observe this over his entire career, and I'm happy to say that he made many of the kicks I sent in his general direction look far better than they actually were.

Many people know Matthew Lloyd the footballer, as there are as many journalists covering the game these days as there are players. My former teammates and I, however, are most fortunate to have known Matthew Lloyd, the boy from Avondale Heights, who is still a great friend to many of us.

My introduction to Matthew Lloyd was as a sixteen-year-old when he was the gun centre half-forward for the Western Jets in the TAC Cup. I was a Geelong Falcon wishing I could jump as high as the bloke from Avondale Heights. After admiring his work in games between the Falcons and Jets, I met him at the draft camp of 1994. The saying that you only get one chance to make a first impression is particularly apt here. Matthew was by far the friendliest person I met at the draft camp. At that stage he already knew he would go to Essendon, while I had no idea whether I would go, if anywhere at all.

After what, for all aspiring footballers, is a particularly nerve-racking time in the lead-up to the draft, I was lucky enough to be drafted to Essendon. With hindsight, it was no great surprise that one of the first people to call me was Lloydy. With excitement evident in his voice at the prospect that we would play together, I immediately started to dream of the endless possibilities that awaited us, but also of the great club where we would be playing.

I moved to Melbourne from Camperdown and did my final year of schooling with him at St Bernard's, and we caught the bus to training. From that time to playing together for fifteen years and achieving the ultimate as members of the 2000 Premiership team, everything has changed and yet nothing has really changed. Throughout his career, success never altered Lloydy's attitude or his attention to detail, which I am sure is due to the foundations and values instilled in him by his family: his parents and his siblings, who were and still continue to be a huge support for him, and his own family of Lisa, Jaeda and Kira.

All sportsmen endure ups and downs, and it can be a lonely world when things aren't going to plan. Lisa has been with Matthew since the very beginning and has always provided unwavering support. This support, which Lloydy often acknowledged when the opportunity arose, highlights how close his family is.

However, to be successful in anything, the drive must come from within. In the case of Matthew Lloyd, his desire for success defined him: it was insatiable. His work ethic, his preparation and his will to win and destroy his opponent was as strong as that of any player I have played with, which includes players of the calibre of Mark Thompson, Mark Harvey, James Hird and Dustin Fletcher, all men who played in premierships during eras of sustained success at the Essendon Football Club – and who demanded at times that blood be spilt. Lloydy, while mild-mannered off the field, was nicknamed 'the Velvet Sledgehammer' for good reason, as Chad Cornes and Brad Sewell will attest. His ruthless streak goes some way to explaining why he was as good as he was.

When players retire they are asked what they miss most about being involved in a football club, and their answers differ. In Lloydy's case, I know he won't miss the anxiety in the lead-up to a big game – he was always confident that he would play well but never entirely sure – or the prospect of rooming with 'the Human Chainsaw' – me – on an interstate trip. That only happened once: fortunately for both of us, I had my own room from then on.

I think Lloydy will miss the unique environment a football club provides. Going to work every day with your mates. Working towards a difficult goal that can only be achieved on one special day. The change-room banter that enables old guys to feel young, even if it's only for thirty minutes every Monday morning. That is what I believe he will miss most.

Lloydy is a great who gave his all for the red and black. His legacy will live on long after he does, and it is already a legacy that is shaping the Essendon Football Club and the current group of players. Never one to mince his words, Lloydy tells a story that is both insightful and extremely honest, which is especially fitting, given that the honesty of the playing group is something all teams strive for.

Introduction

MY BODY WAS TELLING me I had another season in me, possibly two. My mind, however, was telling me a different story. I had an offer on the table from the Essendon Football Club for season 2010, so any decision about playing on was in my hands, as our coach Matthew Knights kept telling the media at the time. I understood what was expected of me as a player, what the game plan was for the year ahead and where it was proposed I could slot into the team.

Deep down, though, I knew in the first couple of minutes after my clash with Brad Sewell that I was playing my last game of senior AFL football. I didn't have the mental energy to revitalise myself again. It was the right time to go, and I knew it.

Football had pretty much been my whole life up to that point – I couldn't remember a time when the game wasn't dominating my thoughts in some way. Perhaps that is still true today. Walking into the Essendon Football Club on 22 September 2009 to tell Matthew Knights and Paul Hamilton that I would not be accepting their contract offer was not easy. I was the captain of the club and I loved playing for the Bombers, but my time was up.

When I told my manager, Andrew Neophitou, that I planned to reject the contract offer, I expected that he'd try to talk me out of it. The money on offer was not what I had been on previously yet it was still very lucrative. But I knew I simply couldn't do it anymore.

I started questioning whether I still wanted to play on in early 2008, and as I again contemplated the end of my career my mind went back to that time. I'd lost confidence but had found a way to win it back and return to the top of my game, although it had taken almost everything I had.

We had played Carlton in Round 3 that year, and I'd had a pretty poor first half before turning it around late in the match. I kicked four to help us beat the Blues, and while I was pleased, I was also a bit concerned that I hadn't been able to get away from Michael Jamison too well. But I'd got the four goals and we had won the match, so I let those thoughts slip into the back of my mind.

But I woke up the next morning and couldn't walk – my calf was aching and sore. I must have taken a knock during the game. I had always been a bad bleeder. Some of my teammates could go out and have a drink after a knock or a corkie, but I never could. I had to do everything spot-on otherwise I'd miss a game from a fairly innocuous knock. I often went into games with pads and Panadeine tablets to help take the edge off the pain I was suffering.

This time, though, I hadn't even been aware of the knock until the next day. I missed Round 4 against the Bulldogs as a result of the knock and I nearly missed the match after that too. Knighta had a team rule that you had to train twice during the week or you couldn't play. John Quinn, our fitness coach, didn't really agree with the theory, but it was the rule of the senior coach and we had to live with it. We'd never had anything like that under Kevin Sheedy, who'd always given me up to the last minute to prove my fitness, but under Knights, if I wanted to play I had to train.

So I hobbled around at training on the Tuesday night just to give myself an opportunity to play in our Round 5 fixture, which was on the Friday night against St Kilda, who were shaping up as a really strong side early in 2008. I managed to train again on the Thursday and was passed fit enough to play the game.

It was a crucial match for us. We were sitting just outside the eight on percentage, with two wins and two losses. But we were a team starting from scratch with a new coach at the helm and we'd struggled against the better sides, losing to Geelong by ninety-nine points and to the Dogs by thirty.

I lined up on Max Hudghton, who was a pretty explosive player off the mark. I'd had some good battles with him over the years. He was older than me but he still had his pace. I always had a complex about my pace. When I was a young player I'd been described as 'explosively quick' or 'deceptively quick', but I'd never seen myself as that. I felt I beat my opponent more often by reading the play than by using pace.

But the night couldn't have gone any worse. I was blanketed by Max and we lost by six goals. I even got a few Bronx cheers towards the end of the night, which didn't help my confidence. I had a shot late in the game but I missed and the crowd jeered. I hadn't kicked a goal and we'd been beaten convincingly.

I never coped well with a poor game at the best of times,

but this was worse than usual. I tossed and turned all night, thinking about how badly I'd played. I did my rehab the next morning with the boys at the club and when I got home I just sat down, flicking through the paper.

Lisa could see that I was tired from not having slept well, but she could also tell I was pretty worn down and stressed about footy. 'Are you all right?' she asked me.

'I'm gone,' I replied.

'What do you mean?'

'It's not only last night,' I said. 'Two weeks ago, on Michael Jamison, who's a bloke I've never had much trouble with, I was struggling off the mark. That's what a full-forward has to do. I'm in trouble.'

I broke down crying, and Lisa started crying just from seeing me in tears.

'I know I'm contracted for next year,' I said, 'but I don't know about it. I don't know if I can do it.'

Lisa said, 'I think you need to start some counselling. You need to start talking.'

I'd never been someone who talked about my problems or feelings – I'd always fought myself out of everything. I'd had form slumps with my goalkicking but I never even contemplated going to see a counsellor or someone at the football club about it.

The next week we played Collingwood on Anzac Day and were thumped to the tune of twelve goals. We were getting smashed in the press both individually and as a team; people were even saying we didn't deserve to have the Anzac Day match with performances like that. I had kicked three but hadn't played that well.

The next Monday, Lisa and I went for dinner at Tania and Greg's, Lisa's sister and her husband. One of the other guests was a family friend of theirs named Father Justin, or Justin, as he liked to be called. As the night wore on, he asked me how I was going. As I always did, I said I was okay, but everyone at the dinner table that night knew full well that I couldn't have been flatter. I was looking pale, tired and depressed. Everyone could see through me, including Justin, who I'd only just met.

At the end of the night, he said, 'I'm here as someone outside the club and your family if you ever need to talk and get your frustrations off your chest.'

For the first time, I agreed to get help. I went to see Justin and I poured out my heart to him. We spoke a lot about my feelings and emotions, and eventually he asked me, 'Do you love this game?'

'I'm not sure if I do,' I replied. 'It's become a bit of a chore.'

I also rang my brother Simon, who is a sports psychologist, as things were becoming desperate for me in my immediate football career. He told me, 'The last thing you can do is walk into your footy club and have your head between your legs. You're the captain.'

Any time I was around the footy club, I tried to act bulletproof, although I was starting to get embarrassed about my form. I was able to carry off the facade for a bit. One of the best things about your teammates is that they'll never bring up your form. We actually didn't talk much footy. I avoided people who I thought might ask, 'Geez, what do you reckon is going on?' I was just waiting for the next game, but the next game would come and nothing would change.

In the lead-up to Round 12, John Quinn called me into his office and said, 'Let's talk.' He's one of the great people that I've worked with. Over my fifteen years at Essendon I must have worked with hundreds of players and staff members, and if I was asked to form a new club I might take five or six players and maybe two or three staff members with me. John is definitely one man I would want on my side. (Greater Western Sydney and Kevin Sheedy obviously feel that way too, which is why they have hired him to be their fitness guru.)

'You need a circuit breaker,' John said. 'Do you really think it'll just happen next week, and if it doesn't then the week after?' I think John was tired of me not wanting to talk about my problems to anyone; this was his way of coaxing me to get things off my chest.

Not long after my talk with Quinny, Matthew Knights called me into his office. I had sensed that he was starting to get frustrated with me too. I'd always been a full-forward, and I could sense that he was thinking that the young Jay Neagle was going to be a full-forward of the future. Maybe he wasn't sure if I was going to be part of the club's next premiership team.

When he began to talk, he said 'I think you need to start playing . . . ' I knew I was under the pump. My initial thought was: 'He's not going to drop me, is he?'

But Knights continued, 'I think you need to start playing on the half-forward flank, starting this weekend,' he said, to my great relief.

My form was so patchy that it was hard to argue. I'd had a bad one at Etihad Stadium against the Hawks the week before. Lance 'Buddy' Franklin had kicked nine down one end, while I had only managed five or six touches. I'd kicked two goals but had no impact. The team spirit had been as low as it gets. We lost by fifty-one points, and I'll never forget how emotional many players were at the way we were playing and where we were heading as a side.

After the match I sat in front of my locker and saw Paddy Ryder bawling his eyes out over how badly he'd been beaten by Buddy. In my opinion, he'd been thrown to the wolves, one-out on Buddy all night, with little assistance from other players or from the coaches' box. Sometimes coaches like to let a kid get the experience, but it also has the potential to set a player back a long way, which was my concern for Paddy at the time.

The delivery and opportunities I'd been getting hadn't been great, but the worry for me was that I was actually shying away from wanting the footy, which is when you know you're in a bad state of mind.

Knighta had told me on the Tuesday that I'd be playing half-forward on the Friday night against the Eagles, but in the days after our conversation I got the flu. He rang me on the Friday afternoon and said, 'If you're not right, maybe it's best you don't play.'

In the lead-up to the game, Mike Sheahan had written in the *Herald Sun* that I was finished, even though I still had eighteen months left on my contract, which I'd signed after I did my hammy. His comments were all motivation for me. I still had so much pride in my club and my own playing standards. I was still working with Justin and I felt in a better space mentally. I'd walk out of those sessions feeling so much better for just getting it all off my chest, which I'd never done before. My mind was getting ready for footy again.

When I heard Knighta's suggestion, I thought to myself, 'You know your value in the team isn't great when you get a call like that.' Pretty much my whole career it had been, 'We'll give you to till the last minute because we just want you playing,' because of the value I brought to the team. Not now, though. Knighta didn't seem fussed whether I played or not.

I said, 'No, no, I'm playing – I'm right.'

I played the half-forward role, as we'd arranged. Darren Glass picked me up as usual. He wasn't going to someone else just because I wasn't in the goal square, the opposition still saw me as the most dangerous forward.

I started the match well. I was laying tackles, and even though I didn't kick any goals in the first quarter I still had eight touches. We'd lost eight in a row at this stage, and Knighta came out at quarter time and said, while looking at me, 'You are setting the scene for this team.' That was exactly what I needed at that point.

If only he had done that a bit more to inspire me and the rest of our players. It gives you such confidence when you feel your coach is on your side and right behind you. Perhaps people thought that, at that stage of my career, they could leave me to my own devices, but I needed care and support just like anyone else.

I was in the zone that night with my workrate alone. I was into every contest from the outset and I started to feel like the rest of my game was coming back. I had been saying that for weeks, but I hadn't been getting my hands dirty and getting to enough contests. This game was different. Maybe it was because I had hit rock-bottom.

I had thirty disposals against the Eagles, took a hanger and kicked two late goals, and suddenly I felt alive again. I had been a recluse for seven weeks and was avoiding anyone except the people who I knew loved me and wouldn't judge me.

After having a big impact in the Eagles match and with the team having a long overdue win, I regained some self-worth. We'd won a game and I was happy to get the papers out at the cafe the next morning. I was back, but it hadn't been easy. I then put six or seven quality games in a row together as the team got on a roll. As for so many others, for me football was so much between the ears.

Having been through all that in 2008, as I sat there at the end of a frustrating 2009 season I asked myself whether I had enough energy for another fight. And I didn't, not for Essendon and not for any other club either.

1

Sleeping with Footballs

'He didn't need to be coached a hell of a lot.'

Merv Keane

YOU COULD ARGUE THAT football was in my family's blood, but there was more to it than that. It was in our whole lives – it was a part of every day, even in summer when we mixed it with cricket. Even when I lived in Scotland as a boy with my family and we explored other football codes. It was always there, and it still is.

These days, I work with the AFL, Channel Ten, SEN and *The Age*, and all my work is focused on football. My eldest brother, Simon, is an assistant coach and head of development at Fremantle. Brad, who is two years older than me, is the recruiting and list manager at Freo and works closely with senior coach Mark Harvey, an ex-teammate and very good friend of mine. Even my sister, Kylie, has found her way into 'our' world – she has worked for Channel Nine and *The Footy Show* for the past ten years. Mum and Dad – Bev and John – are now keen Fremantle supporters – they always follow their boys.

Mum grew up in Seddon and supported Footscray. My

dad played a lot of footy when he was young. He grew up in Yarrawonga and played in the Ovens and Murray League before joining Carlton under Ron Barassi in 1965. He was a half-back flanker in the days when eighteen players had fixed positions.

Into 1967 he had played twenty-nine games when he broke his arm. Barassi slotted the full-forward from the seconds into his spot, and that was kind of it for Dad at VFL level. He started to get a bit frustrated at Carlton and he left.

He was offered more money to play for Eaglehawk up near Bendigo than he was getting to play in the VFL, so he took the offer and moved. He also had the chance to switch to North Melbourne, but he went to the country instead and never looked back.

After he finished playing, he coached, so the three of us boys spent a lot of time around football clubs with him. One of his claims to fame as a coach was that he had a fifteen-year-old Doug Hawkins in his team at Braybrook, and Dougie ended up a champion footballer. He was a great mentor and coach for me as well as for Simon and Brad. How many other fathers of three-year-old kids would tie a long piece of string to their foot with a balloon attached to the other end to teach them how to drop the ball onto their foot properly? It taught me not to slam it down like I used to do at an early age. That was genius from Dad!

Kylie wasn't really into the footy when we were young, but for us boys spending so much time talking, watching and playing football was awesome. I was never happier than when I was running around kicking a football. Some of the people from Dad's clubs still talk about us.

Mum was as influential as Dad at that time, but they were never pushy. Once when I was playing in a representative junior game, my laces kept coming undone because I couldn't tie them up too well. Dad came out at one of the breaks and was down at my feet doing up my laces when the coach said, 'Will you just go off and let your son do it for himself?' I think that probably hurt Dad a little, because he was never the type of person to get in the way of the coach of the side. Anyway, right throughout my career I was meticulous about how my laces were positioned on my foot, as I felt it affected the way the ball came off my boot.

Even when he was my coach, Dad was big on showing respect to the other coaches. I had a go at him one day because I thought he was being too hard on me. I yelled at him, 'Stop being harder on me than the rest of them.' The next minute I was off the ground. He said to me, 'You don't talk to coaches like that.' He was very big on respect and the way we carried ourselves; in fact, I think both Mum and Dad instilled that in us.

They used to juggle going to our matches, and I can't remember not having one of them at a game of mine, apart from the odd interstate match later in my career. I'd be in the under-10s, Brad would be in the under-14s and Simon in the under-18s, and one of them would be at every single match.

I was very highly strung even as a young bloke, and they'd say the right things to help me get over the disappointment of a bad day. It was never 'You should have done this' or 'You should have done that'. I remember them saying that 'as long as you're working hard, you'll be alright'. They'd often come up to me after the match and say, 'You may not have had your best game, but you worked hard.' That was their way of getting me up for the next game, I guess.

Being the youngest of four, I was always up against it. We lived in a court in Avondale Heights and we used to play matches in the street with all the neighbourhood kids, some of whom were a lot older than me. But that didn't stop me getting into it. I'm not sure I really understood the physical differences between myself and someone older, like my brother Simon, who's seven years older than me. I still hit them and I still tackled them. To me, even in street footy, if they had the football they were fair game.

I always went to sleep with a football when I was young. I took it seriously even then – it was more than a game to me, and it was the same for the rest of the boys in the family. I can remember my mum and sister trying to stop the footy talk at the dinner table once, but after five minutes of silence they gave in. We lived and breathed football.

When I was four my family moved to Scotland, where we lived for three years. Dad was an engineer with the Department of Defence and was offered an opportunity to live and work there. I had discovered footy by that stage as well as the Fitzroy Football Club, who I grew up supporting. A family friend from the Avondale Heights Football Club – Peter Markham, or 'Pugs', as we called him – took me to a Fitzroy game as a youngster. He was a diehard Fitzroy fan. After Bernie Quinlan kicked a massive bag of goals that day, Fitzroy became my team and Quinlan my first football hero. I wasn't upset at going to Scotland, as I had the chance to play a couple of other codes of sport as well as still kicking the AFL footy around.

Over our three years in Edinburgh we lived in three

different houses in the suburbs of Balerno and Currie. They are right next to each other, though, so we had continuity with our schooling and sporting clubs. I was a skinny kid but the Scottish boys were even skinnier, so when I lined up to play rugby against kids who were older than me you couldn't really tell. I played rugby for the Currie Rugby Club and soccer for my school in Balerno.

Soccer – or football, as they call it over there – was a big thing, and we got right into it. At one stage Simon convinced me he was the goalkeeper for the Heart of Midlothian Football Club, who play in the Scottish Premier League. I believed him, probably because I followed Aberdeen in that league and Liverpool in the English Premier League. Eventually I worked out he was tricking me.

I was a defender in my school soccer team and we won our Grand Final one year 5–1; the goal our opponents scored was actually an own goal by me. I guess I was telling the coach that I wanted to be down the other end – some things have always remained constant.

Another thing that has never changed was that I had a huge fear of failure. In fact, it is one of the things that still drives me. Sometimes it was a good thing as it meant I prepared and practised really thoroughly, but at other times my obsession would eat me up.

I remember playing pretty well in a round-robin rugby tournament, but when we got to the Grand Final my anxiety about this last big game overwhelmed me. The other kids probably thought I was sick. Mum had to go over and say, 'Sorry, but Matt's too tired – he can't play this game.' I was pretty hard on myself and demanded a lot also.

But I was pretty good at rugby, and through playing both it and British bulldog I learnt how to tackle and run through packs, which became handy when I started playing Aussie rules football a couple of years later. There was also a game called conkers, where you'd pick chestnuts and tie them onto a piece of string and then whack each other on the knuckles and see who cracked first – for the wimps you'd just crack each other's conker. You'd add up your scores to see how many people you had beaten in a day. It doesn't sound like much fun, but it was!

I have great memories of going to school in big gumboots, walking through the snow. I made great friends in Edinburgh. Mum and Dad said people were crying when we left because they'd lost our sporting talents. I came back to Australia with a full-on Scottish accent, so I got laughed at in both places – when I'd arrived in Scotland they couldn't believe my Australian accent, and back home they must have thought I sounded like Billy Connolly.

I'll go back there one day for a holiday; I'd love to catch up with the people I met. As a family we made some great friends, and they tracked my career from over there. My parents still swap Christmas cards with them. One of the boys from next door, Andrew Oldcorn, became a golfer on the professional tour and we followed his career too.

It was in Scotland that I started to become aware that I was a natural with ball sports (although I am a very one-dimensional tennis player, all forehand, and my golf is so bad that it's legendary around the Essendon Football Club for all the wrong reasons). With Simon and Brad playing sport too, our years in Scotland were a great time of our lives.

When we returned to Australia in 1986, we moved back into our home in Avondale Heights where I went to school at St Martin's Catholic Primary school. That was a fantastic school. As we got older, my brothers and I all went to St Bernard's College in Essendon, while Kylie was not far away at Ave Maria College. I still marvel at how my parents paid for all those school fees, but through it all they not only gave us the best tuition but amazing life opportunities. I travelled the world as a young kid, including one time to Disneyland, so there was plenty we did as kids that many others could only dream about.

I was eight years old when we settled in at home again, and I had a bit to learn about being Australian. My best mate in the court we lived in was Shaun Wilkinson, who is still my best mate and a godfather to Jaeda. He was a mad cricketer but at that time I'd never played the game, so he taught me how to play. I became a fast bowler and joined the Avondale Heights Cricket Club, where I had a ball.

I was just as obsessive with my cricket as I was with footy. I didn't really do sport in half-measures and I certainly gave it my all. I loved Glenn McGrath. When new blokes came into the Test team and took a few wickets, I'd latch onto them – it was all about McGrath. Mark Waugh was my real cricket hero, although I didn't buy a Slazenger bat like he used because I didn't think it was good enough brand. I actually bought the one his brother, Steve, used, a GM. I loved that bat and I still have it.

I wasn't a bad batsman but bowling was my strength. I had a snarling fast ball and I'd let fly with bouncers and scare the opposition out. I didn't swing the ball – I just sent down bouncers and yorkers. I won a couple of competition bowling averages but I had no real tricks.

My brothers loved their sport too, and they were always pretty physical with me. I suppose younger brothers are fair game. If I ever beat them at something, they'd say, 'You're not allowed to play anymore,' or else they'd beat me up. They could work me up, though, and I liked to challenge Simon physically even though he was seven years older than me. We used to play a form of chicken in our backyard. I'd say, 'You go down one end of the yard, I'll go down the other end and we'll charge at each other.' He'd always deck me but I'd get up and try to beat him again. We both still laugh about that and can't believe we did it.

Brad was only two years older than me so we were much closer in size, but he still liked to assert his authority. When we played billiards he always had to win the last game, otherwise he'd punch me. One day when I was about thirteen and he was fifteen, he punched me in the back of the head. I turned around and dropped one on his chin and as he fell backwards, he smashed his head back on the door. 'I'm in trouble here,' I thought, but he didn't come after me. He must have realised that I'd grown up a bit, as I don't think he ever tried that sort of intimidation on me again.

I learned so much about physical contests from both Simon and Brad, which taught me to stand up for myself. I got a little bit of that from Kylie, too, but in a different way.

There were times when I felt sorry for Kylie in our house. She had no interest in football at all and so she had to take every chance she could to even the score. She was good friends with a Carlton supporter named Boris, and he once took her to an Essendon and Carlton game because I was playing. I think it was my third senior match. He told me later that after I had kicked a goal late in the third quarter he had turned to Kylie but she'd actually fallen asleep! It is funny that she has ended up working in the football industry with *The Footy Show* – at least now she has to pay attention!

Dad loved his sport as much as us boys did, which was great. Playing cricket at the Doyle Street Oval in Avondale Heights, I once hit a big hook shot that smashed into the bonnet of his red Ford Falcon, leaving a massive dent. Dad was doubled over in laughter. He decided not to take the dent out because it was such a good story to tell. He eventually sold the car to a bloke at his work, who also decided to keep the dent and keep telling the story. I reckon the car's still going around with the dent in it somewhere.

2
More than Blood

'Matthew Lloyd is showing exceptional talent as a footballer. This year he not only captained his own side in the finals but also won the Essendon Junior Social Football League best and fairest award.'

Community News, *4 October 1988*

ALONG WITH CRICKET, I quickly got into Aussie rules football when we returned to Melbourne from Scotland. I joined the Avondale Heights Football Club, which used the same ground as the cricket club. I played my first season aged nine and finished second in the best and fairest behind a big Italian kid named Basil Zoccali who was a year older.

Dad was my greatest influence when I was young. I know that, through my career, I had other coaches who did and said things that were influential, but Dad was the person who really got me going in football. From the day he tied a balloon to my foot to stop me slamming the ball down when I kicked, he guided me in many ways.

At some stage he coached all us boys. I had him as my official team coach for two or three years, but really he was always coaching me, in a way. He wasn't domineering and certainly never interfered with my formal coaches, but he did expect a lot from me. His involvement was always very well balanced, which I think stemmed from his love of the game and his respect for people in general.

Mum and Dad were very strict in teaching us how to treat other people and how to talk to them. People at footy clubs sometimes laughed at me because I didn't swear. Apart from telling stories or letting one out when I missed the odd goal, I didn't. I think my parents' life lessons crept into my being because they lived what they said and they are such warm people. That blend of discipline and warmth is a great balance.

Dad always wanted to make the game fun for me, and he did. He used to be the goal umpire when I was young, and he'd be there telling the opposition's backmen to kick the ball in my direction just to see me get another touch. These poor kids would kick it towards me and I'd mark it and have another shot for goal. It was quite funny, really.

I don't remember a lot about those games, probably because I was so young, but I do remember particular stories and lessons.

In the juniors, I played centre half-forward, but if the team wasn't going well I'd go in and play as a ruck-rover. I was tall and skinny but I always had a good mark. Even at that age I loved wheeling onto my trusty left foot. Strangely, I'm the only left-footer in my family.

Dad used to take my stats, as he had done for Brad and Simon, and in one under-10s match I was up to fifty-two possessions in the third quarter so he decided not to bother keeping count anymore. I was interviewed by the local paper around this time, and I said that all I wanted to do was play AFL footy for Carlton.

My brother Simon was the captain of the Carlton under-19s at this time, playing at full-back. I went to watch him play every week. Anthony Koutoufides and Ang Christou were kids in that side. They were probably around fifteen or sixteen then. At one match, a Carlton recruiting officer walked up to Dad and pulled from his wallet the newspaper article about me from the local paper the week before. Its headline read 'Lloyd wanting to follow in his dad's footsteps', and in it I'd said, 'I like different players rather than one club, but if I could choose I'd play for Carlton. That's all I want, to play league footy.' The recruiter said to Dad, 'We've got our eye on your son already.' I was only around ten or so at the time, and this gave me an inkling that I might one day make it at a league club.

Around this time I got to play a game for the Brisbane Bears' Little League team in a match at Windy Hill. No school wanted to represent Brisbane so our school, St Martin's in Avondale Heights, jumped at the chance. It wasn't a big crowd, but it was still a VFL match at Windy Hill. I asked for jumper number twenty-five, which was Roger Merrett's number – he was the Bears' captain and main forward.

The two best players that day got to play for the Bears again later in the year in a combined team. I had kicked a couple of goals and was chosen, and that was how I had my first match at the MCG. It was such a big occasion. All my family was there to watch me but I didn't get a kick. I had the ball at one stage and went for a run – I took three bounces but the third one bounced back over my head. I had a great time, but it's rare that you'd take three bounces in a game and not get a stat for the match!

Playing in the AFL was my dream and I idolised anyone who played the game. When I heard people bagging a player and saying he was no good, I'd defend them. These blokes were playing AFL footy and that, to me, was enough. Brad Fox and Tony Antrobus had played a handful of games for Essendon, and they presented me with my Best in Competition award one year, and I was looking at them and thinking, 'These are AFL footballers!' I was awestruck.

I was still idolising professional footballers when I was a little older. Gary Barrow was a guy from Avondale Heights around Simon's age who played six games for Footscray in 1992 and 1993. I saw him a few times at functions or parties, and I couldn't believe I was speaking to this guy who was playing in the AFL. He only played six games but I put him on a pedestal.

I rose through the ranks at the Avondale Heights Football Club, winning the best and fairest for the club in my second year at each level – big Basil would always take it out when I was at the bottom age. When I was in the under-14s I started to become aware that I could perhaps actually play at AFL level.

That year I played a lot of footy with one of my best mates, Danny Sequinzia. Some years later, his sister married Mark Moran, who would eventually lose his life in Melbourne's criminal underworld wars. Mark was a big man and made quite an impression wherever he went. He was a mad Carlton fan but he used to come and watch Danny play in our matches. I was kicking a lot of goals and taking a lot of marks in the junior ranks, and he used to come up to me and say, 'Mate, you are going to play for Carlton. I want you playing for Carlton.'

I went to a lot of Carlton games with Danny and Mark, mainly the Friday night matches, and then on Sundays I'd go to Williamstown in the VFA. Unfortunately, Simon hadn't been elevated from Carlton's under-19s to the main list so he signed to play with Willi. Again he played at full-back, and I remember standing down his end behind the goals and trying to mark the ball whenever it went through. At quarter time and three-quarter time I'd always go out and listen to the coach address the team. Simon played in the Seagulls' 1990 premiership side under Barry Round when he was nineteen. Willi came from forty points down late in the third quarter, and Billy Swan – father of Collingwood player Dane – kicked the winning goal.

Danny's brothers were mad Hawthorn supporters so I went to a few of those games as well. I remember jumping the fence with them at Waverley Park when Jason Dunstall kicked his 100th goal against Adelaide in 1993. So I was fitting in a lot of footy over each weekend – maybe two AFL games, a VFA match and my own game for Avondale Heights. I was a footy fanatic and loved it.

In Year 10 I was also playing for the St Bernard's First XVIII, and again I was a young kid playing against bigger bodies. It was 1993 and Brad was captain of the team. We came close to winning the Sun Shield that year. We were three goals up with five minutes to go against Parade College in the Semi Final but the game ended in a draw, with Parade winning in extra time. They won the final the next week by ten goals. We were shattered but, looking back, they had a fair side. Jarrod Molloy, Daniel Harford and Blake Caracella were their big guns.

At Avondale Heights I was in the under-16s. I loved playing with my mates but I was now at an age where guys who couldn't beat me fair and square would play dirty – they'd kick me in the shins behind the play or punch me at the bottom of a pack, that sort of thing. I got in a bit of a wrestle in one match and the boundary umpire crashed into my back – it turned out he was the brother of the player I was scuffling with. This was the ugly side of local footy. Nothing was ever totally out of hand but I started losing my enjoyment for the game.

I felt that I needed something more. I played out the rest of the 1993 season with Avondale Heights and then decided to look for a new challenge at a higher level.

3

A Junior Jet

> 'This kid wandered through the door with a real hunger, a thirst, a real focus, steely determination . . . I thought he was a special young player.'
>
> *Merv Keane*

I HAD PLAYED FOR some representative sides in the Essendon District Football League and also for the Western Jets under-15s, which had culminated in All-Australian selection at the state championships. I knew I was on the radar of the Western Jets under-18s, and in late 1993 I started preseason training with them. I was just fifteen – probably the youngest player the under-18s had ever had – but I wanted to see if I could make their squad of fifty.

Merv Keane was the Jets' coach and Shannon Grant was their gun player at the time. I'd never seen anything like the training regime – there was so much running. Most of the squad members were seventeen or eighteen and their bodies were much bigger than mine. Training was three nights a week. It was designed to prepare us not just for Western Jets games but also for a career in the AFL.

I was only seventy-four kilograms at the time so I knew I had to hit the gym. The whole preseason was as taxing as anything I'd ever done physically, but I got through it and made it onto the list of fifty, which was a huge thrill. Having tasted the next level of football, I really didn't want to play another year at Avondale Heights in the under-16s.

Kinnear Beatson was the footy manager at the Jets. (He later became the head recruiter at the Brisbane Lions through their golden era and is now with the Sydney Swans.) He introduced me to Shannon Grant, saying to Shannon, 'He's your equivalent, just a year behind, in terms of dominating the juniors.' Hearing that felt good.

I was still playing cricket as I was starting out at the Western Jets. I was playing cricket in the mornings and then Mum and Dad would drive me to grounds around Melbourne to play in the Jets' practice matches in the afternoons.

In our cricket Grand Final in 1994 we'd pretty much won the game when I came in to bat, and because I needed to get out of there quickly to get to my football match I was having a big slog. I either wanted a quick ton – and I never did get one – or I'd be going out. I ended up with seventy or eighty. We then had to get to Coburg to play the Central Dragons. I was playing on David Bourke, who was pretty highly rated at the time. He was the son of Francis Bourke, the Richmond champion in the 1970s. I was starting at full-forward, and I remember our fitness coaches giving me extra back work during the warm-up because I couldn't bend over. I'd done a heap of bowling the day before, as well as the batting I'd done that morning.

I had actually started to develop stress fractures in my

back and I was advised to give cricket away if I wanted to make a career of footy. So pretty much straight after we won that Grand Final I quit the game.

I played in a lot of trial games during my preseason with the Jets and I was holding my own against the older guys. When Round 1 came I was picked in a forward pocket. I had half-expected to have to go back to Avondale Heights until I was good enough to play for the Jets. If some Jets players got selected for the Victorian Teal Cup team midway through the season, then there would be more opportunities for me to get a game. But now I thought, 'I'm in for Round 1 and I want to stay here for the rest of the year.'

I had never had any serious injuries before but that was about to change. During that Round 1 match, Shawn Lewfatt, who went on to Essendon with me, went for a big hanger on my back and drove me into the ground, breaking my nose. I was crying in the rooms after the game due to the pain and shock. My nose was operated on and I had the plaster on it for two weeks.

While I was recuperating Merv spoke to Dad and me and suggested I should perhaps go back to play local footy again. But we weren't too keen on that idea as I knew I wouldn't get anything out of playing there anymore. So we told them that I might move to another club, like the Northern Knights.

Our strategy worked and Merv put me back into the team for Round 4. I kicked five goals in that match, as did Shannon Grant, and we had a big win against North Ballarat. Both the team and I went from strength to strength from that time on.

When the Teal Cup squad was announced, I was amazed

to find my name on the list. Great things were happening for me at a rapid rate – a lot faster than I had ever imagined. The Vics' Teal Cup team that year is the one I regard as the greatest ever. In 2001, of course, Chris Judd, Luke Hodge and Luke Ball led the team, but in 1995 I played with Daniel Harford, Shannon Grant, Kane Johnson, Anthony Rocca, Paul Licuria and Jeff White, who all went on to great AFL careers. We won all our games at the carnival by around twenty goals and I made the under-18 All-Australian team as a sixteen-year-old.

I returned to the Jets and had a pretty good year. I was fourth or fifth in the best and fairest and I kicked fifty goals, which was a good return. If the recruiters hadn't been looking at me before, they were now. It was hard not to get caught up in the hype, but Mum and Dad kept me grounded.

I reckon I was still immature emotionally then – when dealing with injury, for instance – but in a broader way I was more advanced than most others my age. I was naturally able to set the bar high for myself. I think my desire to succeed was far greater than that of most guys my age, who were thinking of sneaking out for a party on the weekend while I was mentally preparing for my game the next weekend. I'd come home from school and try to have a twenty-minute nap before training with the Jets because I wanted to steel myself for a big session. I was aware that my body probably wasn't ready for the loads I was putting onto it.

Both my new coaches that year – Merv Keane at the Jets and Rod 'Curly' Austin with the Victorian team – were awesome and I loved playing under both of them. In many respects, they were perfect coaches for that level of footy. I especially loved the representative footy because I got to play with the best players from all clubs. It wasn't as restrictive as club football – it was just fun.

You can't give young blokes learning how to play a complex game plan. At their age, it's about the basics – use the corridor, hit the ball hard at the stoppages, nothing too over the top with set plays and the like. Essentially, coaches at that level are trying to find out what these young players can do.

Curly would say, 'Mate, if you get tackled from behind trying to take three bounces, then no message will be coming out. Go out there and show your flair. We won't accept selfish efforts – it's got to be team first – but if it's your time to go and you get the chance to take a hanger, go for it.'

Merv could have a hard touch at times, but he also developed his players really well and I learned so much from him. He also had a caring side, which I saw when he was concerned about whether I was emotionally ready for this higher level of footy.

I think Merv's relationship with Sheeds helped me to get to Essendon. The age at which a player could be drafted to the AFL was seventeen. As I would be too young to nominate for the National Draft at the end of 1994, I set myself for another season with the Jets in 1995. But this was the year in which the Fremantle Dockers were entering the competition, and the AFL had introduced a rule that if a club lost an uncontracted senior player to Fremantle then it could choose a sixteen-year-old as compensation in the 1995 Preseason Draft.

That opened up possibilities for me. The order of the compensation picks in the 1995 Preseason Draft began with the team that had finished last in the 1994 season and moved up the ladder. So, if each of the bottom clubs lost an uncontracted player to Fremantle, the order would be Sydney, Fitzroy, St Kilda, Brisbane, Adelaide and then Essendon.

Not every club wanted to lose an uncontracted player to Fremantle, though, and it seemed that Sydney, St Kilda, Brisbane and Adelaide all had that attitude. Fitzroy, though, was looking to move a guy named Michael Dunstan to Fremantle to get the number-one pick of the sixteen-year-olds.

Some guys from Fitzroy – the first club I ever met with – came over to our house. They sat down with Dad and Mum and me and said, 'We want to take your boy as the first pick in the draft.'

Dad said to them, in a respectful manner, 'We don't want him to play for Fitzroy. We're not happy with where the club's heading and what the future holds for Fitzroy.' Even though I had grown up barracking for Fitzroy, I was fully behind what Mum and Dad thought. I wanted to play for a more stable and powerful club.

They said, 'We let a crying Brad Johnson go last year because he said he wanted to play for Footscray, and there's no way we're going to let that happen again this year.'

Then Carlton called Dad. He only told me this quite recently, but they said to him, 'Sign for one or two years with Fitzroy and we'll get Matthew across in a year or two's time.' Mind you, Carlton was savage on Ian Collins – one of their own – who, while he was working for the AFL around this time, had changed the requirement to qualify for the father/son rule from twenty games to fifty games. Before that

Carlton would have been able to draft me with no competition as Dad had played twenty-nine games for them.

Momentum was now starting to build. I was even finding my way into the mainstream papers, and even though I was never sure that I would make it to an AFL club it started to feel like it might happen. I picked up the paper one day and saw a story saying Essendon wanted to give up four players to get me as a sixteen-year-old. All I could think was, 'I'm going to be on an AFL list!' I didn't realise at the time that I was probably rated as the best junior in the country.

Two days after Fitzroy had visited, Noel Judkins, the recruiting officer at Essendon, rang and asked me, 'How would you like to play for Essendon?'

'That would be unbelievable, because I live fifteen minutes from Windy Hill,' I said. 'But you finished tenth — how do we get past the other clubs?'

'We're doing a deal with Fremantle,' Noel replied. 'We're going to give up a promising midfielder from Perth, Tony Delaney, plus Dale Kickett, Todd Ridley and Russell Williams. Freo want those four players and they said they won't take any players from the eleventh, twelfth, thirteenth, fourteenth or fifteenth clubs on the ladder.'

Mum and Dad were also keen on the idea because it would make it so much easier for me to manage my final year at school, and Essendon had recently run a similar program for Dustin Fletcher.

I went to the draft camp not long after and saw Tony Delaney, who was doing a talk for us as the next batch of kids coming through. I went over and I said, 'Tony, I'm Matthew Lloyd.' I asked him if he was okay with everything that was being proposed, and he said he was. 'I actually want to go home back to Perth,' he said, which was a big relief for me to hear. The next day there was a big photo of Tony and me in the *Herald Sun* and I started to really believe it was going to happen.

It was all moving so fast. I went from being a fifteen-year-old trying out for the Jets, and within a year I was going to Essendon as the number-one pick in the draft of sixteen-year-olds.

I also met Scott Lucas at the draft camp. He was four or five months older than me so he had nominated for the national draft. When we met, we clicked straightaway and over the years he would become one of my best mates and a person I have the utmost respect for. He's a true family man and a real gentleman.

My parents asked Ricky Nixon to help us out on the management side of things, and he was sensational early in my career. I remember him sitting in the lounge room with Mum and Dad and me, talking through the financial arrangements and confirming where I was going. The love of Fitzroy I'd had as a kid had faded well and truly by this time. Bernie Quinlan had retired, and I'd lost interest in the club when Richard Osborne left at the end of 1992 and Alastair Lynch left the following year. They were the keys up forward and now they were gone and Fitzroy was tumbling down the ladder.

Lynch ended up back in Fitzroy colours a couple of years later when Brisbane and Fitzroy merged. That left me wondering what might have happened if I'd gone to Fitzroy. Would I have ended up in Brisbane or would Carlton's promise to get me there have come off?

After talking it all through with Ricky, we were pretty set on Essendon. All we needed to do was work out the financial arrangements. I was offered a $15,000 base salary, which I thought was just the best. I was going to be *paid* to play AFL footy! It felt like so much money.

When Essendon took Scott Lucas at number four in the National Draft in late 1994 I rang him and said, 'We're going to Essendon!' We were both pretty happy. Blake Caracella (pick ten), Justin Blumfield (pick sixty-two) and Gary Moorcroft (pick forty-five) were also taken in that draft and we would all play in the 2000 Premiership team. Sean Lewfatt, who played with me at the Western Jets, was chosen at number twenty-eight; he had as much ability as any of us but never really had the workrate and didn't play many games.

There were a few others from the Jets, including Shannon Grant, who got drafted that year, and plenty of the guys I played for Victoria with also got the call-up. It was pretty exciting, although all the talk had made me a little nervous. There were newspaper pieces written by people like Mike Sheahan that just made the whole thing feel bigger than it was: he said the Bombers were taking a huge risk. Noel Judkins was sure it was the right thing for the club, though, and he worked hard to keep me at ease. He told me I should just relax, enjoy training and concentrate on finishing off my schooling.

All the newspaper hype and expectation was big, but it was nothing compared to the expectations I had of myself. Not that they mattered, but all I wanted to do was play AFL footy. I would be trying to fit into an Essendon forward line that included Paul Salmon, Scott Cummings, James Hird, Mark Mercuri and Michael Long.

I knew it was going to be hard just to get a game, but I felt ready for the challenge ahead.

'Essendon is expected to draft Western Jets centre half-forward Matthew Lloyd – considered the best 16-year-old footballer in Victoria – providing it completes an intricate pre-draft deal with Fremantle. The Bombers have set their sights on Lloyd, recently named in the ASFL's team of the year.'

Tony de Bolfo and Daryl Timms,
Herald Sun, 5 October 1994

4

The Schoolboy Footballer

'He liked his hair to be in place.'

Dr Bruce Reid, Essendon Club Doctor

My career as an Essendon footballer began with the start of my first AFL preseason training session. It was late 1994 and I was in Year 11 at St Bernard's College. In some ways I was prepared for the challenge, but in many other ways I wasn't.

I was embarking on a two-year program that was going to take me from being a schoolboy footballer to being a regular part of the line-up at the biggest football club in Australia. To me at the time, though, it was simply about playing football and living a dream. And I wanted it straightaway.

I was granted permission to train with Essendon before Christmas in 1994 because it had become clear that the deal to get me to the club was a certainty. My first meeting with Kevin Sheedy and the team was at the Riverside Golf Club, where a get-together was planned. Mum and Dad came down with me because I couldn't drive, and it was good for me to have their support too.

This was when I had my first long chat with Kevin Sheedy. He told me what he thought I needed to do to build a career in the AFL, and one of the first things he said, 'You should have a good enough career to buy a house.' He didn't want to see me waste my income, so he told me to be smart with my money. He said, 'I like to buy a house a year.' I remember hearing one day that he owned about ten houses in Richmond, and I tried to take his advice on board. Two years later I bought a house in Flemington and a unit in Moonee Ponds – I was still only nineteen. Sheeds was as much a life coach as he was a football coach.

The event at the golf club was fairly casual. I was so nervous that I just stood there and waited for people to come and introduce themselves. Some were warmer than others, and to this day I remember my feelings when I met them.

After surviving that get-together, it was down to training. Scott Lucas had joined me at St Bernard's for our final year at school – he moved up from Camperdown, which was past Geelong. Scotty and I were good mates by this stage, and I even asked Mum and Dad if he could come and live with us, but that didn't eventuate. St Bernard's had always been a football school and was really a feeder school for the Bombers: Simon and Justin Madden had gone there, as had David Calthorpe.

After school, Scotty and I would catch the bus from Buckley Street outside St Bernard's to Essendon Station. We always sensed that the other kids were talking about us as we headed off to training. I was happy that it wasn't just me – we were doing it together. We'd walk into training in our school uniforms, often to the laughter of our much older teammates.

In my first year, 1995, there were four players still at school: apart from Scotty and I, Justin Blumfield was at Essendon Grammar (where he was taught by Ken Fletcher, Dustin's dad, who had played 264 games for Essendon in the 1960s and 70s), and Shawn Lewfatt was at Assumption. I had played Teal Cup footy against these guys so I knew them well, which made settling in easier.

I had always worn number eighteen in my younger years. Dad wore it at Carlton when he was there and so did my brothers at junior and senior levels. I was lucky that when I got to Essendon it was free due to Todd Ridley leaving as part of my trade with Fremantle. Apparently, Sheeds was happy because he saw a bit of Paul Van Der Haar in me, and he liked giving jumper numbers to players who resembled those of past eras. I did ask for the number though.

That put me next to Peter Somerville in the change rooms, though, and he set about intimidating me as much as he could. He was a big bloke and he started calling me Sweet Pea. One time, I was sitting in front of his locker getting changed; he'd often arrive after me after a hard day on the tools – he was a plumber by trade. He walked in and gave me a mad stare. He crouched in front of me and put his hands on my bare knees, saying, 'Listen here, Sweet Pea, this will be the last time you'll ever sit in front of my locker.' When he took his hands off, he had rubbed all his chewing gum into my leg hairs.

It was a really daunting time for me. There were all these footballers – such as Somer – trying to stamp their authority on this young kid who already had a media profile. Some of them must have been worrying a bit, given what Essendon had given up to get me to the club. It's human nature, I suppose. When I was established as a player, I always paid attention to who we were drafting to see if I would have an up-and-comer challenging me for my role in the side.

Alec Epis (who we called 'Kooka' because he was always talking, just like a kookaburra) was the club's Director of Football, and he was a mentor to so many of us players. He told me once that Sheeds used to say, 'You don't have to worry about this kid Lloyd – he thinks he's going to make it already.' Danny Corcoran, who worked in the football department, takes great pleasure to this day in stirring me up about my confidence when I walked into the club; he says I was sure I'd be playing in Round 1 of 1995. I recall it differently, though. I idolised these blokes and was having to pinch myself that I was even at the same club as them.

Ricky Olarenshaw was the senior player who helped me most to feel comfortable at the club. He took me waterskiing a week or two into my time there. He was brilliant, and we built a friendship that I still value to this day.

David 'Stumpy' Calthorpe was the funny one of the team – he was always making jokes at the other blokes' expense. There was a lot of experience in both our senior team and our reserves at that time. Having fifty-two players on our club list was great as it meant we younger blokes could learn so much from the older guys, such as Peter Cransberg and David Flood. Even a guy like Darren 'Doc' Wheildon had so much to give. He was a real character to play with, but sadly he got hit by a car in King Street in the middle of 1995 after a night out; he never played again.

Mark 'Choco' Williams was coaching the reserves, and he was a character too, but almost at the other extreme – although he did have his lighter moments. He was such a driven man, and we felt it. You could tell at that early stage of his coaching career that he was going to be a very good senior coach. He was a harder coach than Sheeds, who was probably starting to mellow by that stage. Sheeds was trying to protect me a bit, I reckon, as he really wanted me to make it, whereas to Choco I was just another one of the team.

The whole culture at Essendon then was about hardening up. No one was happy that we'd missed the 1994 finals series – especially since we'd won the Premiership in 1993. The goal was to improve from the bottom up, and that began with the reserves and Mark Williams. It was his first year with Essendon after coaching Glenelg in South Australia. Although 1994 had been a bad year for the Bombers, we were seen as having – along with Carlton – the best list of the Victorian clubs, so a lot was expected of us in 1995.

I was conscious of that. I also had a massive fear of failure, and so I was going to work as hard as I could to make sure I succeeded. But I was still a kid in a man's world. Up till then, I had competed against players around the same age; maybe they were a couple of years older, but we weren't too far apart physically.

Now, here we were – Scotty, Blake Caracella, Justin Blumfield and I, all just sixteen or seventeen, with skinny bodies but desperate to play in the big league. There was a lot of laughter whenever Scott Lucas, Blake Caracella or I went into the weights room. Scott and I could only lift the bar – just the minimum plate that the older guys used to warm up. Blake Caracella was worse, though, and that saved us a bit.

My training program was initially quite restricted. Our fitness coach at the time was Loris Bertolacci, who later went on to work with Mark Thompson at Geelong, and he was given the task of easing me into professional training, and of working with me to get some bulk onto my skinny frame. I was probably doing about half the work of the rest of the squad, but the coaches also knew that, once the season started, I'd be playing for St Bernard's on a Wednesday and then for Essendon on the weekend. I wanted to make sure that was for the senior team, not the reserves.

It wasn't really any different for the other young guys. Our training was designed to help us into our careers without giving us a lot of soft-tissue injuries. Scotty and I were doing the three main days of training, which was Monday, Wednesday and Friday, depending on what day of the weekend the game was. Things were still semi-professional then, and while we were at school many other players were at work.

I coped with the training load well enough, although it was still pretty punishing for a young bloke. I remember one early session with Choco called 'the Brick Circuit'. He had me in tears after that one. Basically, it involved carrying bricks while doing a lot of hard running. I was still a pretty skinny kid and hadn't done much strength training at all. At one stage, when we were under the Windy Hill race and Choco had his back turned, I decided to give my arms a quick rest. But he turned around and caught me and was immediately in my face, screaming 'You are the weak link! You are going to cost us games of football!'

That experience almost destroyed me. I was left wondering about my future, and about who could coach me if that was what Choco thought. I broke down when Mum and Dad picked me up, telling them what had happened and what this coach was like.

Soon after, out on the training track again, Choco kicked the footy to me and said, 'Wouldn't you like delivery like that?' He was the type of coach who took you out of your comfort zone and continually challenged you. It wasn't until halfway through the season that I found my way with him.

In the end, I actually came to love Mark Williams as a coach, and I came to think of him as one of the better mentors that I ever had. He knew what needed to be done and he just went about it. He didn't care how I felt, because that didn't matter. What mattered was whether I, as a part of the team, was able to do my job.

While I was generally coping with the demands on me as a professional footballer, I wasn't ready for the changes to my private life that being in the AFL brought. There had been a lot written about me when the deal to get me to Essendon was being done, and while it was great to see myself in the papers, I now see that I wasn't mature enough to handle what it meant for my life.

Pretty early in my time at Essendon, an incident occurred that showed me that I needed to learn how to deal with being a public figure. There were two girls who always used to stand out the front of Windy Hill and approach the players as they left training. I was the new kid on the block and I found them a bit overbearing – I was young and it wasn't something I was interested in. Because I couldn't drive, I'd often have to wait for Dad to pick me up from training, so I'd have to put up with their attention while I waited.

When girls started phoning our house it just freaked me out. I went to Mum and Dad nearly in tears, saying, 'Girls are ringing me!' I was a very intense young man. Aside from that, my brothers could get me so worked up over things like that that I almost imploded.

This side of things wasn't like footy. Football I had a handle on. I was always intense about it, but my feelings were positive most of the time. But to have girls phoning my home or stalking me outside Windy Hill after training left me way out of my depth. I had always wanted to play AFL footy. I'd dreamt of kicking the winning goal after the siren, of premierships and the like, but I had never thought of what it would do to my life.

One night I was walking out of training with Mark 'Bomber' Thompson, our club captain. I said to him, 'I'm going to go a different way because I don't want to walk past those girls.' He pulled me up straightaway.

'Hey, come back here,' he said. 'Don't treat our supporters like that.'

I didn't answer back, although I should have told him how they'd been pestering me. I just copped it from him. He was the captain and a pretty imposing man. I only had to be told things once to get his message. It showed me how passionate he was about our footy club, but also how important the fans and members of the club were.

Bomber's passion came across in all his speeches as captain in that year – in team huddles and at training he spoke with so much authority. I only got to play with him for one year, but I always remember that talking-to he gave me. I can see why he became so successful as a coach. He really commanded respect.

So I took Bomber's comment to heart. I saw that I had to learn how to cope with the attention, and I always tried to treat our fans with respect from that time on. There were times when I was having a bad run that I'd avoid them, but thankfully not for the same reasons as that day.

> 'I was a Delaney fan, but it turned out to be an inspired move by Essendon. They didn't give up much and they got a bloke who was an elite player for ten years.'
>
> Mike Sheahan, 2011

5

Sweet Pea Lines Up

'He applied himself so well, even early in his career – I've never seen anyone work so hard at it.'

James Hird

IT WAS PRETTY EARLY in 1995 when I played my first game in Essendon colours. It was a tri-series lightning premiership played between Essendon, Collingwood and Carlton before the start of the Ansett Cup. There were squads of thirty and each team played two games – like two quarters of a proper match against both sides like this year's NAB Cup series.

We played Carlton first and I kicked three goals on Mil Hanna. I was in shock. I could have been playing for Carlton, and here I was at sixteen kicking three goals in what was essentially a half of footy against them.

We played Collingwood next. After four or five minutes, the ball was kicked to Damian Monkhorst, the Collingwood ruckman. As 'Monkey' was backing up to set himself for the mark, I saw an opportunity and climbed onto his shoulders to take a big hanger over the top of him. After that, I was floating and had a pretty good day. Even early in my career, my day could sometimes be defined by how I took that first mark.

Rick Olarenshaw was immediately up to me after I kicked the goal – he was saying, 'You're a superstar!' I raced home afterwards to watch the news. They showed my grab and spoke about me kicking a few goals, and I thought to myself, 'I'll be a fair chance to play again.' But I had also picked up a corkie.

This was a problem I would have throughout my career. When you get a corkie, you have to elevate your leg and ice it for twenty minutes every two hours. You shouldn't drink alcohol and you have go to the beach the next day to walk in the cold seawater. Some blokes weren't too careful with their recovery – they'd be drinking that night and they'd be okay – but if I didn't do everything right then I'd miss a game for sure.

Without realising what I'd done to my leg, I went out with the boys that night. The Cactus in Moonee Ponds gave all the players a fifty-dollar drink card on entry, but they knew I wasn't old enough to drink so I missed out on that. Because I wasn't aware of how to treat my injury, which seemed so insignificant, I missed our match the next week against Fitzroy – our first Ansett Cup game.

Scott Lucas ended up getting a run but I just sat there and watched. We won the game and Sheeds slotted me into the side in place of Scotty for the next match, against North Melbourne – I think he was keen to give me another chance in the preseason. I wore big pads on my thighs to help protect against corkies, and I ended up wearing them for most of my career if I was recovering from a corked thigh.

In my first real official match, I played on Dean Laidley of

North Melbourne. I'd been hit and niggled before but Dean was something else. I'd never had someone run me up the ground like he did, either. I didn't know then that there's an art in knowing when to follow your defender and when to stay back, but I learnt a lot about it from that point on, after chasing him around for most of the day.

He was mouthing off at me and bumping me all the time, I was spent. But I still wasn't afraid to pull on his jumper when he was running, which he warned me about a couple of times. 'Listen here, kid,' he said, 'I'll give you one more chance, but if you do that again you'll find out what happens in the big league.'

A few minutes later he set off to run down the wing and I pulled on his jumper again. 'I warned you,' he said, and then he dropped his knee into my thigh-pad and hit me right on the spot of the cork, I was trying to recover from. It hurt at the time but I didn't realise just how bad it was. I was enjoying the experience of playing in the big league too much. It was thrilling but also eye-opening: even though I was being spoken about in the media as a 'teenage sensation', I discovered that night that I was out of my depth.

North Melbourne was a powerful side, with the likes of Wayne Carey, Corey McKernan, Mick Martyn, John Longmire, Anthony Stevens, Glenn Archer and David King. Along with Dean, these blokes were giving it to me verbally and physically whenever they could. We lost that match to North, who ended up winning the Ansett Cup, and I now understood much better just how tough and physical the AFL would be. I also realised that because of the hype surrounding me, I would have a target on my head.

In many ways, I was happy to get off the ground with a few touches and to have stayed away from Mick Martyn for most of the game. Mick and I ended up having some great battles and he became one of my toughest rivals.

When I got home the pain from my leg was excruciating. Dean had got me right in the spot of the previous one. Mum gave me an aspirin for my headache, which was probably the worst thing to do – aspirin thins your blood and makes you bleed even more. I ended up with a touch of calcification, where the blood goes hard. At the time, the club doctors thought it was a result of the aspirin, but as my career unfolded I realised that it was just my body's reaction to a corked thigh. I would always struggle to recover for the next match if I copped a corkie.

I was devastated. This second corkie was worse than the first, so I knew I was going to miss games. I thought I'd done enough to hold my place and win a spot for Round 1, but now I would miss the rest of the preseason.

After that match, it was all about recovery. I had to work hard just to be right for Round 1, when we met Fitzroy. The game was at the Whitten Oval in Footscray, which was Fitzroy's new home ground, and I played in the reserves. There was an extraordinary level of interest in our seniors game that weekend as it was Doug Hawkins' first game for Fitzroy, having played 329 games for Footscray.

Mark Williams played me in the back pocket, which I couldn't understand since I'd come to Essendon as a forward. I quickly learned that Sheeds wanted all players to be able to play in any position on the ground. I didn't have a great game in the reserves but the seniors smashed them – Fitzroy didn't even score in the first half. That made me realise how lucky I was to be at Essendon and not Fitzroy – even if I was in the reserves.

I played on Robert McMahon, who was a top-ten draft pick that year but barely managed a game before Fitzroy's demise. I think he kicked a couple of goals on me, even though we won by forty-nine points. But I wasn't a great backman. I even shielded a goal through for Fitzroy because I was so used to being up the other end of the ground! It was almost as embarrassing as the time I'd forgotten to go onto the field for a practice match against Fremantle a few weeks before.

As I ran around on the backline I wondered where I fitted in, but I was working as hard as I could to make it happen. Deep down, I knew I'd rather have been playing forward, and that I would have done a better job. I had dominated at junior levels, but I knew that most of the guys in the AFL had probably done that as well. And under Kevin Sheedy you had to be able to play at both ends. The backline experiment went on for a few weeks and I was really struggling.

Sheeds always talked to me about Chris Grant, Footscray's champion centre half-forward. 'Go and watch him and take some notes,' Sheeds said to me, and I did. I watched Grant floating from centre half-back to centre half-forward, which gave me new ideas about my role as a player. The whole experience also showed me that Sheedy believed I was truly a forward, and that putting me in the backline was all about me gaining flexibility as a player.

I read the play well, which made me a good leading forward, but that didn't work too well for me as a backman. You sometimes hear people say that some backman would make a great full-forward because he kicks well or reads the play, but actually the roles are quite different and it isn't always possible to change easily. I was a forward and I knew it. I was okay if I was floating as a loose man in defence, but I wasn't so good at manning up.

In April 1995 the first Anzac Day game between Essendon and Collingwood was held. I was in the reserves and we played at Victoria Park in the morning and then made our way across to the MCG. We only just made it in for the start, and I sat back starry-eyed, thinking it was just out of this world. The atmosphere was amazing. Sav Rocca kicked nine that day and Hirdy was brilliant, and the match ended in a draw. All I wanted to do was to be playing on this big stage, and this day just reinforced that view.

Two or three weeks later, against Melbourne, a kid from Assumption College named Brad Hall kicked eight on me in the wet at the MCG. I was playing at centre half-back and he just towelled me up. I was starting to take things pretty hard and get down on myself, but after the match I heard Noel Judkins say to Sheeds and Mark Williams, 'You're killing this kid. He can play but you're playing him out of position.' Within a week I was back on the forward line.

I wasn't sure if they were doubting me by then, but I was certainly doubting myself and I was happy to move back to where it felt natural. I was upset because I was getting humiliated, and I was taking that pretty hard. I saw other players who didn't take bad games the way I did, but I just figured they didn't care like I did. I found it hard looking at my parents and my girlfriend because I felt that I was letting them down, and that I was letting myself down too.

I had met Lisa in May 1995 through a mate of mine, Ben. I was still going out with my schoolmates at that stage rather than the Essendon boys, and we'd hang out at the Queensbury Hotel in the city because that was where you could go when you were underage. It was full of boys from St Bernard's and girls from St Columba's, where Lisa went to school. Ben was going out with a girl named Skye and he said she had a friend I'd really like. He took me into the Queensbury one Saturday night to meet Lisa and we hit it off instantly.

She must have been a good influence on me, as four weeks after meeting her I had my first breakout game in the reserves against Sydney. It was Round 10 and I kicked four goals. In the main game, Sydney beat the Bombers, which was a bit of a shock. We had gone into the match with eight wins and a draw and were sitting fourth on the ladder; Sydney had only won three and was fourteenth. Sheeds wasn't at all happy with the performance.

During the next week, Barry Young approached me before our Thursday training session and told me he thought I was a chance to be picked. He had been called in by the coaches after the Sydney match for a chat and had come out a bit worried for his spot. Sheeds never liked anyone to take anything for granted, and he also liked to shake the tree every so often. Anyway, Barry had snuck back into the coaches' room later on. 'I've seen the board,' he told me, 'and your name's on it.'

'You're joking,' I said.

The media had obviously heard something was afoot, because everywhere I went during that training session they were snapping away at me. And they were right. Sheeds pulled me aside during one drill and said, 'You're in.' Dean Wallis was injured and Barry Young had indeed been dropped; Tim Darcy and I were in the senior team. I floated through the rest of the training session, and when it was over I raced inside and rang Mum and Dad.

I got home for dinner as usual. We had a four-seater dinner table, which was a little squeezy for a family of six, so Brad and I used to sit on stools at the bar because we were the youngest. Brad was talking away to me all through dinner that night but I wasn't listening – I was thinking of Saturday. I was in shock. I was going to play a game of AFL footy. I hoped I would do a good enough job to get a second game.

'He was clean, he was a brilliant kick and he had some great marking techniques. He was smart and you could see he had a feel for the game before a lot of other players. He planned ahead and he was able to initiate a lot earlier than a lot of his teammates at training and then in games.'

Mark Harvey

6

Backwards and Forwards

'Teenager Matthew Lloyd joined a select band of AFL players in his debut yesterday and went a long way to justifying Essendon's extraordinary efforts to recruit him later last year. Lloyd kicked a goal with his first kick in league football against the Crows only 30 seconds into the 122 point massacre at the MCG.'

Glenn McFarlane, Sunday Herald Sun, *9 July 1995*

MY FIRST MATCH WAS to be against Adelaide on a Saturday afternoon at the MCG. It had taken me thirteen rounds to get the call-up and I was keen.

Both Simon and Brad had played for the Carton under-19s – I think Brad was still playing there in 1995 when I joined Essendon. Simon had by this time settled in with Williamstown in the VFL, while Brad was still hoping to make a senior AFL list (which he eventually did with Hawthorn). I was playing my first AFL match before them both, but there was no jealousy or anything negative from either of them. It was a great time.

Funnily, I hadn't told Lisa that I'd been selected when I spoke to her on the phone on the Thursday night. I was trying to be modest, I suppose, but she found out from her friend Skye who introduced us, at school on the Friday and she rang me to wish me luck that night. Lisa's father, Frank, had passed away from cancer when she was fourteen so unfortunately, I was never able to meet him. Lisa lived with her mum in Greenvale and footy just wasn't an interest of theirs. She knew of the Essendon Football Club but didn't know about the under-19s, reserves and seniors or how it all worked. What was great was that our relationship wasn't about football in any way. I was quite happy with that!

I was always really nervous before my matches, and the build-up for this was huge so I found it pretty harrowing. In Friday's paper I was named in the forward pocket, next to Paul Salmon. James Hird, Mark Mercuri, Michael Long, Ryan O'Connor and Che Cockatoo-Collins. I was at school all that day and I couldn't stop thinking about it. I would be at St Bernard's one day and at the MCG the next – a pretty big difference!

I had legs like jelly when I arrived at the ground on the Saturday morning. But I was thrilled about what was happening and I soaked it all up. Running through the banner for the first time was an amazing buzz.

Tyson Edwards was my opponent. He was only eighteen himself and playing in the fourth of his 321 games for Adelaide. Every movement was hard work; my nerves and anxiety were making it pretty tough for me.

At the centre bounce, Peter Somerville got the tap out down to Gary O'Donnell, who blasted it inside the fifty-metre zone. The Big Fish, Paul Salmon, got his hands on it but it slipped out the back of the pack. I ran at the ball and slung my boot at it, and it went through for a goal. Twenty seconds into my first game and I had kicked a goal! I didn't care that I hadn't actually got a hand on the ball.

The crowd was going wild and I had all these blokes, my heroes, rubbing my head and jumping on me. 'This is just unbelievable,' I thought.

My next involvement was to dish off a handball. Just as I was about to do it, I caught a glimpse of Mark Ricciuto running at me. He wasn't as big then as he became towards the end of his career, but he was still pretty imposing. I just stepped out the way and he clipped my chin. I remember thinking, 'These are brutal, tough players! I've got to have my wits about me here.'

It was such a massive difference from the level of football I'd been playing. Two years before, I'd been playing for the Avondale Heights under-16s, and I was still a skinny teenager. There was even a massive difference between the Ansett Cup and this: the pace was quicker and the intensity greater. When Ricciuto was coming at me like a steam train I had been moving in slow motion – I was still basking in the afterglow of my first goal. I realised I had to sharpen up.

That ability to step up to the higher level is, I think, what really determines whether a player makes it in the AFL. Some guys are good reserves footballers but can't take that form into the AFL. Danny Morgan started at Essendon with me in 1995; he was getting fifty possessions in the reserves every week. People would say, 'Why isn't this bloke playing?' But when he did get the chance it just didn't work out. My brother

Brad was another in that category. He played just eleven games for Hawthorn and won the Gardiner Medal in 1997 as the best player in the reserves competition. Injury hurt his AFL career, but he was probably one of those in-between players who was unlucky to have had so many quality players at his club as he was trying to break in to senior football.

In the third quarter, Sean Denham put a pass down my throat and I kicked a goal from fifty metres, and then O'Donnell gave me an easy handball over the top and I kicked a third. Salmon kicked eight that day and we won by twenty goals. After the match, sitting in the rooms, I really felt like I was part of the team. Scotty and the other young guys were asking me what it was like. I thought my workrate that day was massive, but later on in my career I understood how far off the pace I was.

It was a great experience, though. I got sprayed with Powerade by the boys and I had a whole host of interviews to do. I'd never really done any before, but people were clamouring to get a word with me. Steve Layt, who did some work on Essendon's magazine and radio station as well as for the local papers, did my first interview; he still talks about that to this day. Plenty more followed before I'd even left the rooms. Later, Tiffany Cherry, who was working for one of the TV news stations, came over to our house and filed a report. I felt bulletproof.

One afternoon that next week, my friend Ben and I decided to take a few periods off school. We went back to Ben's house and played a bit of Playstation instead. While we were there, a phone call came to Ben's house: 'Matthew isn't there, is he?'

'Yeah, he is,' Ben admitted. 'Why?'

'Tim Watson from Channel Seven is at the school. He's here to do a big interview with him.'

We quickly jumped on the bus back to school and I did the interview on St Bernard's oval with hundreds of kids around me. It was a big week. The school later said they'd let me off for wagging, but Ben was in trouble.

There had always been a group of guys at St Bernard's who were probably the 'popular' ones. I'd often hear them talking about me, saying, 'He's alright but he's too slow,' or 'He's soft.' They were always knocking me down. Overnight, though, there had been a change and now they were saying, 'Yeah, I knew he'd make it.' Everyone had jumped on board. It was a brilliant feeling; I was walking around the school and lapping up all the attention.

The teachers were great too, especially my English teacher, Mrs Davidson, who was a mad Essendon supporter. I was enjoying all the attention but I was also a bit embarrassed too. I walked in to her class one day and found she'd bought me a bag of donuts and wanted to talk about the game. You could see all the kids thinking, 'He's getting preferential treatment.' Mind you, that was the only subject I got a B for; the rest of them didn't go too well.

After kicking three goals on debut, and with the club winning by twenty goals, Sheeds couldn't really drop me, although I think he had been looking to bring me in for just the one game. So I was selected to play against Richmond the next Friday night at the MCG, in front of 80,000 fans.

I'd never really played night footy before and I felt the intensity. It was a bigger game than the week before and the crowd was massive. The field was dewy and there was a yellow footy to deal with, and they're always a little different – not that I got to find out too much about it because Sheedy left me on the bench for most of the game. I think I ended up with one handball. Crunch, I was back to reality.

I was so frustrated after the game – which ended in a draw – that as I walked out of the rooms to see my parents, a girl said, 'Well played today,' and I fired back, 'What game were you at?' She wrote a letter to the club the next week about how rude I was, and I was back in the reserves and at school until Round 22.

That was another big game – against Carlton in front of nearly 90,000 people. I was well aware of the rivalry between the two clubs, having been at the MCG in 1993 when the Bombers defeated the Blues to take the flag. But I don't think I understood its intensity for the players until I was one of them. It didn't take long for the soft spot I'd had for Carlton as a kid to harden. Guys like Bomber Thompson and Gary O'Donnell absolutely hated the Blues with a passion. Gary was the most intense, though, and he passed that on to us younger players. 'You should hate these blokes as much as I do,' he said. 'I know they hate us.'

We got done, though, and I kicked just one goal against a backline that included Mil Hanna, Peter Dean, Michael Sexton and Stephen Silvagni. There were no second-rate defenders in that side, and I was only the fifth or sixth best player in our forward line at the time. Carlton only lost two games for the season. But I had played okay. I'd made the most of what came my way without getting in the way of our big forwards.

After finishing fourth in the home-and-away season, we

lined up against West Coast in a Qualifying Final at Waverley Park the next week. I was selected to play my fourth game and kicked 2.3 as we defeated the Eagles by nineteen points.

Sheeds had actually put me in the goal square for the first time during that match, as Paul Salmon was really struggling. He doubted himself, which is never a good sign for a footballer. He was booed off the ground at the end of the match, and I was told later that he said, 'I'll never play in front of this crowd or for this club again.' He was a jovial character but, deep down, very sensitive, and the crowd's reaction really hurt him. The Big Fish was true to his word and left at the season's end, only to be brought back out of retirement by Sheeds after playing at Hawthorn for five years.

The next week we faced Richmond in a Semi Final. It was massive – the atmosphere was more gladiatorial than the West Coast match had been. Then, I'd been able to get some easy touches, but not in this game. Scotty Turner from Richmond was running around like a madman – he knocked out David Grenvold and Gary O'Donnell with big hip-and-shoulder bumps. We were two men short and had only one fit player on the bench, and Matthew Knights was putting on a clinic in the midfield.

At three-quarter time we were down by a point. Sheeds pulled me aside and said, 'Lloyd, I need you at centre half-back.' That meant lining up on Turner, who was the centre half-forward that day and weighed in at nearly 100 kilograms – at least, that's how he seemed to me. I was powerless and he kicked one or two on me before Sheedy moved me back forward.

Richmond got away in the last quarter and would win by

thirteen points. I managed to kick a goal from fifty late in that final quarter, and even though we were about to be knocked out of the finals I felt pretty good. I was still in 'self' mode at that stage of my career: as long as I was kicking goals, I was happy. I just wanted to build a career. My perspective on the game and my role in it changed as I got older and more established.

I didn't realise it at the time, but with Paul Salmon intending to leave and with Scott Cummings getting ridden pretty hard by Sheeds over his fitness and commitment, an opportunity was about to present itself for me. Sheeds was grooming me for the full-forward's role, but I needed to put on some bulk and get more experience.

'Matthew Lloyd is an investment in the future. He just happens to be giving Essendon an early return.'

Stephen Rielly, The Age, *15 September 1995*

7

Building Bulk... Slowly

'Matthew Lloyd is taller, bigger, stronger and wiser than he was last year when he was a sensation. So how good is he going to be this year?'

Mark Harding, Sports Weekly, *13 February 1996*

I FINISHED 1995 HAPPY with where I'd gotten to, although I did think I should have played more senior games. But who doesn't think that if they haven't played them all?

My school footy career was now over, after I'd had three years playing for St Bernard's First XVIII. We'd had a good year, although we'd lost the Sun Shield to Essendon Grammar, which had Ryan Pagan and Justin Blumfield. They held me and Scotty Lucas well, and that had proved to be enough to get them across the line.

I had been a pretty big fish in the pond of schoolboy football, but I was still a very small fish in the AFL. Now, without a game of school football every Wednesday, I could start spending some more time in the gym and focus more on my AFL career.

Scott and I had always looked at Dermott Brereton and

Jason Dunstall as role models. They were the type of combination we wanted to be at Essendon. Scott had been the full-forward for the Geelong Falcons, so we expected him to play the Dunstall role, and we figured I would develop as a centre half-forward like Brereton. Over time, of course, I became the deeper forward and Scott played up the field. We were very diligent and hard-working – very level-headed for our age, I suppose.

I had finished Year 12 by late 1995 too. My TER score was only average, because my mind was elsewhere, but I wasn't too concerned about my results. I was always very conscious of finishing school, and if I was given an assignment I would go and get it done immediately. But when it came to exam time, I struggled. In my psychology exam I was being asked questions about things we'd studied all year, but I don't think I had ever seen them before. Luckily, it was multiple choice; I wrote my name on the paper and guessed my way through. We had two hours to do the exam, and twenty-five minutes in I stood up, finished. I remember there was a cheer around the hall!

I enrolled in a course that you didn't need much of a TER score for and got into that, and Mum and Dad were pleased to see that the name 'M. Lloyd, had made it into a business course'. I was getting interested in property and wondered if I could run a small business, so that's what I had chosen. I never started the course, though.

After I completed Year 12 I didn't really want to do anything but play football. But Dad sat me down and said, 'You should be doing something else as well, away from footy.' It turned out that Ricky Nixon had a friend working at Foxtel who could get me a job, and Dad thought I should take it. I wasn't sure, though.

A couple of days later, Brad said to me, 'Dad's pretty disappointed. I reckon you should look at the job.'

So I ended up working in Foxtel's accounts department in Moonee Ponds, processing people's payments, and I worked there for two and a half years. As football got more professional my work there started to get in the way and I had to give it up. Funnily, years later I was back at Foxtel on a $100,000 deal to appear on the Fox Footy Channel – quite a change from the minimum wage I got working in accounts.

We began preseason training in late 1995. Our session would start at 3.30 pm, and so Hirdy would come past and pick me up. I'd wait for him out the front of Foxtel on Mt Alexander Road, and when he arrived I'd jump in. He had a flashy red sports car, which I thought was just the best.

We'd do skills training, then running and then weights, and after it all Dad would pick me up at eight o'clock. I was three centimetres taller and three kilograms heavier than the year before, and as the year progressed I got even bigger and stronger because I was on the full training program.

I was still being left for dead in the team runs, though. Overall, I was miles off physically and aerobically for what you needed to play AFL footy. I was staggered by Hird's aerobic capacity and big Ryan O'Connor's strength. I'd be struggling to do one chin-up while he was doing them with thirty or forty kilograms hanging off his back.

My goal was to play seniors in Round 1 of the 1996 season, and I worked with Loris Bertolacci, our strength and fitness coach, to build a program to get me there. The club had no specific expectation of me as a second-year player – they were still taking a long-term view – but I wanted it now. I'd played fifteen or so reserves games, and for me that was enough.

We won the lightning premiership that year and I played in all our games and did well. I only kicked a few goals, but I was a good contributor. We celebrated our win, but we knew it was only a teaser. I reckon I was ranked somewhere between twentieth and thirtieth on Essendon's list at the time, so these preseason matches – which allowed sides to field bigger benches – were great for giving me a run.

We fell out of the Ansett Cup in the first game, which is not always a bad thing. As we continued with our preseason, I was hoping I could do enough to get a call-up for the first match against Richmond. I didn't, though, and I played in the reserves at Punt Road Oval. That day we had an American gridiron player named Dwayne Armstrong playing with us, along with a discus thrower named Werner Reiterer. Kevin Sheedy always liked to experiment. At one stage Dwayne grabbed the ball to kick it in after I'd kicked a point – it would have been funny if he wasn't my teammate.

The next week we played a curtain-raiser at the MCG. During the match, I handballed over the top to Dwayne in the goal square – all he had to do was grab it, turn around and kick the goal. But he could feel the pressure of people running at him and he spiked the ball over his head. The whole MCG crowd broke up in laughter like I've never heard at a sporting event. Those types of incidents in the reserves inspired me even more to play with the big boys; I didn't want to be there.

I was in and out of the seniors up until the time I broke my thumb. It was the night the lights went out at Waverley Park in the seniors, but I had been playing in the twos. I just fell a little awkwardly and broke it. I was devastated to have been injured, because many of our senior players were sore from their game, which ran until the twenty-two-minute mark of the third quarter, when the lights went out. The match was to be finished on the Tuesday night, and I reckon I would have got to play as an injury replacement. Instead, I was off having surgery.

I was in a heap of pain after the match. I said to Dad, 'My thumb is absolutely aching,' so we went to our local hospital on the way home. X-rays showed I had a Bennett's fracture, so when I came out I was in plaster. I went in to the club the next day and our medical staff were annoyed. 'You can't just go off and have plaster put on your hand,' they said. 'This is something you've got to do with us.' I ended up missing the next eight rounds.

Missing so much footy felt like the end of the world to me at the time. It was like my career was over. It was my first real injury in footy and I wasn't dealing with it very well.

My thumb was in plaster and the world stank to me because I wasn't playing footy. I was in a cast and working at Foxtel, and I thought, 'Nothing's going well – I may as well break off my relationship as well.' I called Lisa and asked her to meet me at the Red Rooster around the corner from Foxtel on Mt Alexander Road at Moonee Ponds.

She had just got her licence, and we were sitting in her purple Ford Festiva and she asked, 'What's wrong?' She could tell something wasn't right.

I obviously wasn't too worried about skinfolds and dieting

because I was sitting there with a big pile of chips. I said, 'I just want to focus on my footy.' It was the oldest excuse in the book, and I was lucky she just didn't say, 'Okay, it's over.'

She was very upset, though. 'I just don't understand,' she said. 'Why are we breaking up?' She ended up talking me out of it. I had told a bloke at work that I was going to break off my relationship, but I didn't have the heart to follow through with it.

Lisa was amazing. It was only one year into our relationship and she had a full understanding of me. She wasn't just going to accept me copping out. The reality was that I didn't have any reason to break up with her, other than that I was down in the dumps. I think she knew that, and she was right to keep me honest.

'He played a very dangerous brand of footy. He wasn't the flighty mid-fielder running around getting cheap kicks, he put himself in serious situations to get the ball, so he was always at physical risk.'

Merv Keane

8
Looking at a Future

> 'Matt was very good with injuries and extremely diligent and very professional about his rehab, but he was always a sook with his thumbs. I can't remember him missing a game from his back – he could carry that, sore ribs and all sorts of other things – but he could not carry his thumbs. He did – but you had to nearly push him onto the field.'
>
> *Dr Bruce Reid, Essendon Club Doctor*

IN 1996, BEFORE I got injured, I had played in Rounds 2, 3, 5 and 9. Ricky Nixon and my parents began to talk to Danny Corcoran and Sheeds about my future at Essendon, because we weren't very happy that I was going in and out of the seniors.

'Look,' they said, 'if he can't be given opportunities, do you reckon he should go elsewhere?'

'No, no – he's the future of our footy club,' was their reply.

Of course, I was sixteen when I started and I was still only seventeen, but I was there to play AFL footy.

Che Cockatoo-Collins was having a pretty average run in the early part of 1996, while I was regularly kicking fours and fives in the reserves; I was wondering why I couldn't get his spot. Sheeds said he was trying not to wear me out. He pulled me aside one day. 'Roger Merrett,' he said. 'I reckon I burnt him out at a young age. I'm not going to do the same to you.'

Ricky said to Dad that he thought I should move onto a $50,000 base in 1997, but Dad told him to ask for $75,000. When we were at a dinner with Sheeds and Danny, Ricky said, 'Sheeds, we're not happy,' and Sheeds said, 'Next year, he's two years in, he'll get his opportunity, he'll play.' Then Ricky raised the $75,000 figure. 'No problems,' was the reply. We could have even asked for more, I reckon, and we would have got it.

My first game back after my thumb injury was in the reserves in Round 18. That week, the seniors got beaten in Perth by a goal after scoring only one point in the final quarter. We had a big injury list at the time but Sheeds was angry with the team's effort against the Eagles, so I was promoted after playing only one match in the reserves. Mark Mercuri had been suspended for hitting Peter Matera, and Peter Berbakov was dropped, so in came Peter Somerville and me.

In Round 19 we faced Adelaide at Optus Oval, and I decided to wear a glove to protect my thumb. As we were walking to our positions on the ground, Hirdy said to me, 'Don't worry about the rest of us forwards – you've just got to let yourself go.' That was exactly what I needed to hear from a bloke I idolised. 'I'm going to start standing tall here,' I thought. Hirdy was on his way to winning the Brownlow Medal, so for him to say that to me gave me a lot of confidence.

I got a ride on Nigel Smart's back early in the first quarter, and instead of just falling off him, I ground my knee into his head as I was coming down. It was a sign of my confidence that day. I was taking big grabs, playing on and baulking. I had a big day out, winning my first best on ground. I kicked seven goals, took thirteen marks and had more than thirty disposals. It was a massive, massive day – my first breakout game.

What Hirdy said to me that day stuck with me, and when I became a leader on the forward line and at the club it was always in my mind. When I saw that players around me were nervous or not wanting to get in my way – guys like Scott Gumbleton and Michael Hurley – I'd say the same thing to them to try to ease their nerves so that they weren't as hesitant as I was when I started.

After that, Hirdy and I started to form a bit of a bond. A couple of weeks later I kicked the sealer near the end of a game against Sydney. It was my third for the day. Hirdy picked me up, shouting, 'You superstar!' Just the fact the he was accepting me in the side was great for my confidence, and as a result my output started to pick up.

I had three good games in a row and then was a bit ordinary against Footscray in Round 22. I was starting to think of myself as a senior footballer by this time, so I got quite a shock when Kevin Sheedy walked in after our three-point win and said, 'Lloyd, come over here. You're under the pump. It's the selectors – you need to give me a good one this week because I want to pick you.' I could sense that there were others lined up for my spot, and from that day on I knew that I always had to earn my spot, week in, week out.

It may have been Sheeds' way of saying, 'Come on, we

need a big one from you this week.' He had hardly said a bad word to me to that stage of my career. He was telling me I hadn't had a good game, but he always knew how to say things positively. Sheeds told me a story of how Kevin Bartlett would respond to a poor game. 'Bartlett would say, "I was quiet today but watch me kick five next week".' Sheeds wanted me to feel good about myself because he believed in me. I didn't have many deep conversations with him about it, but I knew he was on my side and behind me.

After finishing the home-and-away season in sixth place, we had to travel to Brisbane to play the third-placed Lions in a Qualifying Final. We didn't travel well as a team. I played on a half-forward flank and didn't kick a goal, but I was part of a chain of play near the end of the match that could have changed the result. Ricky Olarenshaw kicked it to me and then I went long to Gavin Wanganeen, who hit the post with his shot. A goal would have won us the game, but instead we went down by a point.

Our next match was a Semi Final against the Eagles at the MCG. We were fortunate because an anomaly in the finals fixtures meant a game had to be played in Melbourne, West Coast was forced to play us at the MCG instead of at Subiaco. We smashed them in front of 85,000 people, which was a huge result as they had had a big win against Carlton in their Qualifying Final the week before.

Sheeds got the scarf and jacket wave going at the end of this match – he did it for the first time in 1993 when Paul Salmon kicked the winning goal against them. He was forever the showman and turned it into a traditional thing for Essendon–Eagles games, a bit like Aka's handstands. I guess

I didn't understand that about Sheedy at the time; all I wanted to do was play footy, and there was our coach wanting us to have a world presence – he wanted us to be like Manchester United. He wanted all the black-and-red teams around the world to unite, and he's doing a similar thing at the moment with the Giants in Sydney. He thinks big.

There weren't many assistant coaches in those days, so Sheeds pretty much had charge of the whole squad, and he was as passionate about promoting his club as he was winning games of football. We were a powerhouse side, though, so no one would have said to him, 'Come on, pull back, we've got a game to be won here.' We were still winning and we had 85,000 fans flock to the MCG to watch us play against an interstate team, so it was hard to argue with his approach.

After beating the Eagles, we were through to a Preliminary Final against Sydney at the SCG, while North played Brisbane at the MCG. There were 41,000 at the SCG that night but it felt and sounded like a million. It is such as awesome place to play footy, especially compared with ANZ Stadium, which is soulless. Our reserves side had already qualified for their Grand Final, and I had played enough games to be allowed to qualify for that, so I went to Sydney knowing that I would be playing in a Grand Final regardless of the outcome.

It was a cold night but the game was hot and fierce. I was playing as a half-forward and was a little bit lost; because the SCG is so small the half-forwards often get bypassed. This was only the second interstate match of my career; my first had been our Qualifying Final a couple of weeks beforehand. Mum and Dad had flown up so they could watch me play, as they always did.

The crowd was one-sided, as you'd expect, and the noise for Sydney – and for Tony 'Plugger' Lockett, in particular – was deafening. They'd been craving success for such a long time and the build-up had been huge. As we ran onto the ground I remember thinking, 'What am I heading into here?' It was intense.

I felt out of my depth in this cauldron. In the first quarter I was on and off the bench, but I was desperate to force my will onto the game. I can't recall who my direct opponent was; there were players like Plugger, Mark Bayes and big Andrew Dunkley running around. Dunkley had a run-in with Hirdy that night and had to get a court injunction in order to play the next week, while Hirdy had a black eye when he won his Brownlow Medal a couple of nights later.

In the second quarter, an Essendon player – I can't recall who it was – was looking to run with the footy but Bayes was chasing him. Because I couldn't find the footy in this game, I figured I could make an impact by laying a big hip and shoulder. I did and we both hit the ground. I felt winded and I couldn't catch my breath afterwards.

At half time Sheeds was ranting and raving because the game was still in the balance – we hadn't kicked a goal in the second quarter. But I was still struggling for breath. I spent most of the break with our club doctor, Bruce Reid.

'Reidy, I can hardly breathe here,' I said.

'No, no, I reckon you're just badly winded,' he replied. 'I reckon you're nervous. Just relax – you'll be right.'

I went back on after half time but I had to come straight back off. I found the doc again. 'Reidy, I still can't breathe.'

He took a look at me again, asked a few questions and

then organised an ambulance to take me to hospital. So I headed off with our physio, Paul Wise, before the game was even over. We went to some hospital in Kings Cross, and the conditions were the worst you could imagine. The pain was excruciating, and there was this woman who kept popping her head around my curtain, saying, 'I want drugs! Give me drugs!' Paul shut the curtain and all I could hear was people screaming for drugs in this Kings Cross hospital on a Saturday night.

A doctor came in and gave me a shot of morphine for the pain and it instantly subsided. He said, 'Just do a few tests for me.' I had to hop on one leg, which felt okay. He said, 'I reckon you're right to go home.'

We had heard by this stage that Essendon had lost by a point – which Plugger kicked after the siren – so there was no need for me to go back to the ground. We headed back to the team hotel and I saw Hirdy there. He was having a beer in the foyer, and he took me through the game. I could hear other players saying, 'He's not looking too good,' and I was a bit vague because the pain was starting to come back.

Mum and Dad had no idea about the seriousness of my knock and had watched the rest of the game, but they came back to visit me at the hotel after the match. They took me upstairs and put me to bed and stayed with me. After a while, Mum had to help me up so I could go to the toilet. I had my head tilted over on the toilet and I called Mum in. She said, 'You're white as a ghost – I reckon I need to call the doctor.'

I looked down and saw that the toilet was full of blood.

Mum called Reidy up, and he only had to ask me one question: 'Is your shoulder sore?'

Through all the other pain, I could feel my shoulder hurting. Reidy immediately knew I had injured my spleen, so he called another ambulance.

At the hospital I had to drink the most disgusting thing I have ever tasted and they did some scans, which showed I had a 1.5-centimetre tear in my spleen. I also had one and a half litres of blood in my stomach. The pain was getting worse, but I was told, 'You've got to lay there and wait while we'll do some more tests.'

A little later the doctors said, 'We feel like the bleeding is stopping, which means we don't need to remove your spleen. Because you're such a young fella, you'll need it to stop you from getting flu and pneumonia. That's the good news. The bad news is you've got to tough this pain out.'

So I spent the next nine days in a hospital in Sydney just riding through the pain. I had gone into our Preliminary Final thinking, 'I'm in either an AFL Grand Final or a reserves Grand Final,' and I finished it abusing nurses and my parents because I was in such agony. The pain was indescribable.

The worst thing was that I was wasting away – I dropped to seventy-six kilograms. Lisa flew up to visit me. We were getting more serious at that stage but we were usually seeing each other only once or so a week. 'She must be keen if she's flying up to Sydney to see me,' I thought. It was a pleasant surprise though.

When it was time for me to go home, the club flew Dad up and we went home business class, so they did everything they could to look after us. But I was told that I could not undertake any contact sport while my spleen was repairing itself, which meant I wouldn't be able to train for three months.

Bruce Reid still rates it as one of the three worst injuries he has seen in his time in football. He said I could have died if I hadn't gone back to the hospital that night.

I already had my contract for the next few seasons in place. And from the way the guys at the club had worked so hard to look after me, I knew I'd be okay. But it certainly wasn't a nice way to finish the season. To make matters worse, we lost the reserves Grand Final too.

> 'Out of all the players I've had in thirty years, that was the most frightening injury I've seen.'
> Dr Bruce Reid, Essendon Club Doctor

9
Self versus Team

'He'd work harder than anybody thought he could and he was always looking for a more professional way in which to go about his business.'

John Quinn

AFTER SUCH A MASSIVE injury, there were plenty of concerns when I returned – not just about my physical state but also about my mental approach. I was skinnier than when I'd first started with the Bombers; we'd start dealing with that as quickly as possible, but would I be able to attack the ball in the same way?

I'd had three months of not being able to do anything physical after that fateful Preliminary Final, and leading up to Christmas I was permitted to do some low-impact exercise. I wanted to get bigger and stronger, but I still couldn't do weights.

My physical recovery was challenging, but I was torturing myself about missing training and part of the preseason. I was hungry to succeed, though, and I wasn't going to leave anything to chance. The arrival of the 1997 season couldn't come soon enough. It wasn't until a few years later that it actually dawned on me how lucky I was to be alive and to still have my spleen.

After Christmas I was starting to get the run back into my legs and to regain some weight, and it took the whole of the preseason for me to get back to a regular workload. I was nowhere near 100 per cent fitness for Round 1, though.

I'd heard the murmurs of people wondering whether I would regain the ability to back into a pack and throw myself into a game. Honestly, though, I don't think I ever held myself back at all. At my first skills session when I returned to full training, it was clear there were no lasting mental scars.

Both our club doctors, Bruce Reid and Ian Reynolds, had assured me that it would take a rare hit to open up the wound in my spleen, and it would have to hit exactly the same spot. Hearing that gave me all the confidence I needed. The doctors and physios were absolutely brilliant in helping me recover, both physically and mentally. We were spoilt at Essendon with the quality of people we had in that department; that was a big reason why we were such a great club.

We were beaten in the first round of the Ansett Cup, so from then on it was just practice matches. That was good for me. The reality is that you'd rather win Round 1 of the main season than win the whole preseason comp, which is mainly about trialling changes to your game plan and preparing your players. If you win, it's a bonus.

My form in the preseason comp was never a good indicator of my season ahead, but I was a confidence player and so I liked heading into Round 1 with some good performances under my belt. My best preseason was in 2001, and I think that ended up as my best regular season too. I hit Round 1 that year thinking, 'Gee, I'm going to be pretty hard to stop here, and so is the team.'

By the time Round 1 of 1997 arrived, I was fully fit and healthy again. But Sheeds wasn't ready to give me a run in the seniors so I played in the twos. I hadn't played for three months, so it was always going to be a big call to play me first-up. Some players come back from layoffs better than others. As a key forward, I needed to have the timing of my leads just right and I needed to feel the ball in my hands. I needed continuity.

It felt great to be back on the ground, even if it was just the reserves. That game was against Carlton, and I kicked a bag. During the match, I felt for the first time that I was starting to get above the reserves standard. I felt like I was a match-winner that day.

So I was furious with Sheeds when he didn't pick me for Round 2. As it turned out, my Achilles was sore and I missed the weekend anyway, and I was afraid that it was going to hold me from getting back in the senior team for weeks. I was okay for Round 3, though, and was selected as an emergency for the seniors against North Melbourne.

We had a few injury worries that week, so when I saw Mark Mercuri limping off the training track on the Thursday night, I thought I was a chance. He was having some groin issues and had to pull out, and suddenly I was back in the team. We had a good win by forty points and I kicked three goals in the last quarter, giving me four for the game, which really boosted my confidence.

It was like I had arrived as a senior footballer. We'd lined up against North, the team that had taught me about playing football in a man's world, and I had done well. Not only had I battled Dean Laidley early on in my career, I'd once had a run-in with Wayne Carey too. I had gone to run through him but pulled out at the last minute, thinking, 'What am I doing? He weighs twenty kilograms more than me!' Carey got stuck into me: 'You weak prick! You dogged it!' He gave it to me for the rest of the day.

So to kick four against North – in a winning team – was as good a result as I could have hoped for. It was the start of a great season for me, although I still wasn't sure that being a full-forward was the best spot for me.

I had always looked at Chris Grant and Wayne Carey as two of the elite players of the competition, and I wanted to be like them: goal-kicking centre half-forwards who were flexible enough to play both ends when needed. My real strength, though, was that I could beat a guy one-on-one by using my body or by timing my leads well, and those skills weren't as important at centre half-forward, where you're in a lot more traffic.

I had never really played full-forward in the juniors but that was where I was starting to carve my niche in the AFL. That was the vacancy in the team that Sheeds wanted me to fill, and although I didn't know it at the time, it was probably also my ideal position. I developed a real passion for the role, and I loved kicking goals.

I started to be targeted by opposition players around that time, and not just the full-backs. In Round 4 we played Geelong. At one stage during the match I flew for a mark, and as I was falling forward Garry 'Buddha' Hocking cocked his elbow and caught me with it. Pain knifed through my cheekbone area. I was filthy with him, as it wasn't the first time Buddha had got me.

He was cited for it but my anger didn't subside. Our footy manager, Danny Corcoran, said to me that if I was so against what he had done, I should be honest at the tribunal about what had happened. So at the tribunal on the Monday night I told the panel how Buddha had cocked his elbow and hit me, how sore my cheekbone was and how there was no need for that type of act on the football field.

All the time I was giving evidence, Buddha was staring me down with the angriest eyes I'd ever seen – he was furious. Once my evidence was given, I was able to leave the tribunal and go home, while he had to stay to hear the verdict. The hearing was at Southbank but I couldn't find my car in the multi-level car park. After looking around for fifteen minutes or so, I was so petrified that Buddha would be leaving soon too – with a hefty suspension and full of rage – so I started ducking behind other cars whenever I heard someone coming past. This went on for five minutes or so until I eventually found my car.

As it turned out, Buddha actually beat the charge, but the experience taught me never to rat on a fellow player.

I told that story recently on SEN and everyone found it hilarious – even Buddha, who we replayed it to before a match involving Port Adelaide, where he is now an assistant coach. He said he had never seen anyone more scared than I was in that hearing. Looking back now, it's just hilarious to think about, but it wasn't so funny when I was hiding behind cars as a skinny nineteen-year-old.

So, after kicking four goals in my first game for the season and then three in my second, I then bagged two and one in Rounds 5 and 6. In Round 7 I kicked five against Adelaide. I wasn't getting the best backman in each team, so I had guys like Martin Pike playing on me rather than Mick Martyn, but that started to change during the course of the season.

That year I played twenty games in a row and felt like a really important part of the side. As my performances grew, I started to put a lot of undue pressure on myself, as did the press, which I was still quite naive about.

If I was playing a little quietly, I used to think, 'I've got to do more to make this a respectable game.' It was frustrating when people didn't recognise my efforts around the ground. As my goalkicking seemed to be the only thing people judged me on, my thought process was that I needed to make sure I kicked goals, and lots of them.

Supporters would come up to me after a game and say, 'Ah, you only got two today.' Even our own fans weren't seeing it when I set up other goals. Although I still wasn't totally confident of my spot in the side – even though, in hindsight, I should have been – I was still playing for myself a little bit then. It didn't mean I wasn't putting in for the team, but if we lost and I'd had a good game, I'd be happy.

So I was really pleased to kick six on a Friday night against the Western Bulldogs, even though we lost. I played on Danny Southern, who was a tough player. His facial hair and the way he ran around, always with his chest puffed out, made him a real favourite with the Bulldog's faithful. He was a ruthless, uncompromising backman, so I was happy to have come out on top. But apart from my goals, I also contributed in other ways that I measured myself on.

I played on some other great backmen during the course of the season: Mal Michael at Collingwood, Brad Scott at Hawthorn, who wasn't tall but was as mobile and tight as a backman could be, Ben Graham at Geelong, who was close-checking but also a great athlete and footballer, Ben Hart at Adelaide, not to mention Mick Martyn, Steve Kretiuk, Andrew Dunkley and the Eagles' Ashley McIntosh, who, in his prime, was one of the best defenders I ever played on.

Late in the season I was starting to develop the ability to grab a game by the scruff of the neck, as I had dreamed of doing since I first watched Bernie Quinlan in the 1980s. I kicked fourteen goals over our last three games of 1997, against Collingwood, Brisbane and Adelaide.

Brisbane was playing as the Lions by then, having taken over Fitzroy at the end of 1996. In our Round 21 match they really needed to stop me, and so they moved Alastair Lynch onto to me to try to shut me down. He was a monster of a man and one of my heroes from my days following Fitzroy, even though he had joined Brisbane before the takeover. It was good, though, to sense that they believed I was the forward at Essendon they had to stop.

Hirdy was pretty much out for the whole 1997 season with stress fractures, which meant that Scotty Lucas and I – both still teenagers – were leading our forward line. Our dream of being the centre half-forward/full-forward combination was now a reality.

It was an up-and-down year for the club, though, and we ended up with nine wins and finished fourteenth. We only missed the finals by a win and half but we'd been hammered a few times and had a poor percentage.

Our last game for the year was against Adelaide at Princes Park. It was Mark Harvey's final match, and it was also the day Princess Diana died. Mark was a great role model for me as a younger player. He was in tears before the game – he just couldn't control himself. I was sitting there thinking about the end of a long year, my twentieth game in a row, and I looked at him and thought, 'I'd love to win for Harvs. I would love to put in a big performance for him.' It was the first time, really, that I stopped thinking purely about my own performance and career. I began to see that playing football was about more than just myself.

The Crows were flying at that time, and they would end up winning the flag that year. I lined up on Ben Hart, who I really rated as a full-back. By now, getting the opposition's best defender was bringing out the best in me. I loved the challenge.

It was a tight match. The Crows got the jump on us but we came home fast: we had a four-goal first half and twelve-goal second half. I managed to get the better of Ben. I wasn't confident in my leg speed, but I was reading the play well and taking marks in the way Sheeds had taught me, so it was all coming together. I kicked the winning goal, which was an amazing buzz, especially as it meant we celebrated Harvs' last game in a fitting way.

Even though we missed the finals, I felt like I'd had a good season individually. I had been aiming to kick three goals a game. A season of sixty goals plus is a good return for a full-forward, and in any season there will only be four or five blokes who do that. In 1997 Tony Modra won the Coleman Medal with eighty-four goals, while Sav Rocca, Jason Heatley and Scott Cummings (who was by then with Port Adelaide) all kicked more goals than me, but I was number five. I had jumped from an eleven-game, eighteen-goal season in 1996 to twenty games and sixty-three goals in 1997. It was a massive step up. I also finished third in our best and fairest.

I went to watch as many finals as I could that year. I was craving the big stage. I'd played in the finals in 1995 and 1996 and I just loved the atmosphere, and that was where I felt I should be.

I went to the Grand Final and watched Adelaide beat St Kilda. I had played with Kane Johnson in the Victorian Teal Cup squad, and I watched him during the game and hoped it would all go well for him. In the end, I thought he was one of Adelaide's best three players. I didn't take my eyes off him after the siren and saw him hugging players and rolling on the ground in pure elation. That success was what I *really* wanted.

It was the same for the Victorian state games. As a kid, I'd watched them and had desperately wanted to play in them one day. After watching Teddy Whitten go around the MCG with his son in a car before the 1995 game and seeing a star-studded Victoria side destroy the Croweaters that day, I craved to one day be part of that elite environment. During the 1997 season that dream had come true when I played for the Big V after only twenty-three senior games.

I'd had a couple of big matches leading into the selection period and I got the call-up. It was perfect timing on my part. I lined up in a pocket next to Stewart Loewe and we went to Football Park and played South Australia. It was an unbelievable atmosphere. The intensity just blew me away, and I imagined that playing in a Grand Final would be similar. I kicked three goals in the first quarter, and we won by less than a kick. I finished with just three for the day, mind you, but I was so happy to have worn the Big V jumper.

I was on the bench when the game finished, and I wish now that I'd taken my tracksuit off for the photos so I could see my Victorian jumper. But there I was with players like Garry Hocking and Robert Harvey, who had hit me lace-out on the chest that night. It was a special match, and a turning point in my career. Playing for Victoria gave me a lot of confidence in myself as an emerging player.

I'd played representative footy before at junior level, but getting a spot in the Big V was great. I loved the concept of playing for your state, and I still do. This was the pinnacle. These were the best footballers in the land, and playing with them was such an honour. A couple of years later, the great players were walking away from the concept and it died.

I had come a long way in a season. I had gone from getting the second- or third-best defender to getting the best. I had tripled my goal output, played for Victoria and secured my spot in the side. Now I had to take the next step, and that meant team success and a Premiership.

> 'I think the real turnaround game for him was the last game of 1997 when he kicked seven or so against Adelaide at Princes Park. We realised we had a pretty special player on our hands then.'
>
> *James Hird*

10

Part of the Team

'I share everybody's thoughts on Matthew. He's got a very bright future and he's certainly got "the package". He's got all the moves, he's a tremendous reader of the ball into the forward line and the side is giving him plenty of space to work in.'

Paul Salmon, Herald Sun, *3 March 1998*

IN 1998 I SET myself the aim of kicking more goals than I had the year before. From three goals a game, I wanted to get to four a game, or one a quarter. I was chasing consistency. That meant I had to nail the preseason and start the season bigger and stronger. And I did.

I was more confident now because I felt like I belonged. I was ecstatic to have finished in the top three in an AFL team's best and fairest – that was huge for me at the time – and I could tell Essendon was happy with what I had produced in 1997. I had received a big pay hike after the 1997 season, and I was also starting to make some income off-field. I could get between $500 and $1000 in addition to my pay from Essendon for turning up at a function. I had picked up a Nike boot contract and was appearing on footy shows in the media. For a shy guy like me, it was flattering, and Ricky had put me through some basic media training to make sure I was able to cope.

By this time, the media was no longer talking about the risk Essendon had taken in doing the Tony Delaney deal; in fact, they were now saying how smart the club had been. I was following Tony's career, but he was having so many soft-tissue injuries that he wasn't performing as well as he would have liked.

I was starting to put on some good size after three years in the gym – I was probably up to around ninety kilograms by then – but my mindset was always more important to my performance than my physical condition. I was a confidence player. I needed that one early touch, one early mark and one early goal, and then the shackles would be off and I knew I'd be in for a big match.

My fear of failure meant I always prepared well. I suppose I was like a batsman in cricket. No matter what form you carry out to the wicket and no matter how good you feel on the day, you still don't know what the first ball is going to bring. I always had a million things running through my head before the siren had even been sounded.

I knew that, this year, my opponents would be coming for me. I had started the 1997 season under the radar of the other clubs, but that wasn't going to happen in 1998. I was now the main focal point of the Essendon forward line after my third season of football.

As a team, we felt we could do much better in 1998. I sensed over that summer that Sheeds believed it was time to transition some of our older players out and to give the younger guys – such as Justin Blumfield, Blake Caracella and Chris Heffernan, as well as Scott Lucas – consistent game time.

As my career progressed, I started to notice when eras at football clubs were coming to an end and when older players were on the wane, but back then I was oblivious to anything other than what I was doing. But Sheeds had decided to start afresh with a newish batch of players; he saw that the bulk of our champion 1993 side wasn't going to be a part of the next Essendon Premiership.

The core of the 1998 team was a little reminiscent of the 'Baby Bombers' of 1993: half our side was new since 1995. Apart from me, there was Caracella, Lucas, Gary Moorcroft, Blumfield, Sean Wellman and Paul Barnard. We also picked up Heffernan and Jason Johnson, who were both selected with compensation picks when we lost Gavin Wanganeen and Scott Cummings to Port Adelaide, and Mark Bolton and Dean Solomon joined us that year too. So much youth at the club meant there was an incredible energy around the place.

That youth was balanced out with players like James Hird, who was our new captain, and Michael Long, both of whom were coming back from injury. There was also Ricky Olarenshaw, Dustin Fletcher – who was still so young anyway – Steve Alessio, Dean Wallis, Peter Somerville, Darren Bewick and Gary O'Donnell.

Sheeds wasn't silly enough to think he could just wipe out a lot of the older players in one hit. Instead, he phased a few out until he had a really good balance of youth and experience. Player-management was one of Sheedy's great strengths. He had foresight for both individuals and for the team in general. I think that this was the main reason he lasted twenty-seven years as Essendon coach – he was able to move with the times, understand the need to refresh and keep looking to the future.

Some people claimed Sheedy had been tanking in 1997 when he realised we weren't going to make the finals, but I don't believe that was the case. He had a bunch of young guys and he wanted to see what they could do, and it was those young guys on the field at the end of 1997 who formed the nucleus of the great side that we became. As it turned out, we beat the eventual Premiers in the final round of 1997, which was a sign of things to come.

So in early 1998 the structure of our new-look side was coming together. I was the bona fide full-forward, while Scotty Lucas was the centre half-forward or centre half-back, depending on the needs of the team. Blumfield and Caracella were starting to play consistently and Moorcroft was coming on strong too. Wellman and Barnard, who had come to the club in 1996 as part of the deal that saw Paul Salmon leave, were both turning into very good players – Wellman was as good a centre half-back as we had during my time at Essendon. As a team, we knew we could perform much better in 1998. Nothing but finals footy was going to keep us happy.

The preseason started well. We played Hawthorn first in an Ansett Cup match and I lined up on Mark Graham, who was a lightly framed backman who often got the job on bigger forwards. I kicked five in the first quarter of that game and was flying for everything. I took a few big grabs and was in one of those unstoppable frames of mind where I was free in my thoughts. By the end of the game I had ten goals, the first double-figure haul of my career.

My brother Brad played for Hawthorn in that game, but he got knocked out early in that match after a slinging tackle from Damien Hardwick. Brad didn't remember too much about the match afterwards, but he was happy for me.

I received a fair bit of attention after my performance, and after a week of 'going down media street', as Denis Pagan used to say, Micky Martyn and a powerful North Melbourne side were waiting for me and I went from chocolates to boiled lollies. Mick was a guy who, early on in my career, really had it over me. I didn't kick a goal that night and we got done. From ten goals to zero in just a few days!

Still, I approached the season feeling confident. My first appearance on *The Footy Show* came in the lead-up to Round 1, in which we would face Richmond. I was trying to be a bit entertaining and show some humour, which was a side of me people generally didn't get to see. In hindsight, I should have left the jokes to Sam Newman.

Matthew Richardson was carrying a shoulder injury into the game, and I said, with a little smirk, 'If Richo shows up to play, Dean Wallis will be waiting for him and will no doubt test out his shoulder.'

Eddie McGuire leapt on my comment, saying, 'Oh, Matthew Lloyd has just said that Dean Wallis is going to test out Richo's shoulder,' and he blew it up into a big thing.

I went home and couldn't sleep. I was thinking, 'What have I said here? What are the coaches going to say?' I didn't realise the Richmond side would use my comments as motivation for themselves to teach me and Essendon a lesson.

At the match, I headed down to the goal square after the coin toss, passing the Richmond midfield group on my way. Paul Broderick came up to me and said, 'You'll be lucky if you can walk off this ground today – we'll have you carried off.'

I could see I was in for a torrid time. Standing at full-forward, I saw the long hair of Paul Bulluss charging towards me. He crashed into me and said, 'You're in for a big day.'

My mindset changed, and I thought, 'I'll fight fire with fire here.' I felt stronger than before and I believed in myself. I knew I had to perform, whatever came my way.

Richmond really set out to test me physically. Bulluss was a good old-fashioned backman – he was dropping his knees into me and mouthing off all the time. He was belting me in the stomach, corking me with his elbow, whacking me in the arm! I kicked three in the second quarter and felt I was standing up to all the physical treatment the Tigers were handing out.

Bulluss continued, though, and I turned to him during the third quarter and said, 'Every time you whack me, I'm going after one of your teammates.'

He stared back at me and hit me again at the next contest. Not long after that, Matthew Knights dished off a handball and I hit him hard with a hip-and-shoulder. He was down and out for five or ten seconds. I turned back to Bulluss and said, 'I told you that was going to happen.'

I didn't mind at all if I hurt someone with a fair and square hip-and-shoulder. In fact, if I hit a player, I wanted to hurt him – I wanted him to feel it. I liked the physical side of the game. Having had all sorts of tactics tried on me since my junior years, I was starting to stand up for myself.

We ended up losing the game, but I felt like I had got through a football war. When I took my jumper off after the game I had scratches all over my body and I knew I'd done well to stand up to the barrage that I took that day. So while it was disappointing that we lost, I took a fair bit of satisfaction out of the match – although I did realise I had to be more careful with what I said in the media. I appeared seven more times on *The Footy Show* that year but I wasn't very controversial after my first outing.

Sheeds was committed to blooding our younger players, and that wasn't always the best option in the short term. We were inconsistent. By Round 7 we had two wins and five losses and were sitting down near the bottom of the ladder, above only Hawthorn, Brisbane and Carlton. Then we won four in a row and were in the eight, and the second half of our season was pretty good.

My form early in the season was okay. After kicking four goals against Richmond in Round 1, I managed five against St Kilda the next week. In Round 3 we faced Carlton and won by a point, although I butchered my chances and kicked 1.5. I was virtually in tears at the end of the match. But worse was to come – the next week I kicked 0.4 in a loss to Freo at Waverley Park.

So in two weeks I had 1.9 and I was starting to doubt myself. Scott Lucas had a huge game against Fremantle with six goals and I couldn't get one. Suddenly my kicking was being questioned and I was questioning myself.

Luckily, Mum and Dad were there to support me. I was still living at home then, and they reiterated to me that it would have been more worrying if I wasn't even getting the shots at goal. 'You're still getting plenty of the footy,' they said. 'Things will turn.'

In 1997 I had kicked 63.30, so my accuracy had been pretty good, but after four rounds of 1998 I had 10.11 – more behinds than goals. If I missed my first shot, I knew I was in trouble for the day. As I lined it up, my legs would be like jelly or cement, one or the other. Actually, it was a pleasant surprise if I had the ball early in a match at that stage of my career, because at the start of every game my body would feel very limited in movement, due to the huge nerves I suffered from.

I always worried about my goalkicking. One year, during an Anzac Day Game, Sheeds sent me out at quarter time to practice kicking for goal while he addressed the team because he was so furious about some easy shots I'd missed. It was more nerve-wracking than kicking for goal in the game – every single person in the stadium was cheering or booing each kick I had.

It was around this time that I started working on my goalkicking with David Wheadon, an assistant coach, and Jeff Simons, our sports psychologist. David put together a video of Tony Lockett kicking for goal on one side of the screen and me on the other. We discovered that my ball drop was far too high compared to that of Lockett, whom we regarded as the best kick for goal in the game. I was a long, long way behind, and I had no routine whatsoever.

Jeff realised that I was stabbing at the footy as I kicked and that my knee was bent. Especially when I was nervous, I would try to steer the ball through the goals, which affected the trajectory of the football. Jeff and David encouraged me to kick through the ball and gain greater momentum during my run-up. With that — and with plenty of practice — I should improve my accuracy.

I broke my goalkicking process down and developed a system. I tried to program myself to do the same thing with every set shot at goal. Even in the AFL, few players have a routine with their goalkicking, which is obviously an aspect of the game that wins you matches. Tony Lockett once said to me that for every ten shots you have, you should kick seven or eight. That stat never left my mind from that point on.

After I had taken a mark, I'd walk back to the point I was going to kick from and put the ball on the ground. It was fourteen paces back, but I didn't need to pace it out because I could do it visually and subconsciously. With the ball on the ground, I'd pull my socks up, straighten my shorts and tuck in my jumper.

I always checked my laces, too. They had to be nice and tight and in the perfect position. In fact, I was paranoid about them. The knots couldn't be too big and they had to be at a certain level. Even before a game, I would be continuously sorting out my laces so they were perfect when I ran out.

Then I would throw some grass up in the air. Altogether, that took about forty-five seconds. As frustrating as it was for others — and a rule change came about as a result of what I was doing — that pause was what I needed mentally. I used to get my breathing steady and drop my heartrate, because usually I had worked pretty hard just to get my hands on the ball. Now that I had it, I was determined to make the most of the scoring opportunity.

So, the grass-throwing pause was partly a ploy to let my body settle — I didn't want my kick to feel fatigued, especially if it was a long one. But it was also practical. If we were playing at Waverley Park or the MCG, I needed to take the wind into account and think about where I was going to aim my kick. I had started testing the wind that way when I was playing for the Western Jets at Ballarat or Bendigo, where there were no stands to provide protection. I found it helped when it was a windy day, but it didn't become a consistent part of my goalkicking routine until 1998.

From there, I just tried to kick through the football. I'd pick out a letter on the advertising boards on the first level of the stand behind the goals. I'd study it, focus on it for the first four or five steps, walking in, and then I'd build my momentum up and switch my focus to the ball drop. I knew I was kicking well when I could keep the ball as still as possible while I guided it onto my foot, and I'd try not to lift my head until after I had finished the kick.

When I wasn't kicking well, the first thing I did was lift my head to see where the ball was going. That meant I wasn't finishing my routine. For me, everything became so structured that I was able to say what part of the football I had hit. If I missed a shot, I could recall later exactly what I'd done wrong. I became quite anal about every shot for goal.

After my terrible game against Fremantle in Round 4 of 1998, I wanted to make sure I felt good going into the next game, which was the big Anzac Day clash against Collingwood. We had a huge rivalry with the Magpies. The fire in our belly came partly from the Bombers letting them win the 1990 flag – the entire competition had poured scorn on Essendon for that. One of the big lines early in my time at Essendon was: 'Who kicked five goals in the 1990 Grand

Final? Essendon!' But the Anzac Day match raised the rivalry to another level.

In many ways, though, the significance of the day overshadowed our rivalry with Collingwood. Sheeds wanted us to understand the Anzac legend – perhaps he hoped some of their spirit would rub off on us and we'd become better people for it. For him, it was about much more than just football. We would have a service at the War Memorial a day or two before the game, so it was a pretty emotional time for all of us.

The match was like a Grand Final to us. Over the years we did put in a few shockers, but at other times we performed above ourselves. Just as Bomber Thompson and Gary O'Donnell had a hatred of Carlton, James Hird had it for Collingwood, and his record against them speaks for itself. There were times on Anzac Day where he looked like he was going to beat them on his own.

In the 1998 clash the first ball hit my hands well, my strike of the ball was good and I kicked an early goal. So I settled well and kicked four straight for the day, although we went down by twenty points.

The next week against the Bulldogs, however, I barely got a touch. I had four kicks in all playing against Steve Kretiuk, who was pinching and punching me all day. I gave away three free kicks as I let my frustration get the better of me. I realised I still had a lot to learn, now that more and more attention was being paid to me. Kretiuk had got inside my head, intimidated me and beaten me hands down.

After the match, Dean Wallis who was out injured at the time and Mark Harvey (who was now an assistant coach) took me aside. Big man Ryan O'Connor had followed me around to protect me the whole game, out of the forward pocket, and I thought they were both coming to console me. Instead, they said, 'You could be chewed up and spat out of the system if you don't start toughening up and doing something about the treatment you put up with today.' I got a shock, but I quickly realised that they were right not to give me the sympathy I was looking for. This was a man's game and I needed to harden up.

They really gave me a stern talking-to about the physicality I needed to show on the field. People around the competition were saying, 'If you can get on top of Lloyd – mentally or physically – you can beat him.' I decided I wouldn't let that perception define me as a player.

Things started to improve from Round 9 onwards, when I kicked three against Melbourne. I found my confidence and my form and was in pretty good touch from that time on. As the home-and-away season drew to a close, we were battling it out with Richmond, Adelaide and West Coast for the last spots in the top eight.

On the Saturday of Round 22, it appeared that we needed to beat Geelong in order to play finals. I kicked six and Hirdy had a big day too, but we lost by ten points. That meant we needed Melbourne to beat Richmond on the Sunday or our season was over.

I went down to Windy Hill with the rest of the team to watch our reserves play, and the beers were on ice in the esky. We had the radio on, and as the day unfolded it was clear that Melbourne would have a big win over the Tigers. That meant we were going to have a final to play, so the beers remained unopened.

It was first versus eighth that year, so we had a big challenge first-up against North Melbourne, and that was the famous 'marshmallow final'. I was playing on my old nemesis, Mick Martyn. All the North fans brought marshmallows to the game and were flipping them at Sheeds as he walked to the bench.

Mick did a number on me again and held me to one goal, so Sheeds sent me to play at centre half-back on Carey for the last quarter, which was a good experience. It was like when he sent me to watch Chris Grant, only this time I was a lot closer to the action.

We went down by eighteen points, but we actually went away from the game feeling pretty good. We knew we weren't flag contenders that year but we had challenged the flag favourites in a final. Sheeds wasn't satisfied with our performance, though, so we knew we'd be in for some toughening up in the 1999 preseason.

My goalkicking work had paid off well. At one stage in the second half of the year I had kicked fifteen goals without a miss, which was really pleasing after my earlier stretch of 1.9. I now had a better technique and a good routine, so my success really came down to my confidence and application.

Tony Lockett had won the Coleman Medal with 107 goals in the regular season, and he was given the full-forward slot in the All Australian team. I was named in the forward pocket after a seventy-goal season, which meant that I was going to Ireland to play for Australia, which was a huge thrill.

I loved my state footy, and now I was about to play for my country in the return of the International Series, which hadn't been played since the 1980s. Leigh Matthews was our coach and Wayne Carey our captain. Stephen Silvagni, Robert Harvey, Nathan Buckley were all in the team – I couldn't believe the company that I was mixing with.

We won the First Test at Croke Park in Dublin by a point, with David Neitz scoring a six-pointer in the dying seconds. The Australian camp was abuzz with excitement in front of 50,000 screaming Irish fans.

At the pub after that match, Wayne Carey stood up and announced, 'Wayne Jackson's offered to put his credit card on the bar!' Jackson, the CEO of the AFL at the time, hadn't said a word but he ended up doing it due to the peer pressure. We partied for the next five or six days and, unsurprisingly, we lost the Second Test.

It was an amazing experience for me to train and play with these guys. I learnt a huge amount about why they were so good. I even soaked up the little things these players did. One night, after spending the evening in the pub, we were all set to jump in a cab back to our hotel when Robert Harvey said, 'Not for me – I'll run home. I've had a few too many beers tonight.'

When I got home from Ireland I was on top of the world. Things with Lisa were great and life was good. After such a big year, I couldn't wait to get into the 1999 season.

> 'As soon as he came in he looked like he belonged. His hands were good, he was a super kick for goal and he just fitted in. I'd say Lockett's probably the best kick for goal that I've seen, but Lloyd's not far behind him.'
>
> *Mike Sheahan*

11

Our Most Painful Loss

'When I first came to Essendon, it was significant that the first knock at my door was from James Hird and the second was from Matthew Lloyd.'

John Quinn

FOR THE 1999 SEASON, Essendon appointed a new fitness manager, John Quinn. He had never worked in football but he came to our club having previously looked after the Tasmanian Institute of Sport, and he eventually trained Olympic athletes as individuals and also the women's 400-metre relay teams that included Cathy Freeman.

John was pretty upfront about how he saw his role. He was going to toughen us up. 'You'll see me like Hitler,' he said. 'I'm going to work you blokes so hard that you're going to hate me.'

I wasn't sure what to expect, but John lived up to his promise. We were running hills and sand-dunes when no one else was. We started with skinfold measurements in the hundreds but John was expecting sixties. Over that preseason, I think we jumped the rest of the competition in fitness.

My mental perspective had changed too, and I was starting to think more about the team than myself. That was probably because I felt like I belonged in the team. I was in the leadership group and I wanted us to be a strong team. I wanted to play and win Grand Finals like some of my junior footy mates – like Kane Johnson and Shannon Grant – had done. I wanted it to be my time.

Our Ansett Cup campaign lasted only one match, and so we spent our time getting fitter and stronger and preparing for what we expected to be a big year. Hawthorn won the Ansett Cup that year and my brother Brad was a part of the team, which was great for him.

When Round 1 arrived, we hit the season at full pace. We won our first two matches, against Carlton and then North Melbourne. Importantly for me, I started with goals. I got three against Glenn Manton and then three against Mick Martyn, so I felt pretty good. But I still felt like I had more to give.

I had to step up, too, since Hirdy did his foot again against North, which was a huge blow to the team. I saw him sitting on the bench during a team huddle with tears rolling down his cheeks. Since winning the Brownlow Medal in 1996, he'd played only twenty-two matches due to injury, and this latest injury put him out for the whole 1999 season. There was real doubt whether he would be able to come back from yet another setback.

Michael Long took over as club captain, and while he wasn't as charismatic as Hirdy, if he looked you in the eye and said he wanted something from you, you'd do it. He balanced that intensity with great humour, too.

With Hirdy out, I knew I had to be more of a leader on the field. Our next game was at the MCG against Sydney. It was Dean Rioli's first match and Mark McVeigh's second, so we knew we had some good new talent coming through, but I had to stand up and lead from the front.

The Swans got the jump on us early in what started as a pretty tight game. It was four goals to two early – I kicked both of ours. Every time the ball was coming in my direction I was plucking marks in pack situations and splitting the middle with shots at goal. I was playing on Andrew Dunkley, who I rated highly, so I was pretty happy to be doing well.

I kicked four in the second quarter and went into the half-time break with six. Mark Mercuri was playing like a man possessed in 1999, as good as I'd seen even from Hird or Fletcher. He was winning the ball and taking marks above his head, and his delivery was silky smooth. With him dominating the midfield we were getting on top.

After half time, the Swans sent several different opponents to me but I was feeling unstoppable. I knew I'd only get in this frame of mind three or four times through the whole year and so I wanted to make the most of it. When I was on nine goals Mark McVeigh kicked to me and I took a strong grab in front of Gerrard Bennett on about the fifty-metre line. Bennett was arguing with the umpire about where the mark was, so I played on and put it through the middle.

My kick probably travelled about sixty to sixty-five metres, and I remember thinking, 'Yeah!' The roar of the crowd was massive because they hadn't seen a ten-goal haul by an Essendon player since the days of Paul Salmon at his peak. I ended the third quarter with eleven goals.

In the final quarter, Longy, who was an unbelievable team man, was trying to get me to fourteen goals, which was John Coleman's club record. I missed a couple when I was on thirteen, which was a bit of a choke. Darren Bewick copped some flack from the guys when he feigned like he was going to pass to me but kicked the goal himself. He loved kicking one as much as any of us. I ended up kicking 13.4 for the day.

The next day I picked up the paper and saw the headlines of 'Swans want Lloyd as new Plugger' and 'Sydney to make a million-dollar offer for Lloyd'. Tony Lockett was getting ready to retire and it sounded like the club was cashed up and wanting to make me the new face of the Swans.

I was actually having a coffee with Ricky Nixon at the time, but I didn't let the story concern me. The Swans hadn't spoken to Ricky at that stage, so there was nothing to discuss. Later in the day I was driving along Kings Way and stopped at some traffic lights. I couldn't believe it when I saw the Swans on a recovery walk. I put the sun visor down, thinking, 'They won't want to see me again right now.'

Nike ran an ad after that Swans game, reading: 'Matthew Lloyd switched to Nike boots thirteen days ago. Spooky, huh?' We went to Perth the next week and I only got one goal on Ashley McIntosh, who was a full-back I really rated. We had an absolute shocker that day; our score of 3.5 for the entire match was our lowest score in forty-four seasons. We still didn't travel well, but that performance really stung. McIntosh's boot sponsor, Fila, ran their own ad the next week: '13 one week, 1 the next, McIntosh'. It was all in good fun, except it was at my expense.

We then went on to beat Collingwood convincingly in our

annual Anzac Day clash, and I kicked six goals. They didn't have the Anzac Medal that year – it was instituted in 2000, and Mark Mercuri was given the retrospective medal for this game at the 2011 Anzac Day match.

We beat Richmond the next week but I was dirty on myself for kicking 3.5 but I also dropped a few marks I should have taken. Terry Daniher was one of our assistant coaches at this time, and he used to love getting me out to practise my pack marking. He was just as competitive then as he was when he was playing, so I always knew I was in for a good session when he said, 'I reckon you've got to work on your marking.'

The day before we were to play Melbourne, Terry and I were practising. He was whacking my arms to put me off balance like how a defender would, and I hurt one of my fingers. I wasn't going to say I'd had enough, though, so we kept going. I started to favour the hand with the sore finger, and two balls later I dislocated my finger.

Terry was horrified; he really didn't want have to tell the coach or physios that he'd dislocated the full-forward's fingers the day before a match. So he tried to pop it back into place on his own. The pain was incredible – I instantly had a headache and my hand was throbbing.

Eventually, Terry took me to the physio. 'He'll be right, won't he?' he asked. 'You can strap 'em up,' he said in typical TD style.

The physio got my finger back into place straightaway, but we found out later that Terry had done a bit of structural damage to the joint. The physio worked out a way of strapping it to allow me to play the next day, however, and I played on Marcus Seecamp of the Demons. I couldn't take an overhead mark and I only had nine kicks but somehow I ended up with seven goals straight, although we lost the match.

We lost again the next week, to St Kilda, but after that we defeated Hawthorn, Adelaide and Geelong. At the halfway point of the season we had nine wins and three losses, and were second on the ladder behind the Eagles. That was when it twigged that we were actually a chance, although we had lost Scott Lucas with a broken ankle in Round 10. We started to believe that if we got it right we could win the whole show. We were certainly contenders. I had 48.23 at that stage.

In the second half of the season we went on a massive winning streak, losing only one game – again on the road – to Port Adelaide. In Round 17 we played in another classic match against North. It was one of the greatest games I had played in. It was a shootout, which as a forward is what you want to see. I got seven goals and Carey kicked ten, including one of the greatest goals I'd ever seen, a left-foot boomerang from the boundary line. I also kicked a miraculous goal out of midair, but mine was more luck than Carey's. In the end, we won 158 to 132 in a thriller.

North had been a bit of a bogey team for us and was also going very well in 1999, so it was massive for us to beat them. Without either Lucas or Hird, we knew we could win a shootout with a team that boasted Carey, John Longmire, Shannon Grant, Brent Harvey, Matthew Capuano and Corey McKernan.

We were sitting clear on top of the ladder now. Fitness-wise, we felt like we were ahead of the pack, and we were scoring heavily, which meant it was a good place to be a full-forward. We averaged around sixty inside-fifties a match, so I was getting plenty of chances. Flooding the opposition's forward fifty hadn't started at this time, so when the ball came forward it was really just a one-on-one contest. In fact, our game plan required the other forwards to clear out the fifty-metre zone for me. I was enjoying myself immensely: Essendon was a great place to be and I was playing with so many brilliant footballers. In Round 21 I beat my previous best season total of seventy goals, although I'd missed three rounds due to injury.

By the end of the home-and-away season, we had topped the ladder with eighteen wins and won the minor premiership, which was a great honour.

Sydney had snuck into the eight with some pretty ordinary form, and we defeated them easily in our Qualifying Final at the MCG. To this point, I hadn't really played well in a final, so I was pumped to put in a big one. Both Tony Lockett and I kicked five that day. He was retiring at the end of the season and so it was his last match, although he would make a brief return in 2002. I have a photo of the two of us shaking hands and talking at the end of the match; he was such a hero of mine, and that takes pride of place on my wall at home.

That won us a week off. We had a very light training load – in fact, I think we took it too easy and relaxed too much. Carlton, who had lost to Brisbane in the first week of the finals, beat West Coast in week two to win a start against us in a Preliminary Final at the MCG the next Saturday afternoon. North was to face Brisbane in the other Prelim, so it looked like we'd be taking them on in the Grand Final.

As we lined up for the national anthem, Stephen Silvagni

eyeballed me fiercely and I knew he was setting himself for a big one. When the game got underway, Carlton jumped us. We missed some easy shots and they were up by three goals at quarter time. In the second term things got worse. We didn't kick a goal and we were down by four goals at half time.

In the third quarter we had plenty of chances but we missed too many. We kicked 7.7 to take the lead at three-quarter time, but we hadn't put the game away. We knew the last quarter was going to be an arm wrestle. I had kicked a few goals and was having a great battle with Silvagni.

The last quarter was tight but we weren't used to close games and we struggled. Again, we had our chances but failed to take them. With less than a minute to go we were within a kick and Dean Wallis had the ball in the middle. I hoped he'd launch it forward and that someone would take a mark, or even that he might put it over our heads and it would roll through for a score – he had a huge kick and could have done that. You could hear the intensity of the crowd lifting, and I was calling for it long because I fancied myself one-on-one against Silvagni. But then Wallis got run down by Fraser Brown, and Carlton chipped the ball around until the siren went. We had lost by a point.

In 1996 I'd been in hospital after the game and so I hadn't seen Sheeds' reaction, but apparently he was savage. By all reports, he was worse this day. I had never seen him like it. Robert Walls wrote a column in *The Age* in the days after the match saying there had been laughing and joking in the Essendon rooms before the match. I can't recall that, but he was watching the monitors. Walls felt the team was thinking of the next week and the Grand Final rather than our immediate task – Carlton.

A couple of weeks later I talked to Wayne Carey, whose team went on to defeat Carlton in the Grand Final. He said he'd been listening to the radio and thinking, 'Please let Carlton win this game.' The moment the siren went, he said he knew North would win the next week because Carlton had just played its Grand Final against us. Wayne said we would have been a far tougher proposition than the Blues.

Even though it had been another big year for me, dropping out of the finals like we had definitely took the gloss off the season. I got another All Australian selection, this time as full-forward, but I missed out on the Coleman Medal by eleven goals to Scott Cummings, who was with West Coast now. Suddenly, individual honours didn't matter as much as my team, though.

I understood that no individual award could come close to winning a Premiership. This was the game that I look back on now as the worst loss of my playing career – it should never have happened.

We went and watched the AFL Grand Final and the Essendon reserves win their Grand Final under Terry Daniher the following week. About fifteen minutes into the final quarter of the senior Grand Final, it was clear North was going to win. Sheeds and Robert Shaw said to the group at that point, 'Okay, boys, get up.'

We had a restaurant booked across the road. When we walked in, Robert Shaw handed us each a folder, which contained notes on the teams to beat next year and where we needed to improve to beat them. The players just looked at one another. Along with the heartache of our loss to Carlton, which we still had, we saw that we had to begin preseason training in just six weeks' time.

We spent two weeks at Essendon Grammar that off-season working on our new game plan and tactics. Losing in the Preliminary Final of 1999 really hurt, and it still does. But it gave us great resolve to improve. We set ourselves for a mission to win that elusive Premiership in 2000.

> 'Bomber Matty Lloyd has come on so well he is almost twice the player he was last year. He was good last season, but he has exploded into an out-and-out match winner.'
>
> *Wayne Carey,* Herald Sun, *19 May 1999*

12

On a Mission

'You had faith that if you kicked the ball into the forward fifty, he would have read you so well he'd be where you kicked it.'

James Hird

WE ALL WENT INTO the 2000 season carrying a fair amount of pain. We knew we should have played in the 1999 Grand Final and we could have won it. That Grand Final day was termed 'Day 1 of 2000' in our papers. Because we had such a strong forward-looking plan, though, we didn't dwell on 1999 for too long. Every player on the list, every coach and every member of staff was determined not to let an opportunity slip again. Nothing less than a Premiership was going to be satisfactory. We were mean and arrogant and we meant business.

I had set myself the personal goals of kicking a ton and being a solid contributor to the team. I was lifting bigger weights now because I wanted to be stronger; I wanted to control the play on my terms. Peter Somerville had retired and so John Barnes joined us as our new ruckman; he called me 'Conan the Barbarian' because of the weights I was lifting.

Our other young players had also bulked up a bit too, but the main change I noticed was our attitude. We had got ahead of ourselves in the Preliminary Final against Carlton, but that wasn't going to happen now. We were more mature; Hird and Lucas were ready to go back onto the field; and we had Dean Bailey, Mark Harvey, Terry Daniher and Robert Shaw on the coaching staff, with Sheeds overseeing it all – not to mention John Quinn's savage fitness regime.

In January we had a ten-day training camp at Essendon Grammar, where we developed and executed our game plan during intense training and worked on the physical aspects we needed to control during games. It was a big camp; all we did was train and then go home to sleep. We were ready.

We started our Ansett Cup campaign in Darwin and easily accounted for West Coast. It was stinking hot for our second game in the series, which was against the Bulldogs at Waverley, but we had a five-goal win. Next, I kicked six to help us beat Hawthorn; I had fourteen goals from three matches to that point.

In the Semi Final, with Hird on song in his first game back from stress fractures, we destroyed Melbourne before slowing down near the end. I kicked 7.3 for the day and was feeling good. Twenty-one goals in our Ansett Cup campaign was a great return.

We played North in the Grand Final of the Ansett Cup in front of a massive crowd at the MCG. They were the reigning Premiers and had an arrogance about them that used to frustrate us. We knew we had to turn it around physically to beat them. They were a strong and physical team, with Martin Pike, Mick Martyn, Glenn Archer, David King, Anthony

Stevens and Wayne Carey. They were the type of team you'd want to be in and one you hated playing against. When they had you by the throat, they'd rub your nose in the dirt. It wasn't just a physical battering, it was mental too – if you showed any sign of weakness they'd be into you.

As players we felt the rivalry against North Melbourne very sharply, even though they didn't have great crowd support. Collingwood and Carlton weren't bullying us like North was, and it was the Kangaroos we had to knock off if we wanted to climb to the top. More than that, though, North had contempt for us. They acted like we were spoilt rich kids with everything and seemed to believe we lacked their hunger. We hated hearing that, but we knew there was a bit of truth to it.

Robert Shaw put together a video showing everything North had done to us over the years. As I watched the footage, I saw Mick Martyn playing on me and I made a commitment to myself: 'I am going to attack Mick today. I am going to beat him.'

Hirdy, who always had a similar battle with Glenn Archer, set himself the same target as me, although his plan was to run Archer off his legs. The game was played at the MCG because it was too big to be hosted anywhere else. The rock-hard cricket pitch was still in place, and that caused a few issues, including when Joe Misiti got hip-and-shouldered and broke his jaw when he landed on the pitch. Steve Alessio sued the AFL as he believed the cricket pitch attributed to his stress fractures.

But something significant happened during the match that showed what we were all about: Jason Johnson laid one of the biggest hip-and-shoulders you could imagine on John Blakey – his eyes were shut before he even hit the ground. We called Jason 'the Bull,' and it was like Blakey had just been hit by one. That was emblematic of our new attitude – we just attacked North that day.

I gave Mick Martyn a bit of lip, as did Mark Mercuri. We couldn't understand anything he was saying back to us, and so we were taking off the way he was talking. Mick was saying, 'No one, no one says that about Mick Martyn,' which was the only thing we could clearly make out. At one point I danced around him to set up a goal, and again we were in his face. It felt like the whole momentum of the North–Essendon relationship had changed. We had gone from being bullied to being the bullies; we were confident, believed in our ability and were driven to be the best.

Mark Mercuri was brilliant and won the Michael Tuck Medal for best on ground, and we won the match by forty-odd points. We must have annoyed them too. Carey was reported for striking Fletch and Wallis, although the charges were withdrawn before getting to the tribunal. Craig Sholl was suspended for a week for hitting Fletch, and Martyn was done for a week for hitting me. We had got under their skin and they didn't like it.

And we had won. From that time on, we just started smashing teams. We began the regular season against Port Adelaide at our new home ground, Colonial Stadium at the Docklands. I butchered a chance to kick the first ever goal there, which was a record that would have been nice to have. It also would have meant I'd have finished with 300 goals there instead of 299. Anyway, I kicked 7.2 to start the season and we won by ninety-four points, which was Port's biggest ever loss in the AFL.

I could have ended up with more, but Gavin Wanganeen had clobbered me during the third quarter. Hirdy took my kick and put it through – that tells you how hard I was hit if I was letting someone else take my kick at goal. I had to sit out the rest of the match, and it turned out I had a fractured cheekbone. It wasn't too bad, though, and I was able to front up the next week against Richmond, where I kicked seven straight.

The day after the Richmond match, the *Herald Sun*'s headline read: 'Tigers complain to the AFL about Lloyd's staging'. I'd won seven free kicks in my first two games, although only two of those were against Richmond. They had obviously watched my Round 1 match closely, as I'd been awarded five free kicks in that match. I was disappointed that Richmond had complained, but they were right – I was doing it.

I didn't think I was doing anything wrong, though. If I felt like the ball was going over the top and that the full-back was right on my back, I'd fall forwards with my arms out. The free kicks weren't always there, but I felt like I wouldn't get a thing if I didn't make it look bigger, so I did. It was difficult for the umpires because the crowd would go up, and I started getting the free kicks, which riled opposition players and supporters. Once Richmond had made a fuss about it, though, I had massive scrutiny on me every time I went for the ball.

Staging is probably the biggest regret I have in footy. There's no doubt that the stigma of it that I got as a result of that period wasn't great, and it would stay with me for the rest of my career. I was staging at the time, but it didn't last long and then I was still copping it six or seven years later.

It did rattle me, though, because every free kick I was given was heralded with Bronx cheers from the fans. And in fact it probably did me no favours in the long term. After I got all this media attention over it, there were free kicks the umpires should have paid that they were too scared to award me.

There is no doubt the umpires were told to watch me, and they were very conscious of it. Some umpires were better than others in how they handled it. Like players, some umpires were good and others weren't.

While I was under the pump in the media, the positive aspect was that the team was flying. We had a genuinely star-studded team, and it was nasty too. Our backline boasted Fletcher, Wallis, Hardwick, Solomon, Wellman and Mark Johnson. On the wing we had a young buck, Adam Ramanauskas, who was extremely confident and capable. We had a forward line of me, Scotty, Mercs and Hirdy, and a midfield that had the most depth in the competition in Long, Blumfield, Misiti, Heffernan, Caracella and Jason Johnson.

We were unstoppable, and we had a great run of victories. Ninety-four points in Round 1, then forty-three, thirty-six in Perth, forty-seven, twenty-four (after being nearly ten goals up at three-quarter time), sixty-three, forty and sixty-four points. It was Round 9 before anyone got near us, and by then we had a percentage of more than 160 and were scoring heavily. That week we defeated Melbourne by thirteen points, which was the first time someone got close and also the first time during the season we'd scored less than 120 points.

We were winning and winning well, and doing it on the

front foot by sheer weight of goals. That was perfect for a full-forward, and so I was averaging a fraction less than five goals a game – on track for the ton. It wasn't all plain sailing for me, though, since I could have been converting at a better rate.

Such was the mindset of the club that I was pulled up about that even though the team was travelling so well. Against St Kilda in Round 12 and North Melbourne in Round 13 I had returns of 6.5 and 1.4. The coaches clearly wanted to make sure we didn't get complacent about our team success, and so they decided to give a few of us a rev-up.

Robert Shaw played the bad cop to Sheeds' good cop. He organised a meeting after the North match during the week and singled a few of us out. He said, 'Gary Moorcroft, you're not fit enough to be playing in a premiership side.' I was sitting back and feeling pretty content with how I was going, but Robert's eyes fixed on me next. 'You're missing far too many easy shots, Lloyd – you're kidding yourself. You don't rehearse your routine or practise anywhere near as much as Lockett or Dunstall would . . . ' He went on about it for three or four minutes before moving on to someone else.

What he said struck a chord with me. I had my routine down pat, but if I was sore or tired I would sometimes skip my goalkicking practice. I knew I'd been less accurate than in other years, but I still thought I was going okay.

He was right, though – you wouldn't want to lose a premiership by a simple missed shot or by a couple of players not being fit enough to run the game out. It was a turning point for me, and I stepped up my training to another level. No matter how well we were going or how tired I was, I would do my set-shot practice. If it was good enough for Lockett and Dunstall, it was good enough for me.

As a group, we started a goalkicking competition at training, and it became pretty popular among the team. It probably brought another ten blokes out to practise, and it continued for many years. It certainly helped me become a better shot at goal.

In the second half of the season, we really cut loose. The only time we looked under threat was in Round 14 against Sydney at the SCG, which probably got a few opposition coaches thinking. We were strangled by the size of the ground and we couldn't get our game flowing. Aside from that, though, we were flying.

I played my 100th game against Hawthorn in Round 19 and kicked five in a big win. We defeated Carlton in Round 20 to remain unbeaten, and we were starting to think not just about the Premiership but also perhaps of getting through the season without a loss. Our percentage was 164.9 and our average winning margin was fifty-two points. My best return of the season had been the nine goals I kicked against Freo in Round 18, but I'd also three small hauls of just one goal – against the Kangaroos, playing on Mick Martyn, Adelaide, playing on Ben Hart, and Carlton, playing on Glenn Manton. The same blokes still gave me trouble.

What you couldn't tell with some of our scorelines was what Sheeds had been trying from the coach's box. We could have won most of those matches by a lot more if we'd just stuck to one simple game plan. We were a nasty football side – we picked out each team's most significant player (often the captain) and went after him as a team. We were collectively shutting down the opposition's playmakers, but at the same time we were kicking massive scores.

Yet we weren't ready for what the Bulldogs threw at us in Round 21. The Dogs had begun playing with a 'flood' of men in the backline for the three weeks before our game, so we knew it would be a tight and defensive contest. When the match got underway, they put numbers behind the ball and just strangled us. Our forward line was so crowded with Bulldogs players that you could barely see our guys. The game changed that day.

I'd hurt my thumb and couldn't mark the ball cleanly. So I wasn't much use during the Dogs game, except to provide a distraction. We did get out to more than three goals early in the last quarter, but the Doggies stuck to their game plan and were more efficient going into their forward line, and a Chris Grant snap from the boundary line was enough for them to get over us.

It was a pretty torrid game, too. There was an all-in brawl at one stage and a couple of suspensions were handed out. Fines were given to fourteen players for engaging in a melee. Not me, though!

Sportsbet had been running a book on when and if we'd get beaten. No team had really challenged us to that point, so Sheeds was pretty upset with the loss. He was always aware of the history of the game, so he would have been thinking, 'We're going to do something that's never been done before.'

Even after the loss, people were still asking 'if this was the greatest team that's been put on the park', which was Bruce McAvaney's call during the Grand Final telecast. That loss to the Dogs put a bit of doubt in our minds, but it also served to focus us on what we had to do. We knew now, 100 per cent, that we couldn't slacken off one little bit.

After the game, I went to Bruce Reid and said, 'I'm struggling with my thumb – I'm not sure if it'll be right for Round 22.' I was probably getting caught up in the pressure of everything as well. But Reidy said, 'No, we'll make you thumb guards, and I reckon you'll be fine to keep playing.'

I spent a lot of time during the week getting used to the guards which I wore under my hand taping. A big part was getting used to how it felt to guide the ball onto my foot, as the way I held the ball changed. It was unusual. I played the next week with the thumb guards, though, and I got a couple of goals in the first quarter. In the end, I actually played the rest of my career with them because my thumb ligaments had been damaged so many times over the years.

In the final rounds of the regular season we recognised that we had started to come back the field a little bit. We knew that the finals wouldn't be as easy the first twenty-odd rounds had been. Collingwood was a tough slog in Round 22, but we got over them by nineteen points. We finished the home-and-away season five games clear on top of the ladder, with just that one loss and a percentage of 159.1.

> 'A lot of my instinctive play was eventually to just go long to Lloydy. Once he took the mark, he very rarely missed. You walked back to the centre of the ground and got ready for the bounce.'
>
> *James Hird*

13

Premiership Glory

'I remember training with Lloydy when he was young and being out there at goalkicking practice. I wouldn't take any credit for teaching him anything but just when you train with someone for so long, you feel emotionally connected with their career. Getting the hundreds goals was great, and winning a Premiership with that whole team was very special.'

James Hird

THE 2000 SEASON INTRODUCED a new finals system, so instead of the top side playing the eighth in week one, we were to play the fourth-placed team – the Kangaroos. We knew we needed to be on top of our game to beat them.

I went into the match with ninety-four goals. Once I had made it into the high eighties I had started to struggle a little – I'd only kicked one against Carlton, two against the Bulldogs and four against Collingwood. I had won the Coleman Medal but now I was up against Mick Martyn again.

During the week, I was starting to think about the century too much and it was getting to me. I realised I needed some form of guidance. I had a friend who knew Tony Lockett's manager and he arranged for me to fly to Sydney to meet with Plugger. We spent the day together at Fox Studios and he was unbelievable – he gave me everything and anything I asked for, he spoke about his home life and asked me to come and spend a day on his farm if I ever wanted to get away from the Melbourne city lifestyle.

Plugger talked about goal number 100 as being no different to any other. It was just another goal, he said, just a number. According to him, it was no different from going from zero to one or from one to two. 'Just forget about it,' he told me.

So I went into the match feeling much more settled. Luckily for me, we were on our game as a team and put on one of the purest displays of footy that I had ever seen – it was like the Harlem Globetrotters.

I had kicked four goals by three-quarter time, each one was significant because it was on Mick Martyn and we led by a country mile, more than 100 points in fact. So at three-quarter time I was on ninety-eight goals. Addressing the team at the break, Sheeds said, 'We've got the week off next week – you've got to clear out the forward line for Lloyd. We've got to get that 100!'

What Sheeds had said petrified me, in a way – I didn't want to hamper our team plans for the week off. I was aware of what the delay caused by the crowd rushing onto the ground could to do a team's momentum; losing a little momentum when you're 100 points up seemed much better than losing it in the first quarter of the Preliminary Final in two weeks' time.

When play restarted, Hirdy was waving his arms and

shouting at anyone in the forward 50, 'Get out, get out!' Two or three minutes into the final quarter, Gary Moorcroft hit me lace-out. Ninety-nine goals – 'Just another number,' I told myself, but the buzz around the ground was electric. I could hear a hush every time I moved towards the ball.

About eight minutes further in, Longy swooped on a ball around the fifty-metre line and put it down my throat. I knew by the way he moved where it was going, and it was perfect delivery. He had been feeding me all day, and he seemed to care more about the 100 than me. No one at Essendon had kicked the 100 goals since Geoff Blethyn in 1972, and before that John Coleman in 1952.

As I took the mark it was like 80,000 cameras went off. The security guards lined the boundary with their backs to me as the crowd surged down to the fence. I was twenty-five metres out on a slight angle. As I was going back for my kick, my teammates who were closer to me than normal were smiling – they were all getting ready to be a part of history.

I went through my normal process. As I was running in, I could see people already starting to jump the fence, but I kept my focus. I pulled the kick a little, but the ball swung back and went through quite comfortably. I turned to jump on Hirdy and Bewick, and within no time it was just claustrophobic and I was surrounded by security guards and tens of thousands of spectators.

I was being patted on the head and seeing people I knew, guys from Avondale Heights, school friends – even my mate Danny, who I ran out with for Dunstall's ton. I even high-fived my brother Brad. It was surreal – it was like a reunion on the MCG!

It was an amazing feeling. I finally got off the ground and was sitting in the dugout with some security guys having a chat until the ground was cleared. When I came back onto the ground I felt like one of The Beatles – the crowd went mad. I kicked another goal later and I felt a tweak in my quad. I hoped I hadn't done some damage because I'd cooled down in the dugout, but it was okay.

We kicked a cricket score that day – 31.12.198 – which was the highest score ever in a Final. I was definitely relieved to get the ton, but now we had to get on with the business of winning a premiership.

We trained hard over the next week and then tapered off in the second. Melbourne had beaten Carlton in their Qualifying Final, so the Demons also had week off. Carlton hammered the Lions to set up a Preliminary Final with us, while the Kangaroos just edged out Hawthorn to make the other one against Melbourne.

We knew Carlton had the ability to lift, as they had in 1999, so we were a little nervous about facing them. During the week, the Carlton president, John Elliott, and club legend Stephen Kernahan tried to play some mind games: 'Yeah, we can get them in the finals. We've done it before.'

But we weren't going to let it happen again. While the first half was relatively tight, we blew them away in the second half to make the Grand Final against Melbourne, who had dealt with North quite easily.

I had a nervous wait after the match. Glenn Manton would always back into me looking to always have a touch on me, and during the match I had dropped my shoulder into his back when he wasn't ready; it really knocked the stuffing out of him. The goal umpire said, 'I saw that.' I'd kicked four goals on him and sledged him a bit through the day, as his holding tactics had often got the better of me. I now feared I was going to miss the Grand Final.

There were a few articles on it the next day, and I knew it would be looked at. Matthew Drain, our football manager, came up to me during training on the Monday night and said, 'Don't worry, you're safe.' I had crossed the line a lot during 2000 and got away with it, so it was a huge relief to hear that.

If I'd missed the Grand Final it would have been my first time out of the seniors in thirty games. I would have had trouble lining up for Essendon in 2001 after such a huge blow – I would have felt like I'd let my teammates down. Jason McCartney missed a premiership in 1999 after whacking Clark Keating, and I didn't want that kind of devastation in my life.

After being sure I was playing, I had a great Grand Final week. We had car parades and around 10,000 people at our training sessions. We knew Melbourne was in pretty good touch; like the week before, we had to stay on our game despite all the distractions. I went to the Brownlow Medal dinner on the Monday night and polled fourteen votes. When you're lining up in a Grand Final, though, the last place you want to be is at a Brownlow Medal function, so we all left as soon as the formalities were over.

There were seven or eight guys at Essendon who had played in the 1993 Premiership, and they talked us through the week. Longy, Wally, Hirdy, Joey, Mercs and Fletch all made sure we understood that this was a Grand Final – we could leave nothing on the table.

We had a dinner at the Essendon Hall of Fame on the Thursday night, and Sheeds spoke really passionately, tracking the history of our footy club and the Grand Finals we'd won. After that, we had a very clear desire to be a part of Essendon's sixteenth Premiership. Standing on top of the steps at the Treasury after the Grand Final Parade, the reality of what lay in front of us was obvious. There were people as far as the eye could see, and I couldn't even look at the Melbourne players due to my dislike of them. They were standing in the way of what we desperately wanted, and I could feel the tension brewing between the two playing groups. This was big.

Grand Final day was different to other matches. I had to turn my phone off because there were all sorts of requests coming through for last-minute tickets and the like, and I just didn't need that. It was a beautiful sunny day and I left early for the ground.

Our team routine was different too. We weren't allowed out on the ground for our warm-up because of the pre-match entertainment, so I went out an hour earlier than usual to have my practice shots with Ady Schwegler. He was our property steward but he was much more than that – he was always ready to go when I wanted to take my warm-up shots, and he became a close friend. Colin Hooper always belted the footies at the players' hands to sharpen our reflexes before a match. We were all creatures of habit and we wanted nothing to change on the biggest day of our lives.

When we were about to run onto the ground we were like dogs at the starting gate. We were ready and focused. We ran up the race to a huge roar, and then went through our banner before stopping for a photo. Lining up for the national anthem, I was so nervous that I could hardly sing a word.

Anthony Ingerson lined up on me, and Hirdy had Alistair Nicholson. We were a tough forward line to match up on as Scotty Lucas had kicked more than fifty goals that year as well. Hirdy snapped a beautiful goal in the first two or three minutes to get the first goal of the game after David Neitz had blown a chance early in the match. Kicking the first goal of the game was a mental win for us – their skipper had missed one, while ours had got one.

Blake Caracella's nickname was 'the Skunk' because no one ever went near him. That was because he was such a smart footballer, but we'd say to him, 'Do you smell or something?' He got clear and kicked a couple in that all-important first quarter. Late in the quarter, Mark Mercuri ran too far but the umpire didn't call it; the ball spilt out of his hands in a tackle and I boomeranged it through for a goal. I was stoked to get a goal in the first quarter of a Grand Final – getting one early always helped my nerves settle.

Dean Wallis was awesome in defence. At one stage he reset his own dislocated finger because he was so determined not to miss anything. Early in the match he fixed up Brad Green – and later got three weeks for it – but Green didn't do much for the game from there.

Longy was of the mindset that seven years between drinks was too long, and he left nothing to chance. His crunch on Troy Simmonds was sickening, and he was later suspended for four weeks; in today's football he probably would have got eight. Longy could easily have broken Troy Simmonds' neck, he hit him so hard. I ran in to fly the flag when the resulting fight broke out. I couldn't fight my way out of a paper bag, but I was shaping up to Daniel Ward just to look the part.

Sheeds had me playing further up the ground on Ingerson because he was their best defender and liked playing out of the goal square. The first quarter was a bit of an arm wrestle, and then we missed a few easy goals and I was worried we might kick ourselves out of it. Then Paul Barnard came off the bench and kicked a couple and we were off. We were up by seven goals at half time.

Mark Johnson was getting stuck into the forwards at the long break and looked to be panicking, but our midfield was well on top and kept providing us with chances after half time. We had kicked 10.16 to that point.

Justin Blumfield and Steve Alessio kicked a couple of important goals after half time to put the game beyond doubt, and then we were able to enjoy the last quarter and what was about to happen. I kicked a goal with five minutes to go in the match, which was as enjoyable a goal as I ever kicked. It was pure elation, and I got a huge bear hug from Hirdy after it. I looked at him, smiling and laughing, and said, 'We've won this Premiership!'

When the siren went, even though we had the match sewn up, the wave of euphoria was staggering. It was relief, it was joy, it was everything, and I'd achieved it with the greatest bunch of blokes. Seeing John Barnes and Dean Wallis standing there crying because they'd done it as best mates was special. Barnes had come across from Geelong after losing three Grand Finals. Everyone had different emotions, depending on where our careers were at; mine was relief that it was over and that we had achieved what we should have the year before. The mission had been completed.

We had changed our footy on a number of levels. Our nasty backline and skilled forward line was the new model, and we took fitness and strength to a new level. The other teams needed to have negating techniques to stop key forwards like myself – as the Bulldogs had done – but in the end we had a good balance between defence and attack.

That night was one of the greatest of my life. While in the old days players would sit down and have a beer after every game, in 2000 we didn't do much of that. We were focused only on what we wanted to achieve and how we were going to do it. That's one of the reasons Grand Final night can be such a big thing. It was perhaps the one time all year we sat down as a group with our wives, family and friends and enjoyed what we had achieved.

We went to the Tennis Centre and there were 10,000 Essendon fans there, and when I came up on stage it was to chants of 'Lloydy, Lloydy' – it was brilliant! I'd kicked 100 goals, won a flag and a Coleman Medal – life couldn't get any better!

Our celebrations went well into the night and the next day. I hadn't drunk at all during the season but I made up for it that night. As a result, I don't remember as much of it as I should. I do remember Lisa having to escort me to my room – I was in a world of hurt. The next day we had to front up for a parade where we were given the keys to Moonee Ponds, and Dean Solomon and Chris Heffernan bought one of those big buckets of KFC, which we all tucked into, to try to get through the day. We felt invincible, on top of the world, and it felt like that for the next month.

About eight of us – well and truly under the weather – had to go to the tribunal the following Tuesday because of the melee that had broken out during the match. I copped a $2500 fine. Hirdy tried to contest his melee charge but failed, so he ended up getting fined more than the rest of us, which we all had a good laugh about as we sat at the back of the tribunal room.

All the memorabilia the team had signed earned us $125,000, which we used for a team trip to Ibiza in Spain. There's no doubt the scrutiny we faced back then wasn't like it is now, but one of our strengths as a club was how we carried ourselves in public. Essendon was a good place and didn't have too many off-field indiscretions that made it into the public eye. Obviously, it's changed a little bit of late, but that culture runs from the top down, and that will change again, given that it was people like Mark Thompson and Hirdy who set the agenda and led it. They loved a good time, but they were always aware of the club and how we'd be seen by the outside world. They all loved a good time, but there was a line we knew we couldn't cross.

So off we went to Ibiza. There was a TV show on in Melbourne at the time about the partying that went on in Ibiza, and a lot of our wives and girlfriends were a bit worried about what we'd get up to. Not that they needed to, though. We got up to mischief and had a good time, but that was about it.

Going out knowing it was all paid for was great. I didn't really like the place, though. It seemed like everyone else there was drinking bottles of water because they were all on drugs. I didn't see any of that from my teammates throughout my career – we just drank alcohol.

The nightclub we went to on the first night was a place where something different happened every night at 3am. We were waiting for something special, and eventually the sprinklers came out of the roof and it turned into a water party. Even though we were soaked it was pretty good fun – the only problem was that no taxi driver would take us home because we were too wet. Not much fun at four in the morning!

I was with Sean Wellman, Mark McVeigh, Dean Solomon and Hawthorn's Ben Dixon, and they all looked at each other and said, 'Where are we going to kick on to now?' It was four am, we were sopping wet and so Welly and I got something to eat and went home. I saw the others the next afternoon and McVeigh had his arm in a sling and Solomon couldn't see.

It turned out that they'd gone to another bar that turned into a foam party. McVeigh had jumped off a balcony onto a dance floor full of foam and crashed on his shoulder and broken his collarbone, and then Solly had argued with a cab driver, who sprayed him with mace. I realised I'd made a pretty smart decision to go home that night. We weren't laughing at the time, but now we all look back and just laugh at some of the things that happened on footy trips like that.

After the Ibiza trip, Hirdy and I went to the Olympics in Sydney, courtesy of our sponsor, Nike. We were there with Gorden Tallis, Darren Lockyer, Wendell Sailor, Andrew Johns, Laurie Daley, Steve Silvagni and Matthew Richardson. I had just had the football year of my life, then partied with the boys in Ibiza, and now I was at the Sydney Olympics. I had to pinch myself. I was only twenty-two and so much was happening for me.

Nike organised a boat trip along the harbour to the stadium and we then watched Cathy Freeman win her 400-metre race, which was awesome – one of the great experiences of my life. Then we jumped back on the boat and headed off to the Last Lap, the official nightclub of the Sydney Olympics, where we walked straight in past all the queues.

The talent that was around us was astounding. Tallis, Lockyer and Sailor had all won the NRL Premiership with the Broncos that year, and they spent the night getting stuck into Richo: 'What's Richmond ever done?' they kept saying to him. I couldn't believe the size of those guys. It was freezing cold but Wendell had a muscle top on, and he was just saying, 'Gee, I'm quite warm,' just to show his big biceps and muscles. How much they drank was also amazing – we were supposed to be going drink-for-drink with them but I was slipping a lot of mine over the side of the boat. Hirdy's a better drinker than I am, but he was doing it too.

In 1999, on the night of the Grand Final we'd been studying what we needed to do the next year to succeed. Now, though, we didn't think about 2001 for a month. Knowing we had that flag gave us all a sense of pride. At the time, we thought we'd get the chance to do it all again soon. But it was just as well we enjoyed the one we got. We had worked bloody hard and it was all worth it.

> 'Silvagni regards Lloyd simply as the best full-forward in the competition . . . "The thing about the great full-forwards is that

they're able to turn the game around in five minutes of footy. You can hold them for most of the game, but in five minutes they can kick three or four goals. Matty's one of those."'

Greg Baum, The Age, *22 July 2000*

14

Back-to-Back Is Harder than It Sounds

'An unrepentant Matthew Lloyd has vowed to fight fire with fire this season despite his one match suspension for rough play. The Essendon goalkicking ace warned defenders that he would not be a "soft touch" anymore.'

Bruce Matthews

WHEN OUR CELEBRATIONS FINALLY ended, we had to think about the next season. For us, 2001 would be different in just about every way to 2000. In my opinion, we had lost some of our drive after winning a flag, and the toll the season had taken on the group was also significant. Our hunger wasn't the same. The difference was only marginal, but combined with the other clubs' efforts to catch up to us, it was bound to make 2001 a lot harder than 2000.

I had grown out of my desire for personal stats and recognition, and I was now part of a Premiership team. At the start of 2001 I wanted it all again, but it was harder than before. We were feeling pretty good about ourselves, but the reality is as a group we didn't work as hard as we did the year before. We were starting to look over our shoulder to see who was coming, and there were half a dozen teams lining us up.

I also had to look over my shoulder for other things too. The night before the Melbourne Cup in 2000, I was coming home from Lisa's at around 11pm and stopped to grab $500 from an ATM on Military Road in Avondale Heights; I was still living at home with my parents. We were going to the races the next day with Scott Lucas and Justin Blumfield and their girlfriends.

Just as I grabbed my money from the machine, I turned to see a pair of eyes bulging through a balaclava. This guy had a black balaclava over his head, a black jumper, black jeans and black shoes, and he had something in his hand that he threatened me with. It might have been a syringe or a knife – I didn't get a clear look as he was holding it at my chest level and I couldn't take my eyes off his. 'Give me the lot,' he demanded.

I had been leaning down at the ATM and I don't think he knew how big I was, but I was in shock. I straightened up and, acting on instinct, I open-handed him in the face. He took a step back and I turned and ran. He was chasing me down the road, and I was hysterically screaming, 'Help! Help!'

He was shouting, 'Drop the fucking money! Drop the fucking money!' I ran onto the road and a taxi almost hit me, and that's when this guy, realising there were other people around, bolted down a laneway. The cabbie stopped and took me to the police station, where I sat for the next hour giving them a statement. They sent some officers and sniffer dogs down there, but they didn't find him.

When I got home I had to wake Mum and Dad and tell them the story. Eventually, I went to bed and struggled to sleep. It made the papers a couple of days later, and I didn't get much sympathy around the club. Most of the guys thought it was pretty funny, which helped me get over it, although I have never been to an ATM after dark since. In truth, it was quite a harrowing experience, one I wouldn't wish on anyone.

The Ansett Cup in 2001 had a round-robin format. We played three games and didn't win one. We went down to Port Adelaide by seventy-nine points and then lost to Geelong and Sydney to fall out before the Semi Finals. Brisbane played Port in the Final, with Port winning, which was a sign of the future.

Even though we'd been bundled out, everyone knew the Ansett Cup wasn't serious. The media kept on talking about back-to-back flags and an Essendon dynasty. We thought we could be better than 2000 – why wouldn't we improve? We'd only lost one player over the off-season: Darren Bewick, who had retired.

Our Round 1 match against North Melbourne was to open the season. Robert Shaw got a hold of us leading into that game because he thought we needed a wake-up call. He named a team based on 'who is guaranteed a spot based on preseason form', and when we looked at it we saw that there were about eight spots missing. I wasn't there and Joe Misiti wasn't there either. I hadn't thought my form was too bad. Joey and I walked out of that meeting wondering what we had to do to get a game. Shawy didn't care who you were or what you had achieved previously, he wanted to give us all a wake-up call.

We were still selected for the match, though, and Joe had thirty possessions and won the three Brownlow votes. I kicked four and we thumped North by fourteen goals.

We backed that up with a good win over Port, before losing to Carlton in Round 3. I kicked five goals against the Blues and had thirteen to that point of the season. But a worrying trend started for me in that match, as I began to get suspended a bit. I had skated on the edge before the 2000 Premiership, but now I tipped over it as I tried to physically dominate opposition players and the contest.

I was playing on Glenn Manton, who I called 'The Octopus' because he would wrap me up and seemed like he was all arms. I never seemed to get a free kick against him, and my frustration was starting to get the better of me. Simon Fletcher received a handball from Mants, and I charged at him like a raging bull. I went to hip-and-shoulder him but raised my elbow and clipped his jaw. He went down, which was fair because I had hit him, and I went to the tribunal and copped a week. I was lucky – it could have been more.

Being at the tribunal was a nerve-racking experience – it made me feel like I'd killed someone. We had prepared a case at the club earlier in the day, running through the video and the defence, and then we had to sit down to work out how I should plead. Back in those days you couldn't take an early plea and get leniency, so you nearly always pleaded not guilty just in case. I had done the crime, but I was still hopeful I could beat it somehow.

The umpire's advocate was running the show. I gave my plea and we watched the video again in slow-motion. It looked far more vicious than it had actually been. Then the umpire's advocate started to quiz me. I became defensive and then aggressive, all the while trying to outwardly stay calm. Why was this bloke out to get me? Then when I was found guilty, I just sat there with my fingers crossed hoping for a reprimand or a week at worst.

I'd started the year quite well, so it was hard to miss a week – which turned out to be a good win over Sydney at the SCG – but I was back for the Anzac Day clash in Round 5. I was a continuity player, though – I needed to play week in, week out in order to keep my touch. While we won the match, Shane Wakelin was far too strong for me and I only kicked one goal.

That performance stung me and I hit back pretty hard the next week, which was an 88-point win over West Coast at Docklands. The sun that day was as bad as I can ever remember at that stadium, and I couldn't see the ball as it was coming towards me. I didn't touch the ball in the first quarter. Sheeds took me off and said, 'Sit out the last five minutes of the quarter. You're not attacking the ball, so just sit it out.'

As ever, Sheeds seemed to know exactly what I needed. In the next three quarters I attacked the ball well and I kicked 10.4 – my second ever double-figure haul. I even got the three Brownlow votes in that match, so I guess I responded well.

I rate seven goals or more as a big bag, and I was now starting to do that more consistently. I felt like I was at my physical peak. Up to the start of the 2000 season, I'd only kicked more than seven goals five times and then I did it five times in that season alone. After this game against the Eagles, I felt like I had my touch back – I felt strong and quick off the mark, and the team was still playing great footy.

Our match against Hawthorn in Round 9 was a big game. They were unbeaten at that stage and were coming off a monster win. We were second because of our loss to Carlton, but our percentage was high and we were pumped for the clash.

The match attracted the biggest ever crowd at Docklands to that stage. We'd lost Hird, Fletcher and Lucas leading into it, though, so we were under-manned. I took it onto myself to step up and provide some leadership, which was really the first time I'd done that.

We had a good first quarter and then held them goalless in the second. After that, we ran away with the game. I kicked eight straight, and we felt like we were back where we belonged – on top of the ladder. It was a bit of a come-down to lose the next week in Brisbane, but Hawthorn also lost and we would remain on top for the rest of the season.

The Brisbane loss was a significant one, and marked the beginning of a new rivalry for us. It later emerged that, in the lead-up to the game, Leigh Matthews had said his now-famous line about us: 'If it bleeds, we can kill it.' He was confident that he'd built a team that could to take us on, even though they were coming at us from outside the eight.

We'd lost a Final by a point at the Gabba in 1996, but that had been our last loss to Brisbane until this match. They came out that night and beat us with an approach that looked a bit like ours. They had a tough and angry backline, perhaps the silkiest midfield ever put together, and a forward line with class and power. They played a brand of footy that was tough and uncompromising, and the Gabba became a cauldron for the next three years.

The Lions became a beast of a side and would go on to win

three flags in a row. To be honest, they did what we should have. They were brilliant.

I wasn't happy with my 2.5 against St Kilda in Round 11, but I did well over the next four weeks with six goals, then five, five and six. In Round 16 we faced the Kangaroos again, and it would turn out to be one of the most remarkable matches of all time.

The Kangaroos just blew us away in the first quarter, and we found ourselves ten goals down at quarter time when Hirdy delivered what was the greatest motivational talk I had ever heard in football. He broke the game down for the group, to change our negative mindset. 'Don't look at the 58-point deficit,' he said. 'Let's see if we can break it down and try to strike by the last quarter. Let's win this second quarter by four or five goals.'

But the Roos kicked the first two goals of the second quarter. Matthew 'Spider' Burton actually kicked a crumbing goal – we knew we were in trouble when that happened. That put us sixty-nine points down, five minutes into the second quarter. From that point the whole team lifted, though, particularly Jason Johnson and Hirdy. It was probably the greatest game I ever saw Jason play. I kicked five in the second quarter to help us get back in it, while Hirdy was as brilliant and courageous as ever.

We trailed by four goals at the long break, but we had given ourselves a chance. The goals kept coming for both teams in the third quarter and we faced a fourteen-point deficit going into the last. We were now within striking distance and could finish off the Roos in what was the biggest comeback in the history of the game.

I've watched the replay of this game a few times and I've heard a radio broadcast too. Garry Lyon was commenting and he said, 'We are watching the greatest team that has ever played the game, to have that belief that you can come back from this.' When people ask me today what my favourite game was – apart from the Premiership win – this is it. The feeling around the club and our self-belief was amazing.

We dropped a game to Port Adelaide the next week, and then fronted up to face Carlton at the MCG. Glenn Manton was my opponent again and I was off to the tribunal again, this time for elbowing Micky Mansfield in a similar incident to the one earlier in the year. He dished off a handball and I clipped him with my elbow and got two weeks, which meant that I missed Rounds 19 and 20 when I was on eighty-two goals for the year. The suspension killed my dream of kicking 100 goals before the finals, although I did kick thirteen goals during Rounds 21 and 22 to finish the season on ninety-six. Those three games I missed through suspension definitely cost me, although I won the Coleman Medal by more than forty goals.

We had a shocker in the final round against Richmond, and Brisbane drew level with us at the top of the ladder; they had won thirteen in a row and were the in-form team. So we only won the minor premiership on percentage, which was a bit disappointing, but it was also great given it was our third in a row.

Our loss to Richmond was a worry, though, because it meant we had to play them in the first week of the finals – which meant I had Darren Gaspar two weeks in a row. I had kicked six in the loss in front of 77,000 fans in Round 22, and then I kicked four in our Qualifying Final win, which was also at the MCG but in front of 78,000. We were a different team in the final and we won by seventy points; it was an amazing turnaround in the space of seven days.

Gaspar was holding me for the whole game in the final and I couldn't buy a free kick – it was driving me mad. My fourth goal for the day brought up my ton for the season, which was awesome, but I walked away from the game worried because I had headbutted Gaspar during the match. He had me on the boundary line and he pinned me to the fence and wouldn't let me go, so on instinct I gave him a slight tap to the head to say, 'Get off me.' He fired up and shouted, 'That's not on – that's cowardly.'

So I had to wait until Monday to see whether I had to front the tribunal – it took the gloss off the hundred, that's for sure. I lost weight over the weekend I was so worried – what if I got two or three weeks and missed the Grand Final and a Premiership? It was like 2000 all over again, only this time I knew I was going to tribunal.

Ricky Nixon was still my manager at the time, and he was a great support. Mum was supportive but very disappointed in me. I had moved out of home earlier that year, but on the day of the hearing I went and visited Mum as I needed someone to talk too. I explained the process and the possible ramifications, and she was as stressed as I was. Whenever I got myself into trouble, whether she said it or not, I could tell she was thinking, 'Why would you do something like that?' The hardest thing for me to explain was how things like that sometimes happen in the spur of the moment. You wish you could take them back but you can't.

The media speculation surrounding the incident was huge. I was reading about it every day and a camera would be constantly following me. I had to meet with the club and our QCs to put a case together after I was eventually cited. There were plenty of cameras at the tribunal, too. Alastair Lynch had whacked Darryl Wakelin from Port Adelaide in their final, so there was a chance the two big full-forwards would be outed for each team's Preliminary Final and the Grand Final if the Bombers and Lions made it through.

Considering I'd already had two other suspensions that season, I knew the tribunal wouldn't look too kindly on me. When the hearing got underway, Darren Gaspar gave evidence. He was still quite disappointed and said, 'Yeah, he did it to me and I said it's not on.' I must admit, I was filthy on Gaspar as I was expecting him to look after me, as disappointed as he was. I thought he would have gone a little easier on me, given that a Grand Final was potentially on the line. I knew I'd definitely have done that for an opposition player after my Hocking experience, even more so during the finals series.

I pleaded not guilty, and I had some story to prove it, using whatever we could think of to try to get off or keep the penalty to a minimum. 'There was a photographer there and I couldn't get off the fence,' I was saying. 'I was just trying to throw my weight forward. I just wanted him off me.' Eventually, you genuinely start believing your own stories.

In the end, I got a week's suspension, as did Alastair Lynch, which meant we'd both miss our team's Preliminary Finals but would be available for the Grand Final. The club was disappointed with the guilty verdict and thought about an appeal, but I said, 'No, let's leave it – I'll take it as it is.'

We had Hawthorn in the Preliminary Final, and before the game I made an emotional plea to the players. 'I apologise for not being out there,' I said, 'but if you can do the job, I promise that I'll do all I can to help us prevail in the Grand Final.'

Mark Bolton had come into the team for me, and we had some injury concerns – Hirdy and Mercuri had bad groins. Johnny Hay, who was in sensational form at the time for the Hawks, had a brilliant game on Hirdy, shutting him out of it completely in the Preliminary Final.

We had a six-goal lead at half time but they came at us hard in the second half and it was a nail-biter. Trent Croad let fly in the final quarter from the centre square and it looked like it was going through the middle – Hawthorn would have taken the lead with a few minutes left – but it faded and hit the post. Then Paul Barnard kicked a goal and we were out to a nine-point lead with a minute left. Scotty Lucas kicked another one for us to seal the win.

I had spent the match in the coaches' box. It was such an intense environment, and I was uptight and worried that I'd be blamed if we lost. The coaches were good to me, although I don't know what they would have said if we'd lost. 'You'll have a big one next week,' they told me. I thanked the team in the rooms afterwards and told them I wanted to have a big one for them. We were into another Grand Final – this time against the red-hot Brisbane Lions.

'Matthew Lloyd. Not only a 100 goal full-forward, but an unselfish one too. Reliable full-forwards are rare, but Lloyd averages more than four goals a game as he continues to develop as a footballer. [He is] another extremely marketable player who attracts sponsorship dollars to his club.'

Robert Walls, The Age, *29 June 2001*

15

If It Bleeds . . .

'Matty Lloyd comes in at number three. He is just about the perfect player. He rarely misses a game, averages five goals a game, has an extraordinary conversion rate (105.36) and is selfless.'
    Mike Sheahan's Top 50 Players, Herald Sun, *6 October 2001*

GRAND FINAL WEEK IN 2001 was an easier process for me than the year before. It was my second time, and I wasn't invited to the Brownlow Medal dinner because I had been suspended. We went through the same requests for tickets, parades, media interviews and build-up as a team, but we'd been there before.

Sean Wellman and I went around to Alec 'Kooka' Epis's house for the Brownlow count. Kooka and I had a long-running competition about Brownlow votes. He always said I'd never beat his best of fourteen Brownlow votes as long as my bottom was pointing to the ground. Welly and I were cheering every vote I got along the way, while Alec would laugh if I missed. In Round 21 I got two votes against the Eagles to move to fourteen votes, equalling my result in

2000. But I got my fifteenth vote in the final round to knock Kooka off and we roared with laughter.

We knew Brisbane was going to be a formidable opponent in the Grand Final – they hadn't lost a match since the middle of the year. During the season, Leigh Matthews had said, 'If it bleeds, we can kill it.' It was flattering that he took that approach because it meant he held us in high esteem, but the Lions used his words as motivation. We'd had a tough slog against the Hawks so we knew Brisbane would be fresher than us, but we had experience. We also had some injury concerns, though, and we weren't the same team as we were in 2000.

We started the game well and they missed some easy shots, which was a good sign. Because we'd had a week off and then I'd been suspended, I had effectively missed two games, which would normally have been a worry for me. But I was motivated to get the job done, and I was probably playing the best footy of my career to that stage.

We were twenty points up near the end of the second quarter but lapsed a little at that point. Alastair Lynch marked and goaled late in the second quarter, which meant we led by fourteen points at the long break. I often think back to that moment. If he hadn't have kicked that, could things have been different?

With Hird and Mercuri struggling to run due to groin strains, Simon Black, Luke Power, Michael Voss, Jason Akermanis and Nigel Lappin cut lose in the second half. We still felt we were good enough to beat them, but we couldn't. We had more experience but we had injuries too. Brisbane was good and getting better. They hadn't started the year well, but they had momentum at the right time. You need everything to be just right to win a flag, and for us it wasn't in 2001.

Mercs spent most of the game on the bench and only got a handful of touches, while Hirdy just wasn't himself – he didn't have his usual flow. Scotty Lucas and I had good first halves, but Brisbane swapped our opponents at half time. Mal Michael came onto me and Justin Leppitsch went onto Scott, as we were going well considering the supply was drying up. I kicked one in the third quarter, which was our only goal, but the Lions piled on six and we fell behind.

Scotty and I both kicked late goals in the last quarter – I finished with five and Scotty four – but all that did was cut the final margin back to twenty-six points. After the siren, I sat on the ground, exhausted. I'd just worked hard for four quarters but had nothing to show for it. 'This could be it for us,' I was thinking. 'Will Sheeds start looking to rebuild, or have we got another tilt left in us?'

Michael Long and Dean Wallis retired once our season ended, and we also had to cut a few players because of the salary cap. Longy hadn't been able to play in the Grand Final because of injury. He'd spoken to us before the match and told us how he wished he could be there, but he said his body had let him down and he was going to retire. It was such an emotional moment – there were tears rolling down Longy's face.

Looking back, it probably wasn't the best time for him to tell us that, but that was Longy. He wore his heart on his sleeve and bled red and black, as did Dean Wallis. Club lists were smaller by this time and the salary cap was an issue, so it was hard for a footy club to carry even an icon of the game like him when he had injury concerns. Losing characters like him, players of his quality, is always going to hurt a club in the short term. Longy was such a team man – as brilliant as he was, he was such a selfless player. He is one of the players I enjoyed playing with most.

The pain of the loss was dulled a little by the memory of winning in 2000, but it was still tough. I questioned my own performance – what more could I have done? How, as a team, could we have stopped that Lynch goal before half time? If we'd done that and kicked the first goal of the third quarter we'd have been twenty-six points up; instead, it went the other way and we were up by only eight points.

I was so drained at the end of the day and I had a massive headache. It was a warm day and I'd given my all, but it hadn't been enough. I went to my hotel room during our after-match function and just sat there. Going to a post-Grand Final function when you've lost isn't a lot of fun. In 2000 I'd been riding high and had the night of my life, celebrating like there was no tomorrow. This time, I just wanted to get out of there.

I knew we'd missed our chance to cement our greatness as a team. Now we had only one Premiership from that three-year period of dominance. I should have been at least a two-time Premiership player, and other blokes like Fletch and Hirdy should have had three. It was a dark day.

'He was the consummate professional. He wasn't as spectacular as a lot but he was totally efficient, well prepared, did the right things, was predictable in the way he played and he finished well. So notwithstanding that daggy habit of picking the grass up under a roof, everything about him was professional.'

Mike Sheahan

16

The Time Had Come

In 2001 I had moved out of the family home in Avondale Heights and into a house I'd bought in Moonee Ponds. It was massive but it needed some renovating. It was a good home for a family, and I'd already started thinking about my future with Lisa. But living there alone turned out to be a pile of trouble. When some of my teammates got bored on a late night out they'd come and terrorise me. Their favourite was to wear *Scream* masks and bang on the windows. My house was always getting egged and my car would often be wrapped in toilet paper when I got up to go to training in the morning. The boys obviously had too much time on their hands.

I was very strict with my preparation on match days and the day of a night match I'd always try to get an afternoon sleep, but I'd always have kids knocking at my door to wish me good luck. Being a drop punt away from Windy Hill, everyone wanted to talk about the Essendon Football Club. I started spending more time at Lisa's place in Greenvale than I did in Moonee Ponds.

Lisa and her mother, Mary, were sensational for me through that period. Mary would cook up a storm and treated me like her own son. Along with Lisa's sister, Tania, they are such a close family. I knew the Moonee Ponds house was a good investment property, but I just wasn't enjoying living there. And, to be honest, I couldn't cook. Still can't.

It got to the point where the only time I was spending there was the night before games. Later in 2001 I bought a modern-style townhouse in the 'Melburnian' building in St Kilda Road, Southbank, and that suited me much better. It required less maintenance and allowed me to get out of the fishbowl of the Essendon area. The Tan was across the road so I could do all my off-season training there, and it took no time at all to get to training at Windy Hill.

Lisa was a little nervous that I was going to live in the city while she stayed in Greenvale, but I had a plan. After buying the three-level townhouse, I had it all decked out with new furniture ready for our arrival. I say *our* arrival as, after eight years together, the time had arrived for me to propose.

One night Lisa and I went out to watch a Tom Cruise movie, *Vanilla Sky*. I'd organised for my brother Brad to go to the townhouse to light a whole bunch of candles and deck out the house with roses so all would be in readiness for the big moment when we got home. I didn't have a ring, but I was going to propose that night.

Apart from knocking over a couple of candles and putting hot wax all over my new black couch, Brad did a great job. I'd even asked him to scatter rose petals up the steps to the bedroom. 'I'm only planning on doing this once,' I thought, 'so I'd better make it a night to remember.'

After the movie, I said to Lisa, 'I just need to check up on something in the townhouse – come in with me.' We walked up the stairs, she saw the roses, and as we looked out over the city lights, I asked her to marry me. She was in total shock, but said yes.

I hadn't told anyone other than Brad, so we called both our families and they came over to eat a late dinner and celebrate the new stage of our lives that was about to begin.

17

Cultural Shift

'If you were going to write a story about Matthew Lloyd in the early-2000s you could almost call it "my two left feet", he just wasn't that coordinated with his footwork. Over time he went on he became one of the best – and that's the sort of bloke he is. He just worked and worked and worked and worked at it.'

John Quinn

AT ESSENDON, WE WEREN'T sure what 2002 was going to be like. We'd gone into 2001 asking, 'Can anybody catch us?' But at the start of 2002 we knew that things had changed. We had dropped off a bit and Brisbane had certainly picked up. Maybe in 2001 they were the Bombers of 1999 and on the rise. The only difference was that they had delivered first-up, whereas we had failed in the Preliminary Final of 1999.

The quality of our list started to drop as we began the process of letting players go to stay under the salary cap. Michael Long and Dean Wallis retired after careers with us that had lasted well over ten years and included two premierships, while John Barnes left after two very productive seasons.

Damien Hardwick was the first casualty of the salary-cap cuts. He ended up heading to Port Adelaide, where he eventually snagged a second premiership. I knew he would have loved to have stayed, but he was offered a one-year deal at Essendon; Port Adelaide gave him three. Dimma, as we called him, had been a heart-and-soul player of the club, and the way he performed for Port Adelaide on Grand Final day in 2004 had me thinking what a quality person and player we had lost at the end of 2001.

At Essendon in 2002, there was a widening gap between the hardened senior unit, which had been building for four or five years, and a large group of new and unproven players. Some of those young players, many of us felt, weren't going to make it.

The draft at the end of 2000 had been a poor one. Jordan Bannister, Marcus Bullen, James Davies, Ted Richards and Joel Reynolds, who were all meant to be our future stars, were proving to be fringe players at best. Despite that, we still had a senior core as good as any team: Hird was probably the best and most influential player in the league, Mercuri and Misiti were stars, Fletcher was the best full-back in the competition, while Lucas was becoming an elite player. Where we'd dropped off was at the middle and bottom end, but we thought we could still be a top-four side. Who knew what could happen from there?

I injured a quad in the 2002 preseason and it hampered my preparation for the whole year. It was my eighth season and I was a lot bigger than when I had started. I was up to ninety-four kilograms, which meant I could stand my ground against the monster full-backs, but I was still looking to run with the midfield group at training, which wasn't smart.

I was starting to feel some mental strain, too. I had a strongly competitive nature and was pushing myself to the limits on the track, but I was probably also showing the first signs of the fatigue AFL footy can bring. I'd played 142 games as a 24-year-old and was one of the most experienced players at the club.

Paul Salmon had been brought out of retirement to help out Steven Alessio in the ruck. He had played full-forward when I was starting out, but his role in 2002 was clearly as ruck support. In any case, I felt secure in my role with the team because I was now established and was coming off the back of two seasons of more than 100 goals.

When my quad was right, I was allowed to play in a trial game with Bendigo. Dean Solomon and Paul Salmon also played in that game, and a lot of the senior guys were there to watch us have a hit-out. It was good to finally play with Salmon as a peer. I'd kicked my first goal in AFL footy when the ball had slipped off the back of his hands, but I didn't get to play many games with him before he left for Hawthorn.

Lining up for Bendigo meant I also got to play against my brother Brad, who was playing for our opponents, Williamstown. The match was at three pm on the Friday a week before our Round 1 game against Geelong. For me, it was just about getting some touch and I got what I needed out of it.

It wasn't a good match for Solly, though. Just before half time, he changed direction and did his knee in what looked like a nothing incident. He was one of the toughest guys I ever played with, and I'll never forget his scream as he went down. It was tough for the senior group to see one of the most popular players in our team go down. The mood around the club slumped.

Again, we hadn't won a game in the preseason competition. We had showed patchy form but we weren't worried. We went into Round 1 feeling good despite losing Solly for the season with a ruptured anterior cruciate ligament, and we rolled Geelong by fifty points. I ended the day with six goals, which was a great return considering that I'd only played half a game leading into it and was opposed to Matthew Scarlett.

The talk in the media was that Essendon and Brisbane were a cut above the rest of the competition, but things were changing and they hadn't picked up on the subtle shift in power. We were a more fragile team – a couple of injuries would hurt us, whereas in previous years we'd had enough depth and confidence to cover most losses. There was always a risk, too, that our players might get complacent and drop off in performance. Essendon had missed the finals the year after winning the 1993 Premiership, so we knew how important it was that we stay on our game if we were to win another crack at it.

In Round 2 we played Richmond while Brisbane played Hawthorn – so both the Grand Finalists from the year before were playing the teams that lost the Preliminary Finals the year before. We both had really strong wins. Ours was by fifty points and the Lions got up by more than 100. So Brisbane and Essendon sat at the top of the ladder with massive percentages. We were miles in front of everyone else and were scheduled to clash at the Gabba in Round 3.

We felt clearly superior to maybe ten or twelve clubs at that time. When we played those clubs, we walked onto the field feeling we were already in front. With the other teams it was not so clear-cut. Against Brisbane, we knew we were going to have to fight, and the reality was that we still didn't travel well. We played our best footy at Colonial Stadium and had a poor record on the road.

Before the game, we looked for the positives to motivate ourselves. We talked about the lost Grand Final, which had a lot of meaning to those of us that were there, but little to the others – such as Mark Bolton, Robert Forster-Knight, Aaron Hennemen, David Hille, Damien Peverill and Joel Reynolds – who weren't on the field six months earlier.

I don't think we realised at the time how strong Brisbane was becoming. They had what might be the greatest midfield in history. You just couldn't contain all of Akermanis, Lappin, Black, Voss and Power. And because we couldn't hold all of them, how were we to cope with the huge amount of ball heading towards Jonathan Brown, Alastair Lynch and Daniel Bradshaw in their forward line? Who should Dustin Fletcher take?

One of the things you notice when you are measuring your own performance is the confidence of the teams you play. As they get more of a sniff, they start talking a lot more. You could see it with the Australian cricket team. When they were at their peak, you couldn't shut them up, whereas now you don't see them talk a lot on the field. That probably allows other sides to gain some confidence against them.

I had a tough tussle with Mal Michael and Justin Leppitsch

that day. Leppitsch was sitting just in front of me, looking to cut off my leads, while I'd have Mal coming at me from behind with big spoils. I got three goals, though, and I was still leading the goalkicking, although we were well beaten by a far superior side in the Lions.

We had to try to find some positives in the loss, and there was no better coach than Kevin Sheedy for that. We played Adelaide at Colonial Stadium next and bounced back with a big win, and I kicked six. We weren't a quick side but we did move the ball pretty well; we had pretty good foot-skills compared to other teams. Those strengths suited Colonial Stadium, especially with the roof closed. We struggled out on the MCG when it was blustery.

I was travelling okay and we only had the one loss from four matches, but I was starting to feel the mental strain. I had a massive desire for the team to keep succeeding. My personal expectations were enormous, which sometimes I felt was a negative, but more often than not it was a good thing. It kept me on the edge. I had kicked 100 goals in the previous two seasons, and that was my goal again. With eighteen goals after four games, I was on target.

Our traditional Anzac Day match against Collingwood was next, and the weather was shocking. I played on Shane Wakelin again and kicked two goals, which was half our team's total for the day as we went down by thirty-three points. Mark McGough from Collingwood excelled and the Collingwood players were far more desperate than us. They played the wet conditions much smarter.

We went to Subiaco the next week to play Fremantle, and our entire season was turned on its head. Hirdy was chasing a long kick, following the flight of the ball as he always did. Spike McVeigh was coming in too, also with his eyes on the ball, and he was pushed by a Fremantle player. As he was falling forwards, Hirdy was on his hands and knees looking to scramble for a mark and Spike's kneecap crashed right into the top of Hirdy's head.

I was oblivious to what went on afterwards because the game was still going on, but he headed off the field with blood pouring down his face and his head pretty much caved in from the impact.

Hirdy wasn't our only concern, either. Freo had a kick-in from a behind just before half time and it went to my opponent, Shane Parker. I went over to slow him up and got my finger caught in the sleeve of his jumper. 'Geez, that hurt,' I instantly thought. When I tried to clench my right fist after that, all my fingers would bend apart from the ring finger, which stayed straight.

With all the commotion about Hirdy's injury, I played out the half, although I couldn't really attack the ball. At half time the medical staff were preparing to send Hirdy off to hospital because his injuries were so severe. I was sitting at my locker and looking at my hand when I saw Ian Reynolds, one of our club doctors, walk past. 'Ian, can you have a look at my finger?' I said. 'I can't bend it.'

As he strapped it up, he said, 'I think you're in a bit of trouble, but do you think you can you play out the game?' I did, but I couldn't mark the ball and had no influence. I went up to Ian afterwards and said, 'What have I done to it? Can I play next week?'

'No, Lloydy, this is an eight-week injury,' he said.

I was stunned – I had thought it was just a bad dislocation.

'The tendon in your finger has been ruptured,' Ian continued. 'The tendon is like a broken rubber band – the longer you leave it, the further it will creep up your forearm. That would be disastrous and would have long-term effects.' Ian said we'd deal with it when we got back to Melbourne, and he strapped it in a special way to stop the tendon moving too much on the flight back from Perth.

The mood on the way home was as low as I could ever remember. Not only had we lost the match, we had also lost me and Hirdy, who had had to remain in hospital in Perth. We were both expected to be missing for a while – eight weeks for me, and we simply didn't know about Hirdy. It seemed like the whole year was over.

We had our recovery session at ten am the next morning. The coaches had sensed the vibe and wanted to get on top of it as quickly as possible. They decided to use our injuries as an opportunity to motivate the group – who was going to step up? The younger blokes would have to stand on their own two feet.

I went to see a surgeon, Greg Hoy, the next day and we spoke about what needed to happen. While the pain from the surgery lasted a while, the most frustrating thing was that I had to wear a cast for seven weeks with my wrist angled forwards, to keep the finger in the right position. It was like the Lleyton Hewitt salute.

Hirdy had it worse than me, though. He stayed in Perth for a week or two before he could fly home. The doctors had to peel his face back so they could rebuild his bone structure – they said it was like he had been in a car crash.

I had two hours of rehab every day with Carmel, the wife of one of our physios, Bruce Connor, and I had to do more finger exercises at home. I had to shower with a plastic bag over the cast because it couldn't get wet, and Lisa had to drive me everywhere because I couldn't. It was the most frustrating injury I'd ever had.

It was hard mentally as well as physically. I'd had the spleen injury in 1996 but I hadn't missed a game because of it, since it had happened in the last game of the season. I missed six when I fractured my thumb in 1996, but now I had to sit out eight weeks with this finger injury. This was the downside of footy, but injuries were inevitable.

While I was out injured, I tried to be as supportive of the other players as possible, and to assist the forwards. I made an effort to find the guys who needed a boost and to have a chat with them, and I looked out for things during the game that I could talk to them about. I spent some time in the coaches' box, which was very interesting.

I was also spending a lot more time with Lisa. We were getting ready for our wedding later in the year so I became more involved in that. She stopped going to the footy when I wasn't playing. She didn't have a great interest in the game in general – she didn't even know there was a defensive end since all she looked at was our forward line!

Lisa was doing a show on the Fox Footy channel called *Living With*. She was on it with a rotating panel of past and present players' partners, and they'd often be quoted in the papers. I was on the edge of my seat during the show hoping that she and other wives didn't give away too much.

Hirdy's battle to come back from his injury was awesome.

In his weaker moments – he had a huge amount of pain to deal with – he was saying it was all over and that he didn't know how he'd be able to play again. By comparison, I was lucky. I had my surgery and was able to jump on the bike to keep my fitness up, and I could stay around the team, but he couldn't.

With injuries like that, you just want to be healthy again as the pain is off the charts. It's not about playing footy – you just want to feel normal again. The spleen injury I suffered was just like that. This one for me was more annoying than painful, but I couldn't even get sweat on my finger during my rehab on this one, and that didn't help the recovery and I started to worry about my career after starting the year feeling so secure.

Both James and I were worriers – Bruce Reid reckoned Hirdy was worse than me. It meant we were able to pick each other up emotionally, though, because we each knew what the other was thinking. I'd see the crinkles in his forehead due to the stress he was under and know what I had to do to lift his spirits.

When he got back to Melbourne, he started to feel better about life. After a few weeks we both headed up to Alec Epis's farm at Woodend for a day. During the drive there and back, I told him about my mindset prior to that Fremantle game: I'd been feeling flat and was going through the motions a bit. When the injury happened, I had realised, it had come at a time I was putting so much pressure on myself to perform at a high level that it was getting to me.

He said, 'Remember that old saying? Everything happens for a reason. Maybe the injury is telling you something.'

After serious injuries, we both knew we had to appreciate our health while we had it. He said we couldn't take playing in the AFL for granted, because when you're on the sidelines with injury it's a very lonely place.

We spoke about how we wanted to make an impact as soon as we hit the field again. Little did we realise it that would be in the same game against the Bulldogs in Round 14. Afterwards, I often thought it was ironic that we missed the same amount of games because I'd only hurt my finger and Hirdy had smashed his head in.

'The mighty Bombers, the usually cocky Bombers, are in shock and disarray. Essendon is eighth, with just a 50 per cent win rate, and so many injuries even St Kilda is sympathetic ... Six rounds in, there is genuine doubt about Essendon's ability to mount a challenge this year.'

Mike Sheahan, Herald Sun, *6 May 2002*

18

The Prodigal Sons' Return

'There was a ruthless edge to him particularly when he evolved as a leader. He didn't want to have any passengers playing in his team; he wouldn't stand for poor discipline.'

Mark Harvey

To the guys' credit, they had performed really well without Hirdy and me. They won five of the seven matches we ended up missing, and the club was sitting fifth on the ladder after Round 13. It showed the strength of the group, which perhaps owed something to what we had built over the previous three seasons. Paul Barnard thrived throughout this period.

Once Hirdy and I realised there was a possibility we could return to the team in the same week, we worked hard to make sure it happened. We were both selected to take on the Bulldogs in Round 13. It was a big Friday night match, and I started on a half-forward flank. The idea was to give me more opportunities to take uncontested marks and not have my finger whacked too much. I had to wear a special glove that held two of my fingers together for support. I took a couple of strong grabs, and once I knew my finger was fine I was suddenly feeling eighteen again. I kicked a goal early in the second quarter, which gave my confidence a boost.

I was playing on Steve Kretiuk that night, and he was playing rough – every time I went near the ball he'd drop into me with his knees. When I kicked my third goal I was up in his face; he was bending over and I crashed into him, and when he stood up I gave him the old 'Come on!'

Kretiuk was the wrong bloke to do that to and I could see his eyes rolling in anger. As we headed back to the goal square he started smashing my hand, trying to hurt me. I just let him do it because I knew my finger was okay, and I didn't want him thinking I was going to try to protect it. The Essendon cheer squad was going crazy at him and it became a huge story that week.

As I saw it, all's fair in love and war. I was fine with what Kretiuk had done and I was quite embarrassed with the coverage it got. I was on the field and my hand was okay. As I saw it, you do whatever it takes to get an advantage so long as you don't thump someone. It did upset Lisa and my mum, though. But I knew I'd crashed into his back – I'd made him angry, so I'd brought it on myself.

It had been a great game, and that was getting lost in the craze over Kretiuk. I had kicked five goals and Hirdy had won twenty-five possessions in a near best-on-ground performance. Late in the game we were down by a point when a long bomb was fired in my direction. Kretiuk was defending me but he slung me to the ground. I was awarded a free kick, which meant I had a kick for goal after the siren to win the match – it was the stuff of childhood dreams.

There were about seven blokes on the mark, jumping up and down, and there were blokes on the side too. I was about twenty metres out, on the wrong side for a left-footer. I stabbed at the ball and tried to caress it through, but as it came off the boot it veered to the left and went through for a point. The match was a draw but it felt like a loss to me because it was a goal I should have kicked. I had missed my chance to have a fairytale comeback and I was down on myself for it.

I hadn't followed my routine properly and I suffered for it and let the team down. Even a missed kick at goal that meant nothing to the outcome could keep me awake at night, so you can imagine what this one did to me. I chewed over it for at least two days. I hoped those two premiership points wouldn't cost us a spot in the top four or worse at the end of the season – we were only just inside the eight at that stage.

I was happy with how both Hirdy and I had gone, though. It was great to be back, and the fact that we returned in such good physical shape was a credit to the fitness team at Essendon. But coming up for our second match – against West Coast over in Perth – wasn't easy. I was that sore after my first match back and could hardly move. That is why it is often said in football that the second match back is often harder than the first.

Hirdy attacked the ball in exactly the same manner that had made him such a champion – arguably Essendon's greatest player. It was as if was he wasn't wearing a head guard and didn't have plates in his face. It took three or four weeks for me to find consistent form, though, and we were up and down as a team. We actually lost four of the next six matches after Hirdy and I returned.

I was only a bit-part player with one or two goals a match during that run. Our return was hard on the rest of the players, especially the guys who'd done such a great job without us and who were pushed back to the twos when we returned. In that six-week period I struggled – I only touched the ball six times in the loss to Brisbane, and I copped a corkie that held me back against Adelaide and I only got five touches in that match.

I'll never forget that Brisbane game. I took a big mark in the first minute or two and kicked a goal, and I mouthed off to Justin Leppitsch afterwards. I was trying to get myself going, I suppose. When the next ball came to us, he dropped a knee into my quad. He did it well and it looked discreet enough. By the end of that first quarter I couldn't run because of the bleeding in my leg, and that finished me for the day. I sat out the rest of the match with an ice pack, having learnt another lesson on why I shouldn't mouth off.

Sometimes, you get yourself up for a game that you shouldn't be in, and the Adelaide match the next week was one of those. I didn't train all week and I only just got through the final session. Sheedy and John Quinn didn't question me when I said I was right to play. I thought I was okay, but really I wasn't and Nigel Smart beat me hands down.

My failure in that match stung me into action, and I was desperate to finish the season well. I knew I had to start leading harder at the ball again and crash the packs. I recovered well during the week and was fine to play our next game against Collinwood.

My first mark of the match was good, and from there I got the better of Simon Prestigiacomo and kicked five. I even got two Brownlow votes. What I learnt then was how much footy is a battle between the ears. It was my first good game since the Bulldogs match, and the whole team played well to beat the Pies, which put us back in the eight. We felt like we were back on track.

Luke McPharlin at Freo was a player who always made me nervous because of his leg speed and his athleticism. But I went into our Round 21 clash with confidence and won the duel. Then we beat Carlton in the final round and people started to say we were hitting our straps at the right time. Scott Lucas was playing brilliant footy after recovering from injury – he was often the forgotten man of our forward line, but he dominated the final round of the season.

We had finished the year in fifth place, just two points behind Collingwood, and we believed we could make an impact in the finals. I worked out that even if I had kicked the goal to beat the Bulldogs, we still would have missed the top four on percentage, which was a massive relief to me.

Finishing fifth, we had an Elimination Final against West Coast at Colonial Stadium and I went into the match full of confidence. I got into a clash with Peter Matera in the first quarter and I got a big gash when he whacked me and I had to go off for stitches. He was a bit quicker with his hands than I was, and he had hit me pretty hard.

As soon as the stitches were in, I was back on the ground. Not long after, I was running to a contest and Adam Hunter from the Eagles was running the other way. The ball bobbled up between us and we both turned our shoulders to protect ourselves and win the ball. We clashed heads and that was it for me.

I've seen the incident on tape – which is how I can describe it – but I don't remember a thing about it. I was out cold for three minutes and I'd swallowed blood, so Reidy had me on my side to make sure I didn't choke. The first thing I remember after coming to is hearing someone crying – it was Lisa, who was in the front seat of the ambulance. Our family and friends have had a laugh since, saying that the first question Lisa asked when I opened my eyes was, 'Does he still remember he's getting married later this year?'

I was nauseous and constantly vomiting blood after the clash, which was a huge concern. I later found out that bleeding on the brain had caused that. Simon and my parents came into the hospital after watching the rest of the game, which we had won. They were raving about Scott Lucas' game and that it was probably the best they'd ever seen him play. He had started at centre half-back but had moved forward when I was injured. Scotty was the difference in the match.

So we'd won the elimination final and were still in the fight, but I was in a pretty bad way for a couple of days. I wondered how boxers can cope with the knockdowns they cop. Our next final was in Adelaide against Port, but Reidy said pretty early in the week that I wouldn't be playing. I felt lightheaded and unsteady on my feet, and it took me the whole week to feel normal again. Port had topped the ladder but had then had a shock loss to Collingwood, so they were fired up. The match didn't go well for us and Port ended our season.

I was glad the year was over. It had started well, but with injury and poor form I was happy to put it behind me and look ahead to 2003.

It had been a rough year on the field, but at least I had my wedding to look forward to. We had chosen to have it on the 9th of November, just in case we made the Grand Final and everyone went away after the season. I asked John Quinn if I could have a honeymoon as well, given that we'd be back in training by then, and he said, 'Sure, go. But once you get back, you're mine.'

The wedding was great, although I was pretty nervous. We were only twenty-four. Lisa felt like I'd taken too long to ask her, but to me it still felt like we were so young. I was fine throughout the preparations and at the church, but my biggest stress was the speech at the reception and then the dance. We'd had a few lessons but I was still hopeless. I think I needed some grass to throw to get my heart-rate down!

Lisa's father, Frank, had died of cancer when she was fourteen, but I knew she would be thinking of him. Her uncle Pat walked her down the aisle and her brother-in-law Greg gave a speech on behalf of the father of the bride. So it was a day full of emotion, but it was the best day of our lives to that point.

The joy I felt was quite different to winning the Premiership – that had been the outcome of a lot of hard work, and in many respects the hard work was only just starting for us. We had about 140 people at the reception, including many of my closest teammates at Essendon. Eddie McGuire was the MC and, as you would expect, did an unbelievable job. Eddie actually cut a holiday short to help us out, so we were very grateful to him and Carla for that.

I had done a deal with *New Idea* to cover the wedding, and because Lisa worked with Fox Footy channel they filmed the wedding and made a program about it. I copped a bit of flack from the boys about both of those, but how many people have an hour-long TV documentary on their wedding? It's something special that we can keep and show the kids as they get older.

Lisa and I spent our honeymoon in Vegas, seeing all the shows and playing the casinos. Then we relaxed at our favourite holiday destination, Hawaii. After that, it was back to preseason training for me, and I was the property of John Quinn.

> 'I think when they look back, they'll say he was a really special one.'
>
> *John Quinn*

19

Losing Quality

'Essendon spearhead Matthew Lloyd has left his long-time management group, Ricky Nixon's Flying Start, to join the theatrical-based management company Sports and Entertainment Limited.'

Karen Lyon, The Age, *4 December 2002*

ESSENDON LOST JUSTIN BLUMFIELD, Chris Heffernan and Blake Caracella at the end of the 2002 season due to the pressure of the salary cap. Half of a veteran-listed player's salary doesn't go into the salary cap, and the club thought that Hirdy and maybe one other player could fit into that category that year, but it turned out they couldn't. With that, some players had to be culled. It was a very ugly situation for the club.

The trade period had ended at two pm on a Friday. Before it ended, Justin Blumfield had been on the phone with Sheeds, saying, 'I don't want to play for Richmond but Richmond is offering the best deal.' Apparently, Sheeds said to him, 'You'll be playing seconds next year if you stay here.' That was the desperation of the club at that stage. Sheeds needed the trade to happen for us to be under the salary cap.

It was a pretty messy period in the history of the footy club, and that was starting to affect the culture of the place. None of the players wanted to leave but we were said to be $900,000 dollars over the salary cup. Losing them may have relieved the financial pressure but it didn't help the feelings of the remaining players. We were very disappointed that we lost not only quality footballers but also ripping blokes.

Caracella had been a top-ten draft pick, Heffernan had been number two in his draft and Blumfield had almost won a Norm Smith Medal in 2000. In my opinion, these guys were good enough to win us an extra three or four games a year, and on top of that they were very well liked. As a player who would be there in 2003, though, I just had get over that – I had my own career to fight for – but it was a really tough time.

The changes meant that, by the start of 2003, eight of our Premiership side from 2000 had moved on. I felt that all these player losses were weakening our strength as a club, and the guys who had been recruited in the 2000 draft hadn't cut it. The quality of the guys who left meant the hole was too big to fill quickly.

Our club culture was weakening too. We'd started to become a bit of a party club – not everyone, mind you, but there was a group of players that didn't share the ideals that had taken us to the top, three years earlier.

I thought that Sheeds had started to lose his grip too, as he had started topping up our list with older players who were probably past their prime. We should have been looking for younger players with our later picks in the draft, even guys playing in the VFL; they may not have been ready straight-away but could have had ten-year careers.

In the end, we picked up guys like Matthew Allan, Justin Murphy, Ty Zantuck and Scott Camporeale, who were all near the end of their careers but who would play for the base pay or not much more. I didn't mind seeing different faces from other clubs joining us, and I hoped they would bring good form and some fresh ideas, but it's very rare that a player improves after twenty-seven or older, as some of these recruits were.

Around this time, I started to think about my future too. I was still under the management of Ricky Nixon's company, Flying Start. Ricky had been terrific for me, especially when I was young, but I felt I had had outgrown what an organisation like his could offer me. I had a year left on my playing contract, and I realised that if I was going to make a change, I should do it then so that a new manager could look after my next Bombers deal.

As a footballer, your manager is one of the most important people in your life. What I was really looking for was a smaller and more focused management company. I knew there would soon be some salary-cap pressure, and I realised it would be hard for Ricky to get the best deal for me when he had other Essendon players to factor in. I wanted my next contract to truly reflect where I was at.

I needed a manager rather than a management team. I was still at the top of my game but I was also conscious of life after football, and I knew I needed to start looking at what I wanted to do and how I could get there. After all, I couldn't play footy forever.

Andrew Neophitou was Ricky's CEO when I first joined Flying Start in 1995, and we had hit it off straightaway. Neo, as he's known, has a law degree but found it more satisfying to work for Ricky. I felt very comfortable talking to Neo about how I could better myself – not only on the field but also off also it. He'd left Flying Start by 2001 to join SEL, which was a bigger company operating out of Sydney and we had stayed in touch.

In mid 2002 I went to visit Ricky and Alex McDonald, who was looking after me, and let them know I was thinking about moving on. Ricky said he'd have a look at where he thought I should be and see what sort of opportunities we should be looking for. But that took a bit longer to come than I expected, and as I was waiting for that I made my mind up to go with SEL and Neo, who I had asked to manage me.

My next meeting with Ricky wasn't so pleasant. I had made some notes about the reasons I wanted to move, and as I worked through my points I could see Ricky getting pretty angry. Alex remained calm, and I felt glad he was there.

I had endorsements with Nike and Foxtel, of which they were getting twenty per cent, and then a very lucrative deal with Essendon, of which they got three per cent. I was worth a fair bit to them, so I could understand why they were disappointed when I left. I had been with the company since I was sixteen. But I was more mature now, and more confident. If I made a decision, I wanted action, not fluffing around. I also wanted to know that someone was seriously thinking about my life after football.

I was probably earning about half a million dollars a year, which I thought was fair, given my status in the game, but I did have to pinch myself every now and then at the money I was earning. The decision to move wasn't really financial, though, since Flying Start had done a pretty good job. I did think there was more out there for me, but I was most concerned about the level of care I was getting. And when a promised report on your future doesn't come, you start to worry. I felt that with the amount of money I was paying them – probably $60,000 or $70,000 a year – I deserved better service than that.

The end wasn't pleasant with Ricky. I hadn't expected it to be, but I didn't expect what I got, which included a hand-delivered letter accusing Lisa and me of all sorts of treachery. I paid Ricky out for the season, and Neo and SEL took over my affairs. In fact, SEL looked after me for the first year without any commissions. And I never regretted my decision to move. Andrew has become one of my closest friends, and he has given me exactly what I needed as a manager.

The preseason competition of 2003 – the Wizard Home Loans Cup – was a knock-out tournament, and North did exactly that to us when we played them in Canberra. We weren't fussed, though, and we continued preparing for the season proper.

During those few weeks, though, I was tied up in a controversy over the licensing of my internet rights to the club. It was really just the start of the internet era, my management company had registered the domain name www.matthewlloyd.com.au for me, and we planned to develop and commercialise the website. But Essendon wanted to run its own internet site and have all the players be a part of that. They wanted to acquire my online marketing rights so we came to a fair commercial arrangement with the club.

I was still managed by Flying Start at the time this was

done, while Peter Jackson handled the deal for Essendon. I was 100 per cent sure it was all above board, but details of the deal found their way into the media and the AFL decided to investigate it.

It was pretty full-on – I had to give the AFL all my bank statements, which I thought was a bit much, given that I wasn't hiding anything to do with the deal or the money I'd earned from it. I found the investigation very stressful at the time, especially since the last thing I wanted – for myself or the club – was a breach of the salary cap.

Apart from the stigma a breach would bring to the club, the consequences were great. Carlton had been penalised for breaches in the late 1990s and had lost several early draft picks – they should have had Brendon Goddard, for example. In another case, Essendon didn't have a pick until number forty in one draft because we had breached the salary cap in a previous year and not declared it when there was a moratorium. That was in the back of everyone's minds through this process, as it had been when we'd done the deal in the first place. Imagine if the sale of my internet domain cost Essendon draft picks? It was too much for me to think about.

Ken Wood, the AFL's finance advisor, came to the club and asked me a lot of questions. By this time, Neo was my manager, and so he sat through the meetings with me. Having him involved gave me peace of mind, because I knew I could trust him to deal with it. We gave Wood a statement and all the paperwork he asked for.

The AFL took a while to work through all the details but eventually I got the all clear, but it was a worry I didn't need as I prepared for our Round 1 match against the Brisbane Lions.

I was glad to turn my attention back to the season ahead. It was great just to be playing footy again, and for me it was even better because I could play without my fingers being strapped. I still had the thumb-guards, but my fingers were able to move freely. I felt fit once again and, based on how I'd finished 2002, I was approaching the season with confidence.

20

Back in Touch

> 'Matthew Lloyd ... the only genuine 100-goal full-forward in the game. As such is worth his weight in gold. Lost games and confidence with injury last year but has put in a profitable summer to emerge bigger, more powerful and quicker than before.'
>
> Robert Walls, The Age, *22 March 2003*

WHEN ROUND 1 ARRIVED, Brisbane was far too strong for us again. They were really starting to get the wood on us and they just had too much class all over the ground. The match was at the Gabba, and so we played with the 2002 Premiership flag flying above us as a reminder that they'd gone back-to-back. My touch was okay, though, and I started the year with four goals.

I felt revitalised. After my injuries in 2002, I now knew how quickly and easily you can miss a bunch of games. And I was ready to get Essendon back to the top. I was determined not to just make up the numbers – I wanted to be an impact player again.

I wanted to play the game hard again, but not like in 2001,

when I was doing silly things and getting reported all the time. I wanted to be hard at the ball and at the player. Commentators such as Robert Walls had been scathing about me for those incidents; he said I was trying to be something I wasn't, which was partially true.

I never wanted to hurt an opponent with a raised elbow, but I did love the physical side of the game. I got a buzz out of laying a bone-crunching hip-and-shoulder. Back then, I had probably tried too hard to do that, but now I felt I had worked it out. I looked at Jonathan Brown as an example of how I wanted to play. People would say, 'Big, bad Jonathan Brown', but he really just played the footy hard. Unless he was provoked, he didn't go looking for anything other than the ball. That was how I wanted to play and how I wanted to be seen.

In Round 2 we beat Melbourne to sit at tenth on the ladder with one win and one loss. You never want to start a season with multiple losses, so the win was a good result for us. Then we came up against Carlton on Friday night. We went down by a couple of goals and I got reported again.

Glenn Manton and Stephen Silvagni were gone by then, but they'd been replaced by a young guy named Bret Thornton, who spent the match niggling and scragging like he was Steven Kretiuk. It was driving me mad and I threw a pretty weak punch into his tummy just to let him know I was sick of it. Although the ball was up the other end of the ground, there were so many cameras at the Friday night matches that it was seen.

The incident was shown everywhere after the game, and once again I had to front the tribunal after playing Carlton. I had developed a pretty solid dislike of navy blue by this stage of my career. The headlines were 'A case of the Blues', so the media had worked that out too. A more significant issue was that I wasn't alone in being in trouble: Dustin Fletcher and Paul Barnard had also been reported within the first three rounds of the season.

I told a bit of a porkie pie at the tribunal. I said I had been looking at my teammate Damian Cupido and that I had tried to execute a block on Thornton. The tribunal took that on board and let me off, so I was free to play the next week. I had hit him, but it was really only a light tickle so I would have been really disappointed to have been rubbed out. In fact, I reckon the real reason I got off was because of the lack of force involved – I doubt it was because of my lame excuse at the hearing.

During that week, Sheeds spoke to us about consistency. 'You're playing in patches, fits and starts,' he told us. 'You've got to pick it up.' Against the Bulldogs in Round 4, we did. The game was pretty tight in the first half but we blew them away in the second. I had a good game, which was especially pleasing since I had dodged a bullet at the tribunal. It was good having Cupido in the forward pocket beside me – he was a good foil and he was dangerous himself. He was one of our good pick-ups that year.

The Anzac Day game in Round 5 was a ripper – it's a match I remember very fondly. Hirdy was on fire. He was reading the ball off the packs and kicking goals from all angles – his third quarter was devastating. He was such a great big-game player. I kicked six straight, including four in the second quarter, which was my best ever quarter in an Anzac Day clash. Between us, Hird, Cupido and I kicked sixteen goals, which was a huge return from our forwards, and we had our biggest win ever in an Anzac Day game. We felt like our season was well and truly on track.

Not missing a shot at goal was a great result for me. That year, the old Olympic Stand had been pulled down because they were rebuilding the MCG for the 2006 Commonwealth Games, and the wind just whipped through the place. The swirling conditions made kicking for goal really tricky.

We travelled to Fremantle the next week and, true to form, we lost outside Victoria again. I kicked five on Shane Parker, who, like James Clement the week before, was one of the most under-rated players I ever played on. They were both very good full-backs, so I felt like I must be in pretty good touch to get bags against each of them.

Our inconsistency was very frustrating, though. Even leaving aside the interstate trip, we were losing games we should have been winning. Our depth wasn't there, either; if we picked up any injuries or suspensions it really hurt us. But in both my form and my enjoyment for the game, I felt like I was back to my best.

The next week was my 150th game, and I ended it with a quad injury that would keep me out for the next two rounds. We were comprehensively beaten by Richmond; it was a blustery day at the MCG and we had an absolute shocker as a team. My performance was pretty ordinary – I only kicked one goal – and we had no spark whatsoever. To make matters worse, I had strained my quad muscle during the match.

Because it was a milestone game, everyone who was close to me had come to watch, and I felt embarrassed about our lifeless performance. The next night, Lisa and I attended the Logies, which we'd been invited to because of her show on Foxtel, but I felt awful being there after my terrible game. I did an interview for Bomber Radio while I was there, and I said, 'You can't say I'm at the Logies.' I was concerned about how it would look after such a bad loss. You still have to have a life, though, and I was there for Lisa, not me.

Hirdy and I both missed the next week with injury. Fortunately, we faced Hawthorn, who we'd been beating up for years, and we did it again.

I missed one more match but returned against West Coast at the Telstra Dome, as the Docklands stadium was then called. I was a bit nervous because the strain had been in my kicking leg. When I marked the ball on the fifty-metre line early in the first quarter, I thought, 'This is going to test out the quad,' but my kick sailed through the middle and I figured there wasn't too much wrong. I often struggled after a lay-off, so to come back with six goals and the three Brownlow votes was great.

We lost to Sydney the following week, which meant we were outside the eight at the halfway point of the season with five wins and six losses. Our inconsistency was really hurting us, and we lost the next one as well.

I was struggling to rationalise my good personal form with the team's lack of success. A few years earlier I would have been on cloud nine, but not now. I realised that what I enjoyed most was playing well in a win, and that wasn't happening often enough. We weren't running out our games very well, perhaps because some of the boys were having too many big nights out and weren't committed enough. Some blokes could live like that and still perform on the field, but not everyone could. They were mostly young, single guys, and I didn't want to take the life out of them, but there had to be some limits if we were to play well every week.

I wasn't seeing a lot of the partying that went on because I usually just went home, but I did hear stories during the week. The only time I'd really go out with my teammates was after an interstate game, but even then I'd go for only a couple of hours to wind down and then head back to my hotel room. The days of getting home at four am after going on a bender were a thing of the past.

Matthew Scarlett did a number on me in Round 13. We won, but I contributed only one goal. Some days you're just beaten by a better opponent or you don't get the opportunities, but I was still disappointed because I demanded a lot of myself and was well beaten by a superstar in the making in Scarlett.

Still, after playing eleven games I had forty-three goals, so to be going at four goals a game was a pretty good return. The next week I hit back with eight against St Kilda. St Kilda wasn't very strong at the time, but our sixty-nine-point win gave us confidence. St Kilda only kicked seven for the night and the media made a big deal of the fact that I kicked more goals than their whole team.

As a team, we continued to be inconsistent. When we lost to Adelaide in Round 15, we were outside the eight by a win and a half. Then we defeated Brisbane, which was a great win.

In Round 17 we faced Melbourne, and I found myself facing accusations of staging once again. Late in the game, Alistair Nicholson and I were on the goal line and I was trying to shepherd a ball through for a goal. The ball sailed over our heads but Nicholson and I kept wrestling, and the umpire was shouting, 'Stop it! Stop it!' Nicholson gave me a little tap and I flopped to the ground, and the umpire blew his whistle and gave me a free kick and an easy goal. In a tight match that we eventually won, Melbourne was ropable about the incident.

I did ham it up – there's no doubt about that – and I'd rather have got the goal by marking the ball fair and square. I shouldn't have done it. I wanted to have the respect of my peers, my opponents, my coaches and the media, and given that I had previously been perceived as a stager, the public reaction had a big impact on me. I couldn't blame anyone but myself, but I hated the stigma of being thought of as a stager, which overshadowed the qualities I possessed as a player. I had to move on and try to make amends on the field.

I was conscious at the time, too, that I was approaching Simon Madden's record of 575 goals for Essendon. He always used to joke that 'you shouldn't have a ruckman as your club's all-time leading goalkicker', and I was keen to go past his mark but I kicked just two goals against Carlton the next week.

The next week we faced the Dogs and I needed eight to take the record. Lisa and most of my family came along to watch me, but I wasn't confident I would do it as I'd had a couple of lean weeks. But our midfield had a big day and there was plenty of ball coming my way, and I reached the milestone in the third quarter before going on to kick eleven goals for the day. It was a great result for me and we had a big win.

Breaking that record was a big thing for me and it still gives me a lot of pride to be the greatest goalkicker in Essendon's 120-year history. When I started my career, something like that was just a dream. It was a club that had great forwards such as John Coleman, Roger Merrett, Paul Van Der Haar, Simon Madden and Paul Salmon, and I'm very proud to be up there with them.

Footy is a team sport, but there's no one in the game who doesn't want to do well as an individual too. I never hid from the fact that I always wanted to kick a bag of goals. I wouldn't go outside the team framework, but I wanted to kick as many goals as possible for my team. To get more than anyone ever had at Essendon was pretty special.

I was given the match ball from that game, and I asked Kevin Sheedy, James Hird and Simon Madden to sign it. Madden wrote his tally and the date of when I passed it, as well as a message saying he hoped I'd kick many more in the future. He was our ruck coach, so it was great to have him there to congratulate me on the day.

The Coleman Medal is something I rate highly, and after the 2002 season it was a personal goal I set myself for in 2003. By this stage I was looking like winning it; the only question was whether I could get to 100 goals after missing those two games with a quad strain. I was disappointed with my performance in our final-round loss to the Pies, but it was our only stumble in around six weeks and Collingwood was in good form at the time. I finished the season well in front of Alastair Lynch to win my third Coleman Medal.

After the home-and-away season was done, we had finished in eighth position, meaning we had to travel to Perth to play fifth-placed Fremantle in an Elimination Final. It was their first-ever finals match but defeating them at home was going to be a big challenge, especially given our poor away record.

The team met early in the week to discuss what we could do differently to win a game on the road. We decided to stay in two-bedroom apartments rather than the normal hotel routine, and I roomed with Adam McPhee. John Quinn tried to make the setup as much like being at home as possible. We had hot and cold baths set up and we could go out and get our own food.

I got a knock to my leg early in the match and was off for a fair while. As it was a big game, I did everything I could to get back on the ground and help us win that game. I finished with five but the big-game specialist Hirdy put on a show. He was brilliant – he set up goals, he kicked them, he was smothering, he was tackling. 'This bloke is everything you'd want in a captain,' I thought. It's a big call, but this was probably the best game I ever saw him play. We won convincingly, which was a shock because Freo were going pretty well, but I reckon the occasion was too much for them.

Sydney had beaten Port Adelaide in a big upset – Port had topped the ladder again and only lost four matches all year – and so we had to travel the next week to take them on. I was on ninety-two goals for the year.

It was a cold night over there and we knew Port struggled in big games. We never spoke about Port choking but we couldn't help but think about it. The loss to Sydney had clearly stung them, though, and we were blown away in the second half. In some ways, we were pleased that we'd made it into the second week; I don't think the expectations on us were huge. But if we could have pinched that match then we would have been in another Preliminary Final, which would have been against Collingwood at the MCG.

I'd had a poor game, and Mark Robinson from the *Herald Sun* smashed me. He wrote that 'Lloyd was often called a champion but put in another sub-par performance'. That hurt. I knew I hadn't stood up, but I still didn't think criticism like that was warranted.

I had been slammed in the papers before. Robert Walls gave me my first big hammering in 1999, when he said I never performed well in big games. I had a big final about two weeks later, and then he turned around and said what a sensational year I'd had. In two weeks he'd completely changed his opinion! That taught me to not get too caught up in what the media was saying.

Against Port, I'd played on Darryl Wakelin. Both the Wakelin brothers were tough opponents and played the same style of game, sitting in front of me and blocking my run at the footy. If the play wasn't going well for your team, they'd have you, and we hadn't won much ball in the midfield that night.

Footballers have long memories. A few years earlier, I had given Robbo the cold shoulder after one of his comments about me. That seemed to make him more critical of me, so I soon changed that tactic. He was an Essendon supporter and he wore his heart on his sleeve, and he was probably harder on us than on other teams.

I work with Robbo now, and he has told me he felt I was petulant at times back then. I must admit, I could be a little snarly after a loss. Looking back now, I wonder why I worried so much about what people were saying. But then no one likes hearing or reading bad things about themselves.

I guess I craved respect, and so seeing Robbo's criticism of me in the newspaper grated. I drowned it all out with a big end-of-season party. I walked out of an Adelaide nightclub at six am with Paul Barnard and James Hird and went straight to the airport to catch a nine am flight. It had been a long year that I was proud of, but I was disappointed with how it ended.

The team went to Las Vegas for our end-of-season trip. It was the first year I roomed with Hirdy, and it really happened by chance. I saw him in our hotel lobby and he said, 'I've just checked in and I've got two cards – do you want to room with me?' We had a great time, and we came home with a lifetime of stories and laughter. Vegas was the best place I ever went on a footy trip. After going to places like Ibiza, I wondered why we hadn't just done Vegas from the start.

> 'Lloydy is the cleanest, neatest and most structured person of all time. He's immaculate, I've got to say. I was the messy one, he was cleaning up after me half the time. So he was a very good roommate to have, he'd go to bed early, didn't snore and he was very clean. So I've got to give him a tick there – unlike a lot of his teammates who I've roomed with.'
>
> *James Hird*

21

Reality Check

'Essendon has lauded Matthew Lloyd and Sean Wellman for the "reasonable" approach with which they signed new contracts yesterday before warning that others would have to show the same restraint if the club is to avoid the departure of players.'

Stephen Rielly, The Age, *22 August 2003*

ONCE YOU COME BACK to your club to start the preseason, you start reflecting on the previous year, dissecting particular games and the season as a whole. The last game I played in 2003 was a poor one, and I had to wait another six months to get things back on track. In the first couple of weeks of training I was pretty cut up about that, but the feeling subsided as time went by. I was learning not to carry bad performances with me in the same way I used to.

I'd signed a new three-year deal with Essendon for seasons 2004 to 2006, and I was really happy with it. I was earning the sort of money I had never dreamed was possible when I started my career and cleared $14,000.

Kevin Sheedy's advice about purchasing property had

stayed with me since the day I started at Essendon. Over the first ten years of my career, I was fortunate enough to buy some quality properties in good, safe, emerging areas. I'd sold my Moonee Ponds house after only one year but got out of it pretty well. Lisa and I stayed in our apartment in Southbank until Jaeda was born, and then we moved to Brighton in 2006 to raise our family.

In 2004 we won two matches in Wizard Home Loans Cup but were knocked out in the semis by St Kilda, who went on to win the competition. Our first game for 2004 was against Port Adelaide, but by the time the match came around we were struggling. I couldn't remember a team going into the start of a season with so many injuries, and as a result we had two or three first-gamers against Port and we were smashed by ninety-six points. Only seven of our team had played more than 100 games and we were out of our depth. I didn't get many opportunities but I did kick four goals; up the other end, Warren Tredrea and Stewie Dew got six each.

Sheeds was under a lot of pressure, and he must have been wondering how to refocus a team that had been hammered like that at the start of a season. We had a lot of young guys, while so many of our core senior players were no longer at the club.

We were better against St Kilda the next week but still went down by thirty-four points. My game wasn't great. At one stage I fended off Nick Dal Santo and struck him in the head. The day after the match, I got a phone call from the Essendon management to tell me that the Match Review Panel was looking at the incident, and I thought, 'Oh no, not

Me in the garden at my family home in Avondale Heights, 20 months, December 1979.

Standing in the street in the snow with my siblings in Balerno, Scotland, January 1984. *From left to right*: Kylie, me, Brad and Simon.

My parents bought me this great Aberdeen soccer kit for my sixth birthday, which was spent in Greece.

Playing rugby for the Currie Rugby Football Club in Scotland, 1986, aged 8.

Taking a screamer at my best mate Shaun's house on my brother Brad's back, 1986, aged 8, just after returning from Scotland.

Posing for the *Community News* while playing for Avondale Heights Under-10s. This photo accompanied the article on following in Dad's footsteps.

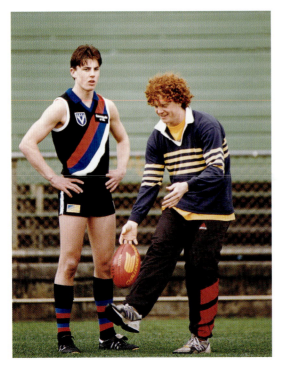

With Tony Delaney late in 1994, around the time the complex deal was done to send him back to Perth to play for Fremantle so I could join the Bombers.

Having a laugh with Hirdy, trying to put him off his shot for goal while the cameras were taking snaps.

My first State of Origin game after 23 games, 1997. Victoria won by eight points. (*The Herald and Weekly Times*/Michael Dodge)

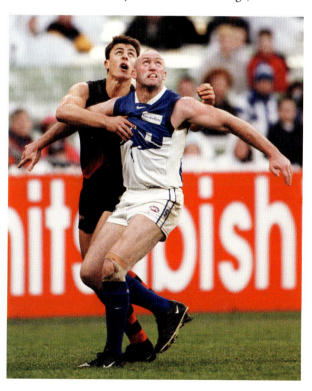

My first big rivalry was with Mick Martyn. He had my measure early on, but in 2000 I was starting to get on top. I kicked seven on him this day and brought up my first ton. (*The Herald and Weekly Times/* George Salpigtidis)

Sharing a magic moment with James Hird and Joe Misiti during the 2000 Grand Final victory over Melbourne. (*The Herald and Weekly Times*/Nicole Garmston)

Inset: holding footy's Holy Grail. (*The Herald and Weekly Times*/ George Salpigtidis)

Celebrating an incredible victory with my Premiership-winning teammates. (*The Herald and Weekly Times*/Michael Dodge)

A billboard on the Niketown store, Bourke Street Mall, Melbourne, January 2000.

Reidy calling for the stretcher after I was knocked unconscious during an elimination final against West Coast in 2002. Lisa wanted to know if I still remembered I was getting married. (*The Herald and Weekly Times*/David Geraghty)

My family on our wedding day, 9 November 2002. *From left to right:* Brad, Dad, Lisa, me, Mum, Kylie and Simon.

My other great support network – Lisa's family. *From left to right:* Lisa's sister, Tania; niece, Kayla; Tania's husband, Greg; nephews, Brandon and Jordan; Lisa; me; niece, Amber; and Lisa's mother, Mary.

My groomsmen. *From left to right:* Mark McVeigh, Simon Lloyd, Brad Lloyd.

With Lisa at the 2005 Brownlow. I always hoped to poll a few votes, but the night was all about the women.

Having a laugh with John Quinn during a training session at Windy Hill, 2003. John was a great mentor to me. (*The Herald and Weekly Times*/Michael Klein)

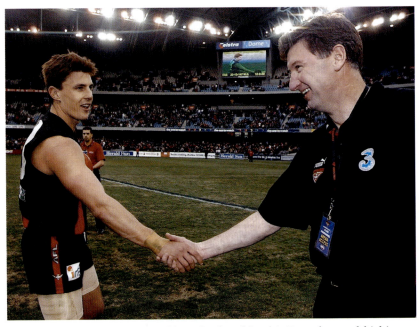

Shaking hands with Simon Madden after breaking his Essendon goal-kicking record with my 576th goal, 2003.

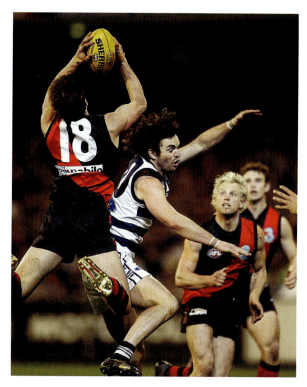

Taking a mark over Geelong's Matthew Scarlett, a great rival of mine, during a 2004 semi-final. (*The Herald and Weekly Times*/Wayne Ludbey)

Having a laugh with Sheeds at training in 2006. He had a wicked sense of humour and loved playing mind games when the cameras were pointed his way. (*The Herald and Weekly Times*/George Salpigtidis)

2008 Mark of the Year, taken during round 18 against Melbourne. (Newspix/ Aaron Francis)

Standing with my parents, John and Bev, after announcing my retirement, 23 September 2009. (*The Herald and Weekly Times*/Fiona Hamilton)

It was a happy but emotional day with my wife and daughters, Jaeda and Kira.

Posing for a shot at the MCG after signing a deal with Channel 10. (*The Herald and Weekly Times*/Michael Klein)

Hanging out with my close friend Scotty Lucas at my daughter Jaeda's third birthday celebration, 15 December 2009.

Kira's first birthday, September 2010.

Kira at 15 months.

A rare footy moment with Jaeda at the MCG. (*The Herald and Weekly Times/ Jon Hargest*)

I thoroughly enjoy my coaching role with the AIS-AFL Academy. *From left to right:* Tom Harley, Brett Kirk, Michael O'Loughlin and me.

again.' By Monday I was heading off the tribunal, and I got two weeks for it.

I wanted to appeal this one, but our footy manager, Dominic Cato, thought it wasn't worth it because it cost $5000 or something like that. I ended up saying to Dominic, 'Do I have to pay this myself? Because if that's what it takes, I'll do it?' That convinced him and we put in an appeal.

Mum was very stressed about it all, and when I saw her during the week she wasn't herself. Eventually, I got her talking and I could sense she wasn't with me on this one. She said, 'I just don't know why you keep doing this.' At the time, I felt like I was embarrassing her, but now I see that she just wanted me to be out there and playing that weekend.

Betting was suspended on our next match pending my appeal, which was heard on the Thursday night. But I wasn't the biggest story that week. Hirdy went on *The Footy Show* on the Wednesday night and said that umpire Scott McLaren's performance the previous weekend had been 'disgraceful'. The *Footy Show* guys loved the controversy and it became a massive story.

As it happened, Hirdy appeared for me as a character witness the next morning. 'This is a big effort for me,' he told me as we waited for the panel's verdict. 'The media are camped out the front of my house because I'm a chance at getting a suspension over my comments last night.' I was grateful to him for coming, and we chatted a little about what lay ahead for him.

As I walked back into the room to hear the result of my appeal, one of the members of the panel gave me a wink. 'Did that just happen?' I thought. 'Was he winking at me?' They then announced that my appeal had been upheld and I was free to play.

I felt like I'd just left prison and I attacked our game against the Eagles with a renewed passion, like I was a free man wanting to make the most of my second chance. It was a high-scoring match and I kicked eight, while Hirdy was so pumped that he hugged a fan after kicking a goal when the game was in the balance. We were delighted to have our first win of the season.

Hirdy copped a $20,000 fine the next week as a result of his comments about McLaren, and a year of attending forums with the umpiring fraternity. My view on umpires was that they had varying levels of form and ability – just like players, some were far better than others. It is such a tough job, and with all the changes to the rules, these days it is getting even harder.

So we moved on. After three rounds I had thirteen goals without a miss, but against Carlton I made up for that with 2.7. I was marking well but my mind was playing games with me that night and my kicking routine went out the window. I was stabbing at the ball one minute and then booting it too hard the next, and I had no real rhythm. I generally found that I would have a bad kicking day two or three times a year, but overall I was fairly consistent.

Although I was devastated after that Carlton game, it wasn't long before I said to myself, 'Well, at least you got plenty of the footy,' and I tried to get on with it from there. It was lucky we had won, or I would have had a few sleepless nights.

As a team, though, we were having a good run and put

together six wins in a row by Round 8. My form was alright, but it was after our match against Fremantle in Round 10, when I kicked five goals straight, that I started to feel at my best. Between Rounds 10 and 13 I kicked 22.6, but then I slowed down against Mick Martyn and the Kangaroos. He got the better of me again that day, but then in the next four weeks after that match I kicked 24.5.

Our match against Hawthorn in Round 11 was a memorable one. Despite the intense rivalry between the two teams in the 1980s, we had pretty much been doing as we liked with them in this era. We would intimidate them physically and mentally – and we'd made sure they knew about it. The Essendon boys used to joke about trying to find someone in the team who had played in a loss against the Hawks; we were on an eight-game winning streak against them, and we'd only lost one of our previous thirteen clashes.

It was more of the same this day. The ball was coming down to me pretty easily and we cleared out to a five-goal lead at half time. Little did we know, though, that at half time a few old-time Hawthorn players and the coaching staff were giving it to their senior players and demanding a better effort. Later it was revealed that Dermott Brereton, who was a club director at the time, had told them to 'draw a line in the sand' and stop letting us bully them.

I went to the goal square after the break and immediately I sensed that things were different. The Hawthorn players were showing plenty of aggression and it looked like they wanted a response. After Mark Williams kicked a goal for the Hawks, the ball was bounced in the centre and a pack formed, with Andrew Welsh and Adam McPhee in the middle of it. Richie Vandenberg jumped on top of them with a bit of a knee, one of our guys reacted and suddenly it was on for young and old.

Trent Croad, who was now back at Hawthorn after a couple of years at Fremantle, was playing on me, and we just stood in the goal square and didn't move. He looked at me and I looked at him, and we both decided to stay out of it. Neither of us thought it was going to explode like that – we were expecting the ball to be bounced and so we were ready for it to come our way. That didn't happen.

From where we stood it looked like a good fight, but we didn't realise how spiteful it was. Jason Winderlich was in the centre of the ground, not really in the fight, and as Campbell Brown was coming off – they were probably dragging him to calm him down – he threw a massive punch into Jason's face. It was one of the worst things I had ever seen on a footy field, and later in the game I said to Campbell, 'What you did was a disgrace.'

We kicked several goals straight after the fight and buried the Hawks again, but the dynamic between the teams had shifted. We felt good because we came out of the fight and thumped them, but a lot of people thought what Hawthorn had done was brilliant because they'd had a go at us. I couldn't understand that thinking. They had thrown a few punches, but who was the better club? We had kicked the next eight goals and won the game.

But the nature of our matches against Hawthorn had changed that day. We knew now that we couldn't physically intimidate them as we had been doing for years. Nineteen players were reported that day and a few Hawks sat in the stands for a while, but you could argue that it was worth it for them as an investment in the future.

My honesty got me into trouble at times, and when I was interviewed on radio after the match I said, 'Today I saw one of the worst acts I've seen in my time in football,' mentioning what Campbell Brown had done. My brother Brad was Campbell's manager at the time, and Campbell's father, Mal, rang Brad and said, 'That's not on – what happens on the field stays on the field. What your brother said is wrong, and I want to speak to him.' From memory, I think there were even threats of legal action thrown into the conversation, but nothing came of it. That is when my rivalry with Browny began.

Against Richmond in Round 15 I had a big day with nine goals and we won, but I carried some regret from the game. It was Hirdy's 200th match, and we used to try to make an extra effort for blokes' milestone games. I was playing on Andrew Kellaway. At one point I let my concentration lapse, and Kellaway got away from me and absolutely creamed Hirdy with a big knee into the ribs while he was spoiling the ball. Hirdy spent most of his 200th at the Epworth Hospital because I hadn't protected him when he was coming back with the flight of the footy. 'I really let my skipper down there,' I thought.

I expected to cop a big spray for it, but I didn't. Sheeds knew that, most of the time, I was going to be harder on myself than he would have been. In fact, I can only remember getting three massive sprays from him in the thirteen years he was my coach. Anyway, I couldn't get out of the ground quick enough to head to the Epworth to apologise for what had happened. Hirdy shrugged it off – 'These things happen,' he said. That didn't change how I felt, though.

I was leading the Coleman Medal by this stage, although Fraser Gehrig at St Kilda was also having a big year. Halfway through the season, when we'd beaten Hawthorn, we were fourth on the ladder. I'd had forty-four goals at that time, while Fraser had been on fifty. Then we'd dropped three in a row before the Richmond win, which we followed with two more losses. By then we were out of the eight, and we bounced in and out with inconsistent form until the end of the year.

My seven-goal game against Port Adelaide in Round 18 was one of the best games I felt I ever played for the club. Hirdy, Fletcher and Lucas were all out and Port was on a roll in what turned out to be a premiership year for them. Chad Cornes was Port Adelaide's best and most influential player at that stage, and at one point I crunched him so hard with a bump that I knocked him out. I was a bit dazed myself, but I had taken it on myself that day to have a physical presence in the game. I also hurt Dean Brogan when he dropped into the hole to cut off my lead; he ended up with cracked ribs. Along with my seven goals, I was taking marks deep in defence and having an impact on the game from start to finish. It was a great team effort that day and it was a sensational win for the club – our best for the year.

After that Round 19 match I had seventy-nine goals, while Gehrig was on sixty-seven. Mike Sheahan wrote an article about me saying I was 'on my way to immortality at 26', because I was about to win my fourth Coleman Medal. He wrote, 'Start inscribing his name on the trophy right now, he's 12 goals clear with four rounds to go, what an achievement.'

The week after that article was published, we played Carlton in wet and miserable conditions at the MCG. Luke Livingston was my opponent that day. During the first quarter, I lost him and was chasing a high ball when David Teague came from nowhere and pinned my left arm. He took me down pretty hard and I smashed down on my right shoulder. The pain was excruciating and I couldn't lift my arm, so I had to go off the ground. The doctors took me down to the rooms, where I had a painkilling shot.

It was my first ever painkilling injection at the footy – our club doctors weren't big fans of the jab – so I knew my shoulder was in pretty bad shape. It was a tight, low-scoring match and for us the finals were on the line, so it was a desperate situation. But the jab didn't really help. I still couldn't lift my arm and I didn't play much of the rest of the game, ending the day goalless.

We lost that match and were out of the eight again, so our next one – against Collingwood – was crucial. But I couldn't even use my arm to drive. So I got a bit surprise on the Monday at Windy Hill when Sheeds said to me, 'All set for Friday night?'

'What do you mean, Sheeds?' I replied. 'I can't even lift my arm.'

'That doesn't matter. James Clement is in good form – he'll come and pick you up and you can keep him out of the game for me.'

I was nervous about the idea and thought I would just embarrass myself and let the team down, but I did end up playing due to the persuasion of the coach. It was the most challenging game I have ever had to play because I was so limited in what I could do. Even though I'd had a jab the previous week, the doctor's wouldn't give me a painkilling injection that day as they wanted my shoulder to improve naturally, so I played without it. I was in agony all day but tried to do the job asked of me. I got a little bit of the footy but I really just ran Clement around. We had a great win that night but I couldn't contribute much. I felt helpless not being able to lift my arm.

So in the two weeks after Mike Sheahan's article, I had kicked just one goal; Fraser Gehrig, on the other hand, had bagged fifteen and had taken the lead in the race for the Coleman.

My shoulder wasn't much better the next week, and I told Reidy that if I was going to play against Sydney, I'd have to have a jab – I just couldn't run around to keep someone out of the game. So I had one and it made a hell of a difference; I played okay, kicking three, although we lost the game. After Round 21, then, we were in ninth place on the ladder but equal on points with Fremantle, who sat in eighth.

That sent us into Round 22 needing to beat the Bulldogs to make the finals, but also hoping that St Kilda beat Fremantle. I privately hoped the Saints could do that without many goals from Gehrig!

As it happened, the Saints did beat Freo and Gehrig kicked four, giving him ninety goals for the season. So I needed seven to catch him, while our team objective was not to get beaten by more than twenty-two points and we would make the eight. I had a pretty average first half with just one goal, but I started the third quarter well, kicking three goals in no time. We started to get control of the game and at three-quarter time Hirdy told the team, 'Clear out the whole fifty – I want this bloke to win the Coleman Medal.'

I kicked a couple more in the fourth quarter to go to six for the day. The crowd was going crazy every time the ball moved forward. With five minutes to go, it was pretty obvious that Essendon was feeding me exclusively, so the Bulldogs planted Rohan Smith as a loose man in defence to cut off my leads. I crashed into him late in the match and dropped a mark, and I missed a few other shots I should have got, so at the end of the game I had fallen one short of my fourth Coleman Medal.

I'm probably more disappointed now about missing the Coleman in 2004 than I was then, because I never won another one. I was just pleased at the time that I'd kicked six, we'd won and were in the finals, and my shoulder held up well.

Towards the end of the 2004 season, Hirdy and Mark Harvey, who was our assistant coach, said they wanted to take me out to lunch. I didn't realise at the time how significant that lunch was going to be for both myself and the Essendon Football Club.

We went to the Royal Hotel in Essendon. There was a bit of small talk for a while, then Harvs said to Hirdy, 'Do you want to get into what you want to talk about?'

Hirdy nodded, looked at me and said, 'I want you to start preparing yourself to be our captain for the 2005 season.'

That really set me back in my chair. I knew Hirdy was getting towards the end of his career, but I figured he'd be our club captain for as long as he kept playing. He was a superstar player and an inspirational leader.

Hirdy was clearly starting to think about his life after footy, but I wasn't ready for this news. He must have been considering his position for a while. He was so selfless and devoted to Essendon that he would always put the club before himself, and he obviously thought this would be the best thing for it.

Sheeds had always planned well ahead with the captaincy of the side. Bomber Thompson had played on for one season after passing on the captaincy to Gary O'Donnell in 1996, and then Sheeds plucked Hirdy from nowhere and handed him the role back in 1997. Hirdy had excelled and become a Premiership captain and an all-time great.

I had never expected the captaincy to come my way. I had been a vice captain for a number of years, along with Sean Wellman, but I felt I was in the role purely because of my football talent. Hirdy was playing so well that it was hard to see him finishing any time soon, and I thought that by the time he did retire a younger player with more years ahead of him would be given the job. If I was to be the main man, I had plenty of learning to do.

'That's taken me by surprise,' I replied. 'I don't really think I'm ready to captain next year. I'm still very insular when I'm not playing well and I don't always know what to say at the right times. I don't think I'm ready for that responsibility yet.'

It was a massive honour to be asked, though. Who wouldn't want to be the captain of his club? But it was something I had to be prepared for if I was going to do it right. I wouldn't do it if I wasn't able to do myself and the club justice.

We talked for a while and agreed to use the 2005 season to get me ready to take over in 2006. That also indicated that the 2005 season might be Hirdy's last as a player, even though he was still playing amazing football.

Not long after that, our club CEO, Peter Jackson, said to me in passing, 'You know you're the man this time next year, don't you?' That showed me the board as well as the coaches were keen to anoint me as the next captain of Essendon.

Because we finished eighth at the end of the home-and-away season, we were up against fifth-placed Melbourne. The top four was really strong that year. Port was on top of the ladder for the second year running, with Brisbane not far behind and gunning for four premierships in a row. St Kilda and Geelong were next, and both were emerging as powerful sides. Of those four, we'd beaten only Port, but we still believed that, on our day, we could beat anyone.

Against Melbourne in our Elimination Final, I had a good first half, kicking four. The whole team played well to give us a lead of five goals at half time, but we let the Demons kick seven goals to none in the third quarter and had to chase them in the last. My kicking had gone awry in the second half; I kicked five behinds, including a bad miss late in the match that should have given us the lead. I was lucky that David Hille kicked a late one to give us the game.

I finished the day on ninety-three goals for the season. As usual, I had been better in the second half of the year than the first. I felt like when other teams and players had been getting tired as the season wore on, I was getting stronger. I don't know why this was, especially as we were winning early in the season, but it just happened that way.

We had to play Geelong in our Semi Final, and I figured that if I had a good day – or if we won and played another final – then I might get to 100 again. Getting through to the next final was probably a more realistic outcome, given that I had to contend with Matty Scarlett, who was starting to give me trouble.

We ended up going down to the Cats by ten points – after kicking only one goal in the first half – and that ended our season. I kicked three goals that night for a total of ninety-six, while Fraser Gehrig kicked his hundredth the next week in the Saints' Preliminary Final loss to Port, who backed up with a premiership win over Brisbane.

Although we didn't know it at the time, it turned out that two eras ended that year. The Brisbane Lions' dominance of the AFL was over, and Essendon would never play finals football under Kevin Sheedy again.

> 'Matthew Lloyd is the last of the goalkicking emperors, but his reign is growing to majestic proportions. Forward lines, once the happy hunting grounds of football royals, have become pinched and parsimonious oligarchies, with more sharing fewer spoils. "His set shots are as good as anyone I have seen," Jason Dunstall said. "His conversion rate is extraordinary."'
>
> Greg Baum, The Age, *29 August 2003*

22

Captain in Training

'We identified reasonably early that he was the next captain. As vice captain he was a great support and he displayed leadership qualities very early in his time at Essendon.'

James Hird

As THE 2005 PRESEASON began, I started to get used to the idea that I'd be the captain within a year. At the time, though, it was clear to me that Hirdy was still the best man to be captaining the club. For me, 2005 was a year to prepare myself for the role, and I knew I had big shoes to fill.

When a situation came up that Hirdy had to deal with, I would think to myself, 'What would I do here?' I also started becoming more vocal around the club, giving more direction to other players, especially on the training track.

We were again knocked out of the Wizard Home Loans Cup early, so we played a few games up in the country and in the suburbs to round out our preseason. We fronted up against Hawthorn at Casey Fields with a big wind blowing to one end of the ground, which made it hard to judge the ball. At one stage the Hawks kicked to Ben McGlynn and I decided I'd go for the mark. McGlynn's a pretty courageous player and didn't flinch, despite the size different between us. My elbow caught him in the face and cut him pretty deeply. Instantly I was surrounded by players like Luke Hodge and Jordan Lewis and it was on again. No one had forgotten the 'line in the sand' match. Hodge was later reported in the game and the rivalry was truly alive and well.

Our last preseason game was against Geelong up at Bendigo, where the Bendigo Bombers play in the VFL. We caught a bus up there as a group. We were looking forward to that match and then having a week off before Round 1.

Angus Monfries was playing one of his first games for the club, and he kicked the ball to me in the second quarter and it fell a bit short. I hit the pack pretty hard and got my fist to the ball to punch it away. Max Rooke was under the ball and my arm hit him in the back of the head; I felt a sharp pain in my forearm straightaway. I gave it a bit of a shake and could feel the bone moving inside my arm, so I knew I'd done something bad.

I played on for a few more minutes, and as I took a mark on Tom Harley I felt an excruciating pain in my arm, so I took myself off the ground. Paul Wise, the team physio who always seemed to be with me through my big dramas, drove me to Bendigo Hospital for X-rays straightaway. Even I could see the problem when the images came back – there was a very clean break in the middle part of my forearm, so it was no wonder I felt movement there.

With my arm in plaster, I got back to the ground in the middle of the final quarter. I didn't want to catch the team bus home so I got a lift with Peter Jackson and our chairman,

Neil McKissock. I went to see the surgeon Greg Hoy the next morning and had my arm operated on a few days later. Again my preparation for a season had been interrupted; the continuity that was always critical to my game had been broken along with my arm.

It was a four-week injury, which meant I might be able to return in Round 4 of the season. We came up against Melbourne in the first round, and that was a pretty emotional night for everyone. The game was played as a tribute to Melbourne player Troy Broadbridge, who had tragically died when the tsunami hit Phuket on Boxing Day of 2004, and the Demons came out and thumped us.

In Round 2 we were better but still lost narrowly to Carlton. I was getting itchy feet – I just wanted to be out there helping the team.

During the next week, Greg Hoy told me that if I was comfortable I'd be alright to play in Round 3. I needed an arm guard to provide me with a bit of protection, though, and Sheeds was happy to give me up until the last minute to declare myself fit to play.

I had a plastic guard made. It was moulded around the shape of my arm and had some soft padding on the inside – a bit like a cricketer's chest guard. We had to send it into the AFL to check whether I'd be permitted to wear it and we got the okay.

The match was against Hawthorn, and it was sure to be another intense physical confrontation. I joined in our final training session for the week and my arm felt good, so I told Sheeds I was right to play. I was pretty underdone, though, and I'd be playing on Jon Hay, one of the best full-backs in the competition.

The conditions were wet and slippery but I set myself to go hard at the footy right from the first bounce. Campbell Brown dumped me in a hard tackle early in the game, which left me in no doubt I was back in the hustle and bustle of an AFL match. The main season is always different to the preseason – practice marches and the NAB Cup are just not the same – and I knew it was going to take me a while to get going.

After Campbell's tackle on me I thought, 'I hope I can just get through this match unscathed.' I instantly corrected myself, though. 'No, I've never gone into a match thinking like that. I've declared myself fit and I'll go as hard as I can at the next contest.'

But Hawthorn's players were running around with a new attitude. Rick Ladson was one who was noticeably harder, pushing me into the fence and mouthing off. The team as a whole had a tougher edge – they'd crossed over the line in the sand. This was the beginning of what the media eventually tagged the 'Unsociable Hawks'.

Not long after, the ball tumbled in towards me and I slid in to get it, hitting Josh Thurgood pretty hard. I turned back to look at him and felt some satisfaction when I saw he was still on the ground. As a hard ball player, you need a bit of killer instinct. I didn't realise it at the time, but I'd actually broken his jaw. The incident really sparked the game – not that it was needed after the 2004 match!

There was no retaliation from the Hawthorn players this time, though, because the game was close and both sides were focused on winning. Both clubs had lost their first two games, so this was a big one. I ended up getting my hands on the footy a bit but I was rusty and kicked pretty poorly. We won in the end, but it was controversial. Dean Solomon had a fresh-air swat at a ball that went through the goals; he missed it but the goal umpire called it good and we got home by two points.

After the match, my arm guard was all the talk. Although we'd had it approved properly before the match, we sent it off to the AFL again after the match; once again, it got the all clear. If I hadn't been wearing it, I don't think the result would have been any different, but we'll never know. I didn't mind hurting players when I went hard at the ball, but I never wanted to hurt someone that badly.

A week or so later I was doing some promotional photos at the MCG for Anzac Day. The Hawthorn players were there, warming up for a training run, and I could hear them sniping at me. 'Too many things have happened to be an accident . . . You're becoming pretty good at those cheap shots . . . ' I had meant to hit McGlynn, although of course I didn't mean to split his face open, but the Thurgood incident had been a complete accident.

I sensed that the rivalry had become personal – it had become 'Matthew Lloyd versus Hawthorn' rather than 'Essendon versus Hawthorn'. As a young footy fan in the 1980s, I'd watched those Hawthorn and Essendon games and loved them – Dermott Brereton running through huddles, Billy Duckworth kissing Dermie, Dermie knocking out Van Der Haar – it was awesome. I never thought that, down the track, I would be one of the protagonists in a new phase of that history.

The next week, on my birthday, 16 April, we had a big loss to Geelong. I still had the arm guard on and kicked five on Matty Scarlett. I also brought up my 700th career goal, which was a great individual honour, but the Cats blew us away after half time.

Then we had our traditional Anzac Day clash with Collingwood. By now, the game was among the biggest of the season, even if both clubs were down near the bottom of the ladder. Hirdy had another huge game, but Andrew Lovett, in his third match for us, put on a clinic and won the Anzac Medal. Even Jason Laycock, who always seemed to be injured, had a big game – probably his best ever for the club.

Lovett was amazing – he had black hair with a white stripe that day and looked like a skunk. He cut his way through packs of Collingwood players with blinding pace, and he kicked five sensational running goals. In the rooms after the game, he came up to me and whispered, 'Do you reckon that will get me an invite to the Brownlow?' We ribbed him about that for the rest of the year. He didn't get the three Brownlow votes that day – Hirdy did – and nor did get an invite to the dinner at the year's end, to his disappointment.

We'd beaten Hawthorn and Collingwood at that stage of the season and dropped three others, and along with those two teams we were in the lower half of the ladder. Essendon fans' expectations were always high. That was one of the things I loved about playing for the club: no matter where we were on the ladder, we were guaranteed four or five games a year with more than 60,000 fans: Anzac Day against Collingwood, Dreamtime at the 'G against Richmond, as well as our matches against Carlton and Hawthorn.

Early in the year, our season was already on the line, but we copped a thumping by Brisbane in Melbourne in Round 6.

Brisbane was sliding down the ladder now, so a loss to a team we regarded as inferior wasn't good. We should have won that match. Maybe at the Gabba Brisbane would still have had the edge on us, but not at Telstra Dome. We were getting overrun, so to me it was clear that we weren't as fit as we used to be, in relative terms.

I was becoming very concerned about the lifestyles of the playing group as a whole. Some players were having big nights every weekend, and I believed that was starting to have an effect on the careers of all of us. If it was just three or four guys, then maybe you can do something about it quickly, but I believed a quarter of our list at least could have been far more professional.

Our younger group of players had never seen success, I realised, and they didn't know what it took to get there. They were in the AFL system, and maybe to some of them that was enough. It was easier to get a game now, I thought, than when I first started. Back then the list held fifty-two players, but now players didn't have to fight as hard for a spot in the seniors. Having smaller lists, no reserves and a salary cap were all making a big impact.

We were an inconsistent team with the ability to pull a good match out of the box every now and then, but we weren't worth much as a whole. And we weren't doing enough to improve. Perhaps we had our heads in the sand, thinking our form would improve as the season unfolded. But we had too much ground to make up.

Maybe we at Essendon had become victims of our own success. During our successful era of 1999–2001, we had changed the way football was played and the way players trained for it. Every team had been training hard up to that point, of course, but when John Quinn came to Essendon the standards were raised. We still enjoyed a drink, but we were training harder and smarter than we'd ever trained before, and I think we caught opposition teams on the hop.

Over time, though, other teams started doing things even better again, and our attitude slipped. We weren't as businesslike or focused. If we won a game, we got carried away and would head into the next game and get smashed. We'd lost our consistency as a group. We knew what we were going to get from some guys every week – Damien Peverill was one and Mark Bolton another – but we also had a lot of guys who were far less consistent, and we were no longer good enough to carry passengers.

I had often challenged Sheeds on issues of player behaviour, and I think sometimes he thought I was too hardline about it. If I was questioning the behaviour of an Indigenous player, for instance, he'd say, 'You've got to look at their upbringing and you've got to accept that they're not all going to be like you.' I was frustrated that I didn't have the backing of the coach, which I needed if I was going to curb what I saw as the declining culture of the club. It was a culture that I thought was now costing us wins.

Double standards had also developed at the club. Early in the season, Ben Haynes and Marc Bullen were suspended for disciplinary reasons – they'd been out drinking and were late for training – but others were escaping the same penalty when they shouldn't have. Just before our match against Hawthorn in Round 3, Jason Johnson and Dean Solomon got caught drinking; based on the examples of Haynes and

Bullen, I figured they would automatically be dropped, but their only penalty was to start the Hawks game on the bench.

Having one rule for some and another rule for others was wrong, I believed. It's hard enough to win games consistently when you are doing everything right, so it's virtually impossible when you're doing things wrong. Only a freak of a player can perform week in, week out when he's not preparing properly. Most blokes will never perform to their optimum potential if they haven't had the perfect preparation, no matter how much natural ability they have.

Perhaps Hirdy as captain and me as vice-captain didn't do enough, but we both tried. We tried to set the best example we could. We trained hard and left nothing to chance, and we played hard when we were on the field. Socially, we were more settled – we really just weren't into the lifestyle of the young single guys. We all got on okay, but we weren't united like other sides I had played in.

Back in 2000, we'd had one vision and one goal that brought us together. We'd also had very good players who were unable to get into the seniors, and that had every player on edge, whether you were in the senior team or not. It was obvious that Essendon in 2005 was a long way from that team.

> 'He's always been respectful but he's always given me the impression that he still sees himself as a kid even though he is such a big name in the game. It was if he didn't quite think he was as big as he obviously was and is.'
>
> *Mike Sheahan*

23

Head

'Football was all-consuming; he could never ever relax.'

Lisa Lloyd

IT ALWAYS TOOK ME a while to get into a season, and I found 2005 even harder after my broken arm. I could sometimes pull a good match out of the box when my preparation wasn't spot-on, like the Geelong game, but it wasn't like that every week. It was a tough slog. I wasn't taking many marks because of the injury, and for me marking the ball well gave me confidence. In hindsight, I perhaps should have come back through the twos, but I hadn't played a reserves match since 1997.

In Round 7 I played Sydney in my fifth game of the season. I took seven marks, which was my best for the year, and kicked four goals, but most importantly I was in the contest. The stats say I had four tackles as well, which shows how my attitude was. We lost by a kick, though, so we only had two wins. Pressure was starting to mount on the club, and especially on Sheeds.

In the next five matches, we won both our games in Melbourne – against Fremantle and the Western Bulldogs – but lost interstate to Port Adelaide, Adelaide and West Coast. We were quite familiar with losing interstate by then, which I think had a more to do with our mental preparation than anything else. We jumped on a plane and seemed to become a different team.

I went into our Round 10 match against the Bulldogs – which was the third game in this run of five – under a lot of pressure. The media scrutiny on me was intense, which was fair enough, given that I was coming off two games with only one goal in each.

The day before the match, I was at an auction putting in a bid for a house when Simon Matthews, our media manager, called me to say that he'd heard the *Herald Sun* was writing a big piece on my form for their Sunday edition. Our game against the Dogs was on the Sunday afternoon.

When the paper was released, someone called me and said, 'Robert Shaw's made a few negative comments about you.' Actually, it had been Tony Shaw and the paper had made a mistake. Robert was distraught and demanded that the paper print a public correction, which they did, but people were talking about my game and how it was on the wane.

So I went into the Doggies game under massive pressure. It was the first time I played without the hard armguard; I had a soft one in its place, which was really for peace of mind more than anything else. I didn't like the full guard much because it affected the way I kicked – which sounds strange, given it was an armguard, but it had an impact.

Early in the game, I kicked a goal and there was a massive roar from the Essendon faithful, who were trying to get me up and about. I ended up having a really good first half. Hirdy was going out of his way to get me in the game. Everyone I played with knew I was a confidence player and needed early touches, but Hirdy was very good at helping me out. As a captain, he was looking out for one of his players. That meant a lot to me. I didn't go on with it in the second half, but it felt like a turning point in my season. It was good to contribute, and that day I contributed to a win, which was a good feeling.

After our losses to the Crows and the Eagles in Rounds 11 and 12, the questions being asked of us as a team and of Sheeds as our coach only increased. Round 12 against St Kilda was my 200th game. I would have liked to have carried some better form into such a big milestone match, but my touch was improving and I felt like success was just around the corner.

My family rallied around me and helped me to celebrate all 199 games I'd played, and not just the ten of the current season where I was well and truly out of touch. The club was brilliant too, and I felt valued. Essendon did a great job with players' milestone games. They made a highlights video, which we watched as a group, and Hirdy spoke with passion. He said I had lifted for others' milestones and so that is what every player needed to do on the field this week for me.

We were already undermanned and we lost Dustin Fletcher before the game as well. That meant Solly got the job on Fraser Gehrig, even though he looked half the size of the monster forward, while Adam McPhee got Nick Riewoldt, who was emerging as one of the top players in the league. Neither seemed the right option, especially with the form those two key Saints were showing at the time. They only had one win more than us but they were playing better footy.

It was great to run onto the ground and see a big banner in my honour, and then to cop all the back-slapping of my mates. The game started perfectly for me: I took a grab early and kicked the first goal. Solly was playing the game of his life on Gehrig and held him to three, while Riewoldt kicked four. Even a guy who hadn't been with us that long, Justin Murphy, played his best game since coming to us from Carlton.

The game itself was tight all the way through, but we got out to a two-goal lead near the end and held on. I kicked an important late goal and we started to wind the clock down by chipping it around. The siren went just after Hirdy kicked it to me, so we had won my 200th game and I had the ball in my hands. I've still got that ball.

It was a shock win for us, given that they were carrying good form and we had so many injuries, and that made it even more special. Overall, it was a good team performance and one that gave us hope. It was also nice to give a few positive media interviews after the game. We had deflected the negative talk, at least for a week.

I hadn't had too many games that year where I was actually satisfied, but after this one I was. We'd had an exhilarating win, I'd contributed and we'd sung the song hard. I was in the middle getting sprayed with Powerade and then I sat down with my family and enjoyed the moment. I was quite emotional. Having both Lisa's and my family in the rooms afterwards to celebrate not only a great win but also my 200 games was a moment I savoured. The happy times at Essendon had been few and far between that year.

The next week we played the Kangaroos and I lined up on Leigh Brown. I took twelve marks after Sheeds gave me a roaming role in the forward line, but the papers all said Brown had beaten me because I'd only kicked two goals. That was frustrating – it showed that a lot of the media didn't see what was really happening in the game.

Regardless, my form was much better. Our next match, a loss against Richmond, was played in torrential rain. I played a more traditional role at full-forward on Gasper and kicked four goals. It was such a tough day for football, and those four were the equivalent of far more in good conditions. I also laid seven tackles, which shocked my teammates as I was definitely no Tony Liberatore.

Against Collingwood the next week, I hit the ball harder than I had done all season. I started on Simon Prestigiacomo and then they sent James Clement to me – both quality players – but I was having a night out and I bagged eight. Scott Lucas kicked five as well, and I enjoyed having a big night with him. It was great night for both of us, and for the club.

But while it was a good win, overall we were still struggling and sat thirteenth on the ladder. We had lost so many players through injury and were a few games out of the eight, so realistically we had left our finals ambitions behind by this stage. Most of us were simply thinking about earning some respectability in the win-loss column, and also about our individual form and the 2006 season. I was also about thinking about the challenges that having the captaincy would bring.

We went to Brisbane next and lost, and then returned for a Friday night match against Geelong. The whole team was frustrated with our performance. We had injuries but that didn't stop us wanting to win.

Sheeds rarely gave a spray to Hirdy, but he did in this

game. Hirdy's opponent, Joel Corey, had about eleven disposals on him in the first quarter, so Sheeds dragged him. Hirdy was probably the greatest competitor I ever played with, and that just fired him up as he was rarely taken off because of his form. He was angry with himself and angry with Sheeds, who was disappointed with Hirdy's accountability and told him so.

When Hirdy got back on the ground, he was on a mission to stick it up Sheeds and Geelong. He kicked an inspirational goal late in the game and turned to the coaches' box and shouted, 'Stick that up your arse!' After the game, that was what made the news – not that we'd won, but the relationship between Sheeds and Hirdy. Were they fighting? Was the pressure getting to them?

Hirdy and Sheeds often disagreed about different aspects of footy but they'd discuss them in private and come to an arrangement on what was best for the team. Sheeds never wanted any animosity between himself and his captain. Against Geelong, the emotions of the night had simply spilled over; there was nothing more to it than that.

It made a good story, though. As a club we were under siege, and maybe that was having some effect on their relationship. A lot of people were asking for Sheeds' head at the time but he wasn't going anywhere. He simply hadn't been happy with the way Hirdy was playing that day, and that was fair enough. All players have to be accountable for their performance.

Even though we were going to have September off, my form had picked up. My second half of the season had been much better than my first, and as a team we were finishing games off better. We were struggling for manpower, though.

Sydney beat us at home and then we had Hawthorn in the Heritage Round. They were wearing mainly blue jumpers, which was odd, and we had jumpers that looked like they were lace-ups even though they weren't.

I started the game at the Hawthorn cheer squad's end and I noticed a pair of twins in their cheer squad who looked to be in their fifties. Early in the match, I had a run-in with my old mate Campbell Brown. He was running in my direction and watching the play at the same time; he wasn't looking where he was going. Instead of stepping out of his way, I put my arm up and he ran straight into my elbow and went down. I know it doesn't sound like a genuine story, but that is exactly what happened.

Anyway, Campbell went down and the impact broke his nose. I don't think he knew what had happened initially, but it didn't take long for him to work it out. These brothers and the entire Hawthorn cheer squad were hanging over the fence calling me every name under the sun. I wasn't the most popular bloke with Hawthorn people anyway, so this just fired them up more. Every touch I got from then on was booed, and when I kicked for goal the rumble was amazing – there were only 32,000 people there but it sounded like there were 100,000 Hawthorn supporters.

It was a frustrating game for me. The Hawks were pushing so many numbers back that our forward line was very crowded. So I started mouthing off at people. I said to Peter 'Spider' Everett, 'You've got a bit of a spare tyre around your waist,' and I kept going with some silly things like that. I was just trying to get into him and at the same time, trying to get myself going, Spider didn't like it though and he was mouthing off at me as well. I gave him a bit of backhander in the chest and he lost it then and we started wrestling with each other as the half-time siren went. Danny Jacobs, who I played with when he was a Bomber, stepped in to help out Spider and they dumped me onto the ground.

I was on all fours, and when I looked up all I could see was Campbell sprinting at me like a raging bull. He had me in his sights and he charged in and landed four uppercuts to the side of my head and eye region. They didn't really hurt, but they were clear hits. The melee went on for a while, and Hawthorn eventually won the match, which was their first over us in a very long time. Campbell got four weeks – one for each uppercut – and I had a black eye and a bruised ego after the loss.

In Round 21 we faced Carlton, and we won by ninety-nine points. Normally, you'd take a lot from such a big win, but Carlton was clearly not playing to win. I don't mean the players weren't putting in – I believe that every time a player crosses the boundary line it is his intention to win – but there were some pretty strange moves from the coaches' box that had the media talking about 'tanking' all week.

Carlton went into the match with eighteen Premiership points from the season – four wins and a draw. Winning one more match would have meant they lost a priority pick in the next National Draft.

As players, you know that you will never be told, 'We don't want you to win.' No team would cop that, but there are other ways to achieve the desired outcome. You can just stop making the moves to win a game. Send your gun players in for early operations to get ready for the next season.

That day, the players we started on were the players we ended with, regardless of what happened in the match. The Carlton coaches would have been sitting there asking themselves, 'Is four points worth losing a Brendon Goddard or a Dale Thomas?' The answer is pretty obvious, and that is why the rule needed to be changed, as it wasn't a good look for our game.

It's an ugly side of the professional game, and for us it was a hollow victory. Carlton, Collingwood and Hawthorn all got priority picks that year because they had five wins or less, and given that Carlton had been excluded from parts of previous drafts because of salary-cap breaches, it was especially important for them.

For Essendon, this meant that even though we finished thirteenth, our first pick in the next National Draft was at number seven. Marc Murphy, Dale Thomas and Xavier Ellis all went as priority picks in the 2005 Draft, and the latter two have been very good players in Premiership wins. If Carlton had beaten us, they would have lost Murphy and maybe also Josh Kennedy, who was later used in the trade to get Chris Judd to the club. The stakes for Carlton were high; a loss was far better than a win for their future.

We finished the season with a loss to Melbourne in Round 22. Early in the game, I landed awkwardly and my ankle blew up and so I had little impact on the game. Lisa and I were going away on holidays four days after the match, so I missed our 'Mad Monday' celebrations because I had to get my ankle right for travelling. I didn't mind too much, though, as I could never keep up with the rest of the boys.

Our season had been a frustrating one. We'd won only eight games, including two against sides that finished in the top eight, so it was clear we weren't worthy of a place in the finals that year.

Before going overseas, I had a meeting with Sheeds. 'If we're to improve next year,' I said, 'I reckon we need to make some drastic changes to the list.'

'Well, here it is,' he said, handing me a team sheet. 'You tell me who shouldn't be here. Who won't be part of our next Premiership side?'

I ticked off ten names, and nine of them were moved on that year, not necessarily because of my assessment but because it was quite obvious who wasn't worth persisting with the following year. I was looking at both their playing ability and their character. If you want to win a Premiership, you've got to have everything right. You've got to have teammates you can rely on. We needed to be fit and committed, and if we wanted to finish games strongly, we had to look at our lifestyles. I knew that the behaviour of some of my teammates was affecting both my career and the success of the team as a whole.

After all that was done, Lisa and I headed off on our holiday to Italy. We knew we'd be starting a family soon, so this was our last big holiday together. It was a fantastic break after what I rated as a disappointing year for the club.

> 'I think you can certainly categorise players into different areas when it comes to leadership in footy clubs. You have politicians and you have diplomats, and I think that Lloydy was just politically ruthless.'
>
> *John Quinn*

24

The Spartans

'The hamstring off the bone... My goodness, that was a nightmare. He could barely sit down and he was in a lot of pain. He had started the season so well and it was his first year as captain, and I thought it was going to be his best season ever.'

Lisa Lloyd

IN LATE 2005, HIRDY told Sheeds that if he was to keep playing he wanted to do his own preseason program. He wanted to start training in December, after the rest of the players. He spoke to our leadership group and said he wouldn't play on if we didn't think that was fair, and he explained why he needed to do it that way: he was looking to grow his business interests off the field.

While it wasn't ideal to have a player like Hirdy doing a preseason away from the club, it was a given that we'd back him. As Dean Solomon said, the service Hirdy had given the club over the years and the way he put in on the field meant he deserved our support, and he got it.

By then he had officially handed over the captaincy to me.

I was never going to be the same captain as Hirdy, but I'd put a lot of thought during 2005 into how my captaincy would be. I felt I was now ready for the role. In a way, it was good for me that Hirdy was away for the first month or two of the preseason because it made the transition easier.

The first thing I wanted to address was the slipping standards of the playing group. I wanted to make all players accountable to their teammates for their actions off the field and for the way they trained. I put a video package together of things like us walking off the ground after a loss. 'Could we have done more that day?' I asked. 'Had we prepared at 100 per cent? How are we seen right now by the football public? As an individual, are you giving yourself the best opportunity to succeed? What do we stand for as a team?'

The boys got on really well, so we didn't need to build team unity in that sense, but we did need to work on our team discipline and on-field structures. I brought in a weekly award called the Trademark. The idea was that all the players would vote for the player who had contributed the most, who had performed the most sacrificial act for the good of the team each round.

Along with the leadership group, I worked on some other motivational tools. We came up with a theme of Sparta. We talked about how a small state like Sparta was able to defend itself through its unity and selflessness. Mark Johnson, Jason Johnson and I put a lot of work into the concept.

All the players signed off on it straightaway, which was a little disappointing because we had hoped for some discussion and input from the whole playing group. I later found out that a lot of them thought it was a bit of a wank but weren't willing to be open and honest about their feelings at the time. That was exactly what was wrong with the club at the time. I wanted input from beyond the leadership group, because often the younger players can be just as influential as their senior teammates.

Once again we were knocked out of the preseason competition in the first round, which had become a common theme. We played a few other matches, which were all about finding some touch and working on some adjustments to the game plan, but we didn't get serious until our final match in the lead-up to the home-and-away series.

Sheeds and the AFL had organised a match against Richmond in Mildura as a tribute to four kids who were killed by a drunk driver there. We flew up on a charter plane with our best available team, and Richmond did the same. I was wrapped with how the team went. We smashed the Tigers by about ten goals but it wasn't just about the score. We showed great unity and determination, which was a great sign for the season ahead.

Personally, I was feeling pretty good. I felt like I was as fit as I had been at the start of 2001 and my body felt great. After our good performance against Richmond, I was looking forward to a very big year.

In the first quarter of the new season – my first official game as captain – I kicked six goals and eight for the match, and we went on to a good twenty-seven-point win over Sydney. I wasn't nervous about the match, unusually for me; rather, I was excited and proud to lead Essendon. That we jumped the reigning premier was a huge feather in the cap for us. The Swans had come back at us pretty hard after we made a good start, and a lot of our blokes had stood tall. It felt like we had put 2005 behind us.

We had placed a lot of emphasis on all our players being accountable. Dustin Fletcher was unbelievable in this game and we gave him our first Trademark award. Things couldn't have started better for me as captain, particularly after kicking six goals in my first quarter as captain of the Essendon Football Club.

Unfortunately, a road trip to the Gabba brought us back to earth in Round 2. Early on in the match, I had a scuffle with Jonathan Brown. He pushed me backwards and I twisted my ankle when I stood on someone's foot, so I played out the game at well below 100 per cent. I played on Mal Michael and kicked four goals, though, giving me twelve for the season to that point. Despite the loss, I felt it was going to be a good year.

As captain, I really wanted to set a high standard on the training track even though I was sore at times. That week, Reidy pulled me up and said, 'Just because you're the captain, it doesn't mean you always have to be out there. You can take a seat from time to time, let yourself recover for next week.'

'No, Reidy,' I said, 'I want to make sure we train the way we have been, which has been at a really high standard.'

Our next game was against the Bulldogs, and for some reason I was extremely nervous about it – far more than usual. I didn't want us to fall behind with two losses after Round 3, and I knew it was important for us to win.

The Bulldogs had Brian Lake at my back and Dale Morris cutting off my leads from the side, and I had kicked just one goal. Just before half time, I was dumped in a tackle over the boundary line and felt a little bit of a twinge high in my hamstring. I spoke to Reidy about it at the break and we did a running test. It didn't feel too bad and Reidy said he'd talk to Sheeds about playing me out of the goal square to keep my running down.

When the game restarted, the field just opened up in front of me as our midfield pushed up the ground – I had sixty metres of clear space in which to run. Nathan Lovett-Murray got the ball on a fast break and I took off on a hard lead. As I always did when I had someone right on me, I arched my back and stuck out my bottom to give myself a bit of extra reach from my opponent.

As I did that, I just blacked out – it was like I'd been shot – and Morris crashed down on top of me, giving me a massive corkie on my hip. When I regained consciousness, I was getting the little flashes you sometimes get when you've been concussed, but I hadn't taken a hit to the head. I had no idea what was going on, but it wasn't good.

I lay there dry-retching and holding my hammy while the play went on around me. The pain from the corkie was bad but I knew I'd done a hamstring as well. All I remember thinking was how I didn't want to be carried off on a stretcher – for a hamstring injury that just wasn't a look I was comfortable with. If I'd known the seriousness of the injury, though, I would have called for the stretcher immediately, but I believed I had simply torn the muscle, and a torn hamstring wasn't worthy of such drastic measures, in my mind.

A couple of trainers and physios helped me off the ground and took me down into the rooms. I was in agony and couldn't do anything with the injured leg – all I could do was keep it straight as the pain was too much if I bent the leg. Dean Rioli, who wasn't playing in the match, came down to see me; he'd done a few hammies in his time. I asked him if he had ever blacked out and felt nauseous when he'd done one, and he said no. I was really concerned now that this was something big.

After the game finished I put on my tracksuit and headed home to start icing my leg. I was in agony and on crutches. One thing that still irks me to this day was that Dominic Cato, our football manager, called me later and said, 'You've set the standards this season, and we're a bit disappointed that you didn't hang around for the after-match meeting to listen to the coach.'

'Dom,' I said, 'I'm in absolute agony.'

'I think that, for the team, you should have stayed.'

'Well, I disagree, Dom,' I replied. 'I was in great pain, and getting started on my rehabilitation was more important at that stage.'

In fairness to Dom, I don't think anyone could have comprehended the pain I was in. Because it looked like just a hamstring injury, they mustn't have thought it was that bad.

I was pleased that the standards and expectations that I'd put forward for the group seemed to have settled into the culture, and Dom was probably just trying to stick to them, but I just couldn't do it. The next day, Reidy and Ian Reynolds, our other legendary club doctor, put a tape measure around my left leg and it was three centimetres fatter than my right one. 'It's full of blood,' Reidy said. 'We won't be able to scan it for a week, as that much fluid will distort the image.'

The Anzac Day match was next, and I watched us lose it from the couch at home, still icing my leg. I eventually got a scan the next week, and Ian Reynolds rang me the night after it was done. He said I may need surgery to fix it, and he'd come and take me the next day to see a surgeon by the name of Julian Feller.

I was shocked and asked Ian how many weeks out I was looking at, but he just said, 'Let's worry about that in the morning.' Given my history as a worrier, that was probably the worst thing he could have said.

So, after a sleepless night, I battled the paparazzi to get out of our apartment block. Word had leaked out that I was in trouble, which was pretty amazing given that even I didn't know how severe the injury was.

One reporter I'd never seen before shoved her microphone in my face and said, 'Is your career over? Have we seen Matthew Lloyd play his last game?'

'No, I wouldn't have thought so,' I said.

When I met with Julian at around ten am, he showed me the scan and started talking me through the injury. 'We could try to let the scar tissue heal itself,' he said, 'but you'll never run the same again. You've detached three-quarters of the hamstring tendon from the bone – there are four parts to the tendon and three of them are hanging off the bone. I feel your best option is to have this surgically repaired. If we do that, you should make a full recovery.'

'Okay,' I said, 'but what does that mean for my year?'

'It's season over, I'm afraid,' he said.

I was in a daze. Four rounds into the year, my first as captain, and my year was over. I went home and told Lisa, and then headed off to see my brother, Brad, play in a milestone match for Williamstown at Preston Oval. While I was driving there, I switched on Triple M and heard Brian 'BT' Taylor open the show at midday with: 'Big breaking news! Matthew Lloyd's season is over.'

Aside from Ian Reynolds, Julian Feller and Lisa, no one else knew anything about my injury. Even I had only just found out the full extent of it. I figured that there must be staff at the hospitals who pass things on to the media. Then Triple M interviewed Sheeds, who didn't know at that stage, and he just said, 'Well, that's news to me.' I could sense he was quite rattled by what he'd just heard.

Then I started receiving phone calls – I had about thirty by the time I got to Preston. I let them all go to voicemail, but when I parked the car I listened to a message from Adam McPhee, 'Please tell me this isn't true,' he'd said. 'I've just heard a rumour you're out for the season . . . I just hope this isn't true.' After that I switched my phone off – I really wasn't ready to talk to anyone about it.

A few days later, I had my surgery and began my painful recovery. I had a massive cut the width of my hand just underneath the crease of my backside, which took a long time to heal. I ended up reopening the wound when I tried to start my rehab too soon. Instead of restitching it, the doctors decided to leave it open. Poor Lisa had to dress the wound three or four times a night and maybe ten times a day as it wouldn't stop weeping. It was a real nightmare of an injury – I couldn't even sit down properly for six weeks or so.

When I was finally coming good, I started my long rehab journey with John Quinn. As always, he was amazing. He knew exactly what had to be done, and I don't know where I would have been without him.

Another source of stress for me at the time was that I was out of contract at the end of the season. I was now twenty-eight and, with my serious injury, I realised there was a very real chance that the club wouldn't offer me a new deal. John Quinn and Bruce Reid were fantastic, and they assured the club I would be fine to play in 2007.

Because of their backing, I re-signed with the club midway through the 2006 season, which was a great relief. It was also the most lucrative contract of my career, which showed me the club had faith in me to regain my peak fitness and form. The only sticking point was that I wanted a three-year deal and they only offered two, but I stuck to my guns and got what I wanted. Getting a good deal with the club was important to me, as I knew it might be my last football contract. As things turned out, it was.

On the field, Essendon was having a shocking time in 2006. By the middle of the year, our season was effectively over. After our win against Sydney in Round 1, we had lost every game, and many by big margins, on our way to fourteen losses in a row.

Instead of going back to Hirdy as the on-field captain, Sheeds had chosen David Hille. Hilly is a great bloke and of the highest character, but I'm not sure if it was the right decision; he may have been too young to deal with what was happening at the club. My role became a mentoring one, so I tried to spend as much time talking about standards, goal-setting and positivity.

There was a front-page article about us one week during our big run of losses – it may have been after our 138-point loss to Adelaide in Round 10 – and I was in the cafe when the boys were looking at the paper. An illustration had parachutes with the Essendon players' heads in them, referring to the fact that our season was in freefall, and I immediately saw the boys slump – their confidence was shot to bits.

If you have lost four games by a total of nearly 300 points and you're sitting at the bottom of the ladder with one win in twelve rounds, it becomes pretty hard to stay positive. I decided to set some simple goals for the team that didn't revolve around winning or losing. 'Okay, this week our goal is eighty tackles,' I'd say. With that attitude, we started to turn things around a bit. We were still losing but the margins were a lot slimmer.

By Round 15 we had lost fourteen matches in a row and sat on the bottom of the ladder. I was going crazy watching the football week after week. I felt like I needed to escape, that I needed a holiday, which sounds strange given that I wasn't playing. But I couldn't stand watching the boys struggle any longer.

In Round 16 we played Carlton in what was dubbed the Bryce Gibbs Cup. Carlton was only one win above us on the ladder and we looked set to battle it out for the wooden spoon. It was thought, at the time, that whichever team lost would take the wooden spoon and get first crack at the National Draft. Both clubs knew that Bryce Gibbs was the best prospect to have come along in quite a while, so the stakes were clear. Lose the match, finish last and get Gibbs.

It was Heritage Round again, and the boys were wearing red shorts – which I was pleased I didn't have to wear. During the week, Dean Solomon had run into Sheeds at training during a drill and injured the coach's shoulder. Sheeds had to have an operation on it, so he joined me on the injured list for the week and Gary O'Donnell coached the senior side. It was the one and only game Sheeds missed in his twenty-seven years with the club, and O'Donnell's only game as a senior coach.

I sat in the box that day with both of them. The match finished in a draw, but we should have won it. Gary was so angry that he punched the desk, but Sheeds said, 'No, it's okay, that's okay.' So Gary ended up with a coaching career of one game for no losses and no wins, which I reckon must be some sort of record.

Of course, Sheeds was thinking of our draft selections, even though by then it had been decided that the priority picks would follow the first round selections. The draw meant that we remained a game below Carlton at the bottom of the ladder.

Scotty Lucas ruined things the next week by playing a blinder against Brisbane. He kicked seven goals and Hirdy got four, in a big win that got us off the bottom of the ladder. Even though it looked like being costly at the draft table, it was great for the club to get a win as it meant so much to the playing group and loyal supporters. In reality, though, everyone just wanted the season to end.

At around this time I did take a holiday. The club understood how I was feeling, which I was appreciative of. I had been diligent with my rehab and I needed some down time. Lisa and I went to the Gold Coast for a week where I listened on the radio as the boys beat Collingwood in Round 19, which gave us three and half wins for the season.

We didn't win another game, although Scotty Lucas

bagged another eight to try to beat the Bulldogs singlehandedly in Round 22 – he was sensational. We received a priority pick for winning less than four games but it came at number seventeen, which seemed a little unfair; the previous year Collingwood had been able to take Dale Thomas at number two. Anyway, we took Leroy Jetta, who these days is showing good potential to be a quality player for Essendon.

Sheeds' mind was already focused on 2007. It seemed to me that he didn't care whether we won or lost in 2006 – he was thinking only about playing his younger blokes and seeing how the list next year was shaping up. It was hard to watch, even if I could understand the logic.

The risk for Sheeds was that he would start to lose the confidence and faith of the players, though, and I think that became a factor towards the end of his time at Essendon. I'm sure the senior players understood that our younger players needed to gain experience, but they were also fighting for their own careers. The players were sick of copping it in the press, week after week.

It was hard for me to watch what was happening. I was a first-year captain and couldn't do anything for my team on the field, so I realised I had to do more off the field. I needed some advice, and I spoke to Nathan Buckley and Luke Darcy, who had both suffered big injuries while captaining their clubs. Bucks said, 'Structure all your training, do all your training around the playing group, be at every meeting, be at every game. You have to be seen.' Darce, on the other hand, felt that the only thing that mattered was for me to get myself right, however I did it. They were both brilliant to talk to, and I took a lot of inspiration from them.

As I got to the end of my rehab, Quinny organised for me to train with Lauren Hewitt, who was getting ready for the 2008 Olympics. That was a great challenge for me. My rehab was moving more slowly than I had wanted, but I suppose a long-term injury always feels like that.

The only great thing that year was that Lisa was pregnant, and that really kept me going. I was able to spend so much extra time with her during the pregnancy, and I realised that I might have missed a lot of that if I had been playing. Going for ultrasounds was nice – a good scan rather than the sort I was used to – and we went for walks together every day.

Despite having that enjoyment in my life, I missed training and playing. I was counting down the days and months until I could return to the field.

At the end of the 2006 season, Hirdy was again weighing up whether to continue playing. He felt that Peter Jackson, our CEO, was steering him towards retirement because there had been so much talk about his testimonial. But I knew we needed him on the field in 2007; if he still had the desire to play, I wanted him with us.

I felt that he just needed some reassurance so I rang him one afternoon and said, 'For what it's worth, I still think you've got it as a player. I reckon you've got so much more to give, and it'd be sad if you were to finish in a year where we win three and a half games and you and I didn't get to play together.'

'All right, that's it,' he replied. 'I'm playing. I'll ring Peter right now.'

I knew we were getting close to the end of an era, and that 2007 was going to be a big year for the club. I was now sure it was going to be Hirdy's last year, and Sheeds' future was also in the balance. There had been talk that Sheeds had said his two-year contract for 2006 and 2007 was going to be his last, but that now he'd changed his mind. There was certainly friction between him and some players, as well as with the board. My relationship with him wasn't as good as it had once been, either. There was nothing nasty, but we'd been together for thirteen years and we viewed aspects of footy differently at times.

It was totally clear to everyone at the club that in 2006 we had sunk to a low point, and that 2007 had to be much better. We had been mediocre for far too long.

> 'The hamstring injury was a major injury. He went from sprinting at 100 per cent to useless in seconds.'
>
> Dr Bruce Reid

25

Fighting Back from the Brink

> 'You had a lot of faith when you had the ball and Lloydy was up forward that you could just go long and he'd be where the ball was kicked. His ability to read the play and understand his teammates was as good as anyone I have ever seen.'
>
> *James Hird*

SUMMER TRAINING FOR THE 2007 season started the day after the Melbourne Cup, and I was pleased to be back and involved with the group again after such a frustrating year in 2006. Actually, it felt like I'd already completed a preseason since I'd been training since June. I had injured myself on my birthday – 16 April – and it had taken until the middle of June before I could walk properly again.

By the time the proper preseason began, I was feeling good. I ran my fastest ever twenty-metre sprint test – 2.93 seconds. I was generally happy if I got under three, and my time was up with the best in our playing group. Jason Winderlich and Alwyn Davey were quicker, but for a bigger guy like me it was a great time. That gave me enormous confidence that I could get back to what I was before, but I still had some doubts about myself.

We didn't go into our 2007 preseason dwelling on the season that had just ended. Just about everything that could have gone wrong in 2006 had, and we knew that by the middle of 2006 Kevin Sheedy had started planning for 2007. Our preseason began well, and we had our sights set on being a competitive unit again.

In early December I started to get a bit of tendonitis in the hamstring that had been injured. The tendon had been screwed back onto the bone, so there was no issue with that but it was a bit sore. All the exercises I'd done to that point had focused on strengthening the injured area and conditioning my body to cope with the rigours of AFL footy again. I was doing Pilates three times a week – which I hated – and I was also doing a lot of stretching exercises and explosive speed work.

One of my biggest worries when I got back into training was that I lost my kicking power entirely. It was my kicking leg that had been injured and the best I could manage when I returned was thirty metres. To my relief, as time went on I started to get my distance back. Before the injury I had been able to kick fifty-two or fifty-three metres without too much strain, and as a full-forward I believed I had to be able to do that.

The tendonitis forced me to miss around three weeks of skills and running work. I was spending most of my time in the swimming pool. One day, I was just about to jump in for a session when Ady, our property steward, ran in and told me that Lisa had just called – she was on her way to the hospital to have our first child. I raced to the Freemasons Hospital in East Melbourne and sat with her as she battled through a seven-hour labour for the birth of our first daughter, Jaeda.

It was so great to be there and support Lisa, and Jaeda was born weighing nine pounds four. While Lisa struggled to cope with the effects of labour, I sat with Jaeda in my arms for hours on end – football and hamstrings were the furthest things from my mind. I thought to myself, 'This is what life's about.' Maybe those initial hours we had together is why Jaeda is such a Daddy's girl. I was ecstatic and tears rolled down my face when I first laid eyes on her.

I had been hoping to play half of our intra-club match the next day, but I decided to give that a miss to spend time with Lisa and Jaeda. For the next few weeks I was running around Windy Hill with my eyes popping out of my head. Parenthood really knocked us both for six. I was trying to support Lisa as much as I could but also putting everything into getting myself back playing footy again. I was tired but I felt great, physically and emotionally.

My hamstring tendonitis forced me to miss a couple more weeks early in 2007, but I came up for the NAB Cup game against Carlton on 24 February, which was more than ten months after the Bulldogs game where I ruptured my tendon. It felt like it was my first game all over again and I felt vulnerable, like I was out of my depth; even though it was only a NAB Cup game, it was lightening fast. My touch was nowhere near it. I kicked a couple of goals but I was as rusty as I'd ever been, which is understandable, I suppose. The old saying that no amount of training will ever prepare you for the real thing was so true that day.

In his first game for Essendon that day, Alwyn Davey kept us in the match with seven or eight tackles. Alwyn changed the way tackling was viewed at Essendon. He set such a high standard that the rest of us had to lift our act in that area of the game. We went down by less than a kick, which wasn't a bad thing for me because it freed me to find my touch away from the spotlight of the NAB Cup competition.

By the end of that preseason I was in pretty good shape. I kicked seven on Brian Lake in a match against the Bulldogs at Skilled Stadium. By then I was able to get off the mark well, and I was also marking and kicking strongly.

The horror of 2006 was now behind me, and I was looking forward to our first game of the regular season, which was in Adelaide against the Crows. It was a sunny Sunday afternoon and we came to play. We were intense and we piled on the pressure, and the Crows crumbled – I think we shocked them. Luckily, I got a friendly handball over the top from Angus Monfries and kicked a goal in the first quarter, which was brilliant. All the boys came over to me; it was good to be back. I ended up with a couple but Scotty Lucas was the star and kicked seven. Fletch was brilliant down back and Jason Winderlich was moving really well, and we had started the season with a rare interstate win. I felt it was one of our best wins since the 2000 season.

In some ways, the long break had been good for me. After so many seasons of playing, the game had probably worn me down a bit. But now I had regained my pure love of kicking goals and playing footy with my mates. It was like being back in the schoolyard. I had missed the competitive nature of the game and the camaraderie with the boys. It was great to be back and to have a win. And I got through the game unscathed.

We backed that up with a win over Fremantle, and I contributed well with 4.1. We carried that form into Round 3 against Carlton, who had won the NAB Cup, and we were eight goals up halfway through the second quarter and playing unbelievable footy. The group was absolutely pumped, thinking, 'We can actually see some light here.'

But then Fevola got hold of us, we went into our shells a little bit and we dropped the game. I ended the day with 5.3, but Fev's 8.2 was the difference. We had kicked seventeen goals for the match but lost in a shootout. Our games with Carlton over the next few years would regularly turn into high-scoring contests, and we would generally come out on top.

The team was gutted. We dropped a game we never should have lost and that hurt us, especially after having worked so hard in the first two weeks.

Still, there was a buzz around the club. We went into our match against St Kilda in Round 4 still full of confidence, and we accounted for them by thirty-one points. It was a pretty intense game but we ran over the top of them in the last quarter, with Brent Stanton, Jason Winderlich and Andrew Lovett running amok. I picked up a bit of a corkie, though, and we had only four days to get ready for our next game which was the Anzac Day clash with Collingwood.

Sheeds and the medical staff gave me until the last possible minute to prove my fitness. I met the docs at Windy Hill on the morning of the game, and I probably made myself believe I was okay. 'It's Anzac Day,' I thought. 'I'm right.'

I played and got through the game well enough. I kicked three but we lost, and I felt very sore afterwards. I could barely run at recovery the next day and I had some soreness in my hamstring. We had more than a week before our next game, which was against the Hawks.

The doctors sent me off for a scan on my hamstring, and it turned out I had strained it on Anzac Day. I think it was due to a poor running action caused by the corked thigh, which would have put too much pressure on the hamstring. It was a whole new hamstring injury, thankfully, and unrelated to the big one. I missed Rounds 6 and 7, which were losses to the Hawks and Kangaroos.

I came back against Brisbane in Round 8 and we smashed them by sixty-four points. That started a run of four wins in a row, which got our season back on track. I was returning between three and five goals a game, which was good. I wasn't as prolific as I had been in 2000 and 2001, but the reality was that we weren't the same team.

The game was changing, too, and team defence was taking over. Sydney had won the Premiership in 2005 on the back of its defensive strategy, and most other teams were developing similar systems of their own. The Hawks had 'Clarko's Cluster', while at Adelaide Neil Craig was placing every man behind the ball. Scoring was getting tougher and eighty goals in the season was probably the new 100.

I was enjoying my role as captain. I was chasing and tackling harder than before, which was an area of my game that needed plenty of improvement. As captain, I knew I had to set a better example in that area. After defeating Brisbane, we won three close ones – Richmond by eight points and then the two Grand Final teams of 2006, Sydney and the Eagles, by a point each. It was an awesome feeling to be back in the eight by the halfway point of the season.

Our one-point wins were full of drama. Against Sydney, in Sydney, Mark McVeigh was over the boundary line when he passed the ball to Adam McPhee, but the boundary umpire didn't call it. McPhee kicked the goal that won us the match and the Sydney fans were furious.

Each year, Essendon plays Sydney for the Marngrook Trophy, which celebrates the impact Indigenous players have had on our game. At the presentation after this match, the crowd was booing so loudly that I couldn't even make a speech. I gave it back to them, saying that we thoroughly deserved the win, and then I held up the trophy above my head in the direction of the boos, which my teammates absolutely loved.

Against the Eagles, we had to resist some pretty intense pressure from the reigning premiers. Dustin Fletcher was amazing on this day. I'll never forget the ball going deep into the Eagles' forward line late in the game; Fletch expertly spoiled the ball and got it to the boundary line without giving away a point. We had the whole team deep in defence for the throw-in, including me, and we hung on.

The next week, against Port, we suffered a bit of a letdown after our one-point wins. That said, losing in Adelaide to a good side was probably to be expected, given our record on the road. From there, we weren't able to put together two wins in a row, and the instability within the club was growing. It was now late June and there was plenty of speculation in the media over Sheeds' future.

As a team, we could pull a good win out of the bag from

time to time, but we weren't consistent. We were a good side but a bit below the best clubs. At the halfway point of the season we were technically only one win away from the top of the ladder, but I felt that didn't truly reflect where we were at as a team.

After Port we had a week off during the split round, which was a mixed blessing. Most of our players were hanging out for a break, but for me a week off was another week missed. Personally, I liked having the footy and being in the contest, so while part of me looked forward to the mental break, I played better with the continuity of games. Generally, the more I played, the better I performed.

We came back from the week off and scored a two-point win over Melbourne. I played on Nathan Carroll, who was a mean-looking bloke with a Chopper Read–style moustache. He used to love getting in my face and he niggled like you wouldn't believe. I missed a sitter from thirty metres, directly in front, and Carroll was into me, bumping me and shouting at me.

I copped it for a while and then I just got sick of it. At the three-quarter time break, as Carroll was jogging away from me, I charged into his back and put him down. The umpire was right there and reported me for rough conduct. It was a nothing incident, but I copped a week for it. To be blunt, I lost a week because of stupidity.

What hurt the most was that I realised my importance to the side. Mike Sheahan wrote a column at the time about Essendon's win–loss record when I played and when I didn't. I was pleased to be having such an influence – I'd played in eleven games at that stage for eight wins. We lost against

Geelong when I was suspended, and I saw how my stupidity had hurt the team.

After playing Geelong, we dropped games to the Bulldogs and Collingwood. The confidence of the team was starting to evaporate. It was a gradual drop-off but it was happening. We had a tough run home too, so our season was looking precarious.

There seemed to be speculation in the papers every day over Sheeds' position, and the week after the Collingwood loss the inevitable finally happened. Peter Jackson called me in one day and told me, as captain, that the board wasn't going to renew his contract for 2008.

Sheeds had needed 2007 to be a really big year in order to save his job, but it had only been passable to that point. In reality, our results had flattered us, and there were plenty of people inside the club who understood that.

Then publicly the board announced that it was not going to renew Sheeds' contract, and so after twenty-seven years with the club this would be his last. I knew Sheeds wanted to go on, so to me it was clear that he was sacked. Putting it any other way was just being polite.

I loved Sheeds – I still do, even though he claims he would have traded me for Chris Judd – but I thought a new coach wouldn't be such a bad thing for the club. Maybe someone new might inject a bit of life into my career too. A younger coach might relate to the younger players a bit better, and as a playing group we were certainly ready to move on.

Sheeds was probably the most influential person that our great footy club had ever had, and for the players who hadn't been with other clubs, he was the only coach we knew. So it was a huge thing for all of us. Yet we felt like we had been drifting under Sheeds, which may be a bit harsh on him but it was our perception at the time. We were excited at the prospect of positive change after years of slashing lists and recycling players.

The board's process for finding a new coach was methodical, and it wouldn't be finalised until after the season ended. So for the last few weeks of the year, we played not knowing who would coach us the next year. We would be heading into 2008 without both Sheeds and Hirdy – the most influential coach in the club's history and its best player.

Understandably, Sheeds' mind would have been elsewhere for the remainder of the season, although he never dropped his bundle in front of the players. There were stories in the press about where Sheeds was going and what he might do. There were TV reports about him having late-night interviews around Melbourne, and we started to go into a tailspin. The end of the season couldn't come quickly enough; it was too big a distraction.

Although we were all pretty sure it would also be Hirdy's last season, his form was great. He played like he always had, making the most of every match. But his body was failing him and he started to get a lot of soft-tissue injuries. He would never lose his ability to influence a game, but physically he couldn't keep playing like he was a twenty-year-old.

He got a bad calf injury in Round 14. This was after the Geelong game that I missed through suspension. Alwyn Davey also broke his arm – it was a nightmare day for the club.

That evening, Quinny rang me and said, 'Can you come around to Hirdy's house? He's talking about retirement and we've got to stop him.' Hirdy had grabbed his bag after the game and stormed out of the change rooms, saying, 'I think I'm done.'

By the time I got there, Reidy and Quinny had Hirdy laughing and there wasn't really much for me to do. He said, 'Okay, I'll do my rehab and I'll try to finish the way I should finish, with a better farewell.' I knew then and there that our Round 21 clash against Richmond at the MCG would be our real chance to farewell him, even though we had West Coast the next week in Perth to close out our season.

We stumbled our way towards that game, dropping games to Hawthorn – who now seemed to have it over us – and Fremantle before beating Carlton, which was always a good feeling. My form had been good. I kicked eighteen goals in four games during that run, and we were a chance at the finals if we could deal with the Tigers and the Eagles.

In some ways, the distraction of the build-up to that last game in Melbourne for Sheeds and Hirdy wasn't good for us, but as a playing group we knew we had to be up for it. Hirdy was the golden boy of our club, and not just because of his hair. He was a warrior for Essendon, putting himself on the line and coming out on top time and time again. We owed it to him to send him out in the right way.

I am a big believer that teams and players lift for big occasions, even if it is minimal – I had seen it for myself in Mark Harvey's last game – and I knew we'd all want to win for both Hirdy and Sheeds. It's rare that a club sees two legends depart at the same time, and I made one of my most heartfelt emotional pleas before the Tigers game.

I grabbed Hirdy by the jumper in our huddle and said,

'This bloke has put this club in front of everything else. It means the world to him.' Hirdy had told me when he handed over the captaincy that, after his family, it was the most precious thing he had ever been given. 'This bloke is Essendon,' I continued. 'He's played his heart and soul out for this club. He'd love to keep going but there comes a time for everyone. So play your hearts out for him today.'

The blokes were welling up as Hirdy thanked me, and he later told me that what I had said meant a lot to him.

We weren't good enough to win on the night, but we left nothing on the table. Every single one of us gave it our all in front of 88,000 people. And they were all there at the end when Sheeds and Hirdy did a lap of honour. The fans all knew that our chances of playing in the finals were slim, so this was their chance to thank them both.

The next week we headed to Perth. Essendon had a good following there, so the crowd was pretty fired up. Unfortunately, my game was a nightmare. My preparation and my system was everything to me, so when anything was out of order it meant bad news.

When we went to run out onto the field for our warm-up, I couldn't find my mouthguard, which for me was like not having my boots on. Our assistant fitness coach, Joel Hocking, ran over to the local chemist to buy one and I quickly had it fitted, but it kept falling out as it wasn't of great quality.

In the first quarter I was running around thinking more about my teeth than the game – my security blanket wasn't there and I felt lost. About halfway through the second quarter, I thought, 'Stuff it! If my teeth get knocked out, so be it. I can't be running around half-arsed like this.' I was on

Darren Glass, though, which made the task of getting into the game even harder.

By three-quarter time we were fifty-two points down, but then Scotty Lucas cut loose and the game turned to us. Hirdy was having a huge impact and had more than thirty possessions. He was still playing like a man on a mission. We cleared out the forward line for Scotty because he was in such good touch. Although we fell short by eight points, it was a mighty effort from everyone. Scotty was unstoppable in that last quarter, kicking seven goals, which the AFL website rated as the best individual quarter of the season.

When the siren went it was a very emotional time. The West Coast players and fans were brilliant. Hirdy and Sheeds walked a lap of the ground while the rest of us stood together and enjoyed our own memories of them. We had missed the finals, which was disappointing, but we all knew the Essendon Football Club was never going to be the same again.

We jumped on a plane home pretty much straight after the game, so we didn't have a chance to reflect on what had happened until the next night. Sheeds had booked a restaurant in Chapel Street and he was there with a group of friends, so a few of us decided to turn up – Hirdy, Reidy, Welshy, Spike and Fletch. We were hurting from the way things had ended for Sheeds, and we wanted him to know how we felt. I was conflicted: part of me wanted a change but the rest of me loved the journey I'd shared with Sheeds. We sat there till one am eating pizza, drinking red wine and having a laugh.

I told Sheeds how I felt and thanked him for all the opportunities he had given me. He had taken me on as a young bloke and played me in the Ansett Cup at sixteen, and then in the AFL finals at seventeen. I told him how I always remembered him saying, 'Play a good one for me this week because I don't want to drop you.' I was a bit emotional, but it was a great night and I'm pleased we crashed his dinner.

The playing group had our end-of-season trip to Las Vegas again, and Hirdy and I roomed together for the last time. He was so relaxed on these trips. At the club, he was always in a hurry rushing off to work or his family – he even did his weights in a hurry. Get him on a footy trip, though, and you'd see him lying by a pool and having a laugh and a joke. In Vegas, no one knew who he was so he was fully relaxed.

He and I spent a lot of time on that trip reminiscing about our time together, about his career and how much influence he had on me. Right from the early days when he used to pick me up from Foxtel because I didn't have my licence, through to him handing over the captaincy to me – the memories were so good. I will never forget us smiling at each other in the last quarter of the 2000 Grand Final when we knew we were going to win.

I was sad to be losing both Hirdy and Sheeds, but I was also excited about the future. The club was financially strong and could deal with pretty much anything as a business. We had good sponsors and a really strong supporter base. I knew other players would step up and try to emulate Hirdy's role, but the void was huge.

'Bring on the new era, though,' I thought. I didn't know what the change would bring, but I was excited to find out.

'Lloydy's very serious when he needs to be but he also knows how to have a laugh. Before games he actually got quite nervous and he needed his own space and was very serious and intense. When he was relaxed, though, he was hysterical. You would often find yourself sitting there laughing with him, at him, around him, because he had a very unique way of making fun of you and the people around him.'

James Hird

26

New Era . . . New Opportunities

'He's got great character. He's a guy that would always stop and have a chat to you, would always return your phone calls, and would always initiate conversation about football and about other things.'

Mark Harvey

THE CLUB STARTED THE interview process for Kevin Sheedy's successor during the finals series, and there were a lot of rumours floating around. Neale Daniher and Peter Sumich were mentioned, Damian Hardwick was listed as a chance, and there was speculation that Bomber Thompson wasn't happy with the review of the Geelong process that had taken place at the start of that year.

Peter Jackson didn't want to wait until after the Grand Final to appoint our new coach, though, because there was only a week between the Grand Final and the trade week ahead of the Draft, so the fact that Geelong went all the way ruled Bomber out.

Matthew Knights was already part of the Essendon coaching team – he was coaching the Bendigo Bombers for us and he knew the playing group well. When he emerged as a serious prospect, we all thought it would be great. The guys who had played under him really liked him, and he had a really good reputation for giving his players clarity about their roles. Sheeds was often the opposite – he liked to keep everyone guessing.

If we were going to go with a coach unproven at AFL level, I thought Knights was a great choice. I had spent a lot of time training with him when I was doing my hamstring rehabilitation and he'd been brilliant. Peter Jackson had forged a strong relationship with him as well, so when it came down to a choice between Hardwick and Knights, he was in the box seat.

The rumour was that Hardwick had lost out on the role partly because of his presentation to the board; there were plenty of people suggesting that Hawthorn had taken his documentation off him and, as a consequence, his final presentation was not that great. Knights believed we had a good list and that we could go somewhere with it, while Hardwick thought it was weak and needed some culling.

In the end, the board went with Knights, and I was fired up and ready to do something special with him at the helm. Peter Jackson had copped a lot of heat for making the change, and Knighta was always going to have a battle to convince some of the fans that he was a suitable replacement, but he could do nothing to change that.

Some of the guys were worried about their future and a few of the delistings that followed shocked us. Sheeds had loved Mark Johnson but he was the first to go, and Jason would have gone too if he hadn't had another year on his contract. Mark put on a barbecue for all of us at the end of the year and it was clear he was pretty cut up about it.

Mark went on to play a season under Mark Harvey at Fremantle, but it was sad to see a club best-and-fairest winner leave in that way. Knighta was very clear about what he wanted. He had others slotted into the back pocket ahead of Mark, and he was straight with him about it.

I'd come off a reasonable season, personally. I'd kicked sixty-two goals despite missing three matches, and the Coleman Medal was won that year with only seventy-seven. I'd even won the Goal of the Year Award for a back-heeled goal against Carlton. Even that had been controversial, since there had been so many great goals that season which weren't simply fluky reflexes like mine was. But I took the award anyway; I mean, it's not like I could have given it back.

So, for the first time in twenty-seven years, Essendon started preseason training with a new coach. I'd had times in the past where my passion for the game had fluctuated, and in recent years under Sheeds it wasn't what it should have been. But now I was up again and it felt good.

With hindsight, there's no doubt Sheeds' time had been up, and we realised that when we walked into training. That first training session under Knighta was structured and precise. Sheeds might have gone fifteen or twenty minutes over time in a training session, but this was to the minute. Knighta was very organised. He explained what the session was going to focus on before we ran out there, and things would go to a tee. I really enjoyed the structure and the dialogue between the players and the coach.

Under Sheeds, the forwards had been given licence to do what we wanted, but under Knighta, even that was given a set structure. We had new running patterns to learn, and we felt like we were on a path to matching a team like Geelong, which was as structured in attack as it was in defence.

In the middle of December we went to Tasmania for a training camp with a group called Stealth Developments, which was a bunch of guys from the Special Operations Group. For the first couple of days it was like a normal camp – we were running sand dunes and stuff like that. It was tough, but then we'd go back to our hotel and have a good night's sleep – nothing we couldn't handle.

After a few days, though, there was a bang on my door at four am. 'Princess, wake up and get your team together!' We stumbled out, knowing we were in for something big. The trainers stood in front of us barking instructions and we started running. It was still dark, and all we had was a flask of water and a bit of food in a backpack. They got us to grab rocks and hold them above our heads as we ran along some streets of Tasmania in the early hours of the morning.

After about three hours of that, we broke into teams of eight and had a huge thirty-kilogram rope that couldn't leave our shoulders, plus a twenty-kilogram jerry can filled with water that we also had to carry. If you called anyone by name, there was a penalty, and those built up along the way. We all had bibs on – my team was red so we were each called Red 1, Red 2, Red 3 and so on. Once in our teams, and having just run for three hours, we hiked up Cradle Mountain carrying thirty kilograms on our backs, which took eight hours. At the top we had to do push-ups and sit-ups – it was brutal. We camped up there, eating lentils and baked beans. It was the toughest experience of my life.

When it was over, I found that, as huge as the challenge had been, I had enjoyed the satisfaction that I got out of completing it. As a team, it was just what we needed to address our slipping standards. We had done similar sessions in previous years and John Quinn had been disgusted at how we'd handled a bit of duress. He had decided to do something tough again and this was it.

Back at Windy Hill, we did a lot of walk-through sessions so we could learn and understand our roles in the new and highly structured game plan. But we started to fall behind – we weren't getting through everything that was planned, and I was starting to worry about that. Knighta was relaxed about it. 'This is a long process,' he said. 'I'm not going to hit you guys with everything now. We've got to get the basics right first.'

Although we were learning the new game style, we weren't executing it under match-pressure intensity, so it was hard to judge whether it was going to hold up when the season began. For example, when the midfielders worked into the forward line, there was a pattern we had to follow. The higher half-forward had to lead up and the other half-forward had to run behind him, and the two blokes in the goal square would do the same. It was taking us a while to get used to all the patterns, and there was no way we were going to be ready for the start of the season. We also didn't know how these patterns would work when we had opponents pushing and shoving us and the midfielders were under extreme kicking pressure.

Knighta could tell the midfielders exactly when they should be rotating off the ground, and he also decided that the key forwards should also come off at a certain time each quarter. This was all new to me. I'd never come off the ground in the past unless I was playing an absolute shocker or injured. There were times within a game that I could get my rest, so putting key forwards and defenders on the bench every quarter didn't make sense to me. In my opinion, it was a waste of a rotation, especially if we had been outplayed and the ball had hardly entered the forward fifty. That's when common sense should prevail and you adjust your rotations. I thought that then and I still do now.

I explained my thoughts to Knighta. 'I feel better the more I'm out there,' I said. 'The stop/start nature of coming off the ground is hard for a forward. Being out there lets me work my defender over, which sometimes takes time.'

'Well, you've got not excuse for not working hard when you're on the ground,' was all he said, 'because you're coming off.' He obviously wasn't going to entertain a conversation about his new approach. I would have loved it if the opposition coach took Matty Scarlett, Steve Silvagni or Mal Michael off me every quarter, but unfortunately that never happened.

One of Knighta's strongest qualities was his workrate – it was enormous. He'd be at the club at six o'clock in the morning and he'd put in days of twelve hours plus. He really got involved with the players, too. As a young coach, he was bumping us out on the training track to get himself involved and doing some running with us during conditioning sessions. I couldn't fault his enthusiasm and passion for the job, but as time went on I started to get a sense that he didn't really like listening. He knew what he wanted, and that was the way it was going to be.

Up to Christmas, my preseason had been pretty good, but then I got a sore hamstring again. I was a bit worried about it so I had it scanned, and it showed I had been carrying a little tear for a couple of months. With that, I began a four-week rehab process and so I missed the NAB Cup and almost all our practice matches. I played half of our final practice match – against the Eagles at Subiaco – two weeks before the start of the season.

Knighta had given players the option of playing in the NAB Cup opener against Brisbane, and quite a few opted out. David Hille was one of the only senior guys playing, and he played really well. Andrew Welsh put on a barbecue and a few drinks at his place for those of us not playing, and so we watched the first NAB Cup game on television. I was pretty impressed that a lot of the things we'd been training towards worked well, and the young group did a good job and came away with a win.

We also beat the Bulldogs the next week but then got knocked out by the Saints. Knighta was happy with how the younger players performed. He once said that the hardest players to coach were the older guys. The younger players, he said, hadn't known anything other than his way, whereas we had a lot of habits that he knew were hard to change. You can't teach an old dog new tricks, and Knighta seemed to believe that. Over time, that would become a real bugbear of his.

'He's always been respectful, but he's always given me the impression that he still sees himself as a kid, even though he is such a big name in the game. It was as if he didn't quite think he was as big as he obviously was and is. He reminds me of Peter Hudson in that respect, it was as if they were both sort of saying, "I'm not a superstar", when clearly they were because their figures *said* they were.'

Mike Sheahan

27

Jekyll & Hyde Football

'I think he handled himself really well near the end of his career. I think when you are there and you think the coach probably doesn't want you anymore you could start talking to the wrong people, but he didn't do that out of respect for the club. He is most certainly the kind of player I'd like to be coaching now.'

James Hird

ONCE THE PRESEASON WAS done, it was probably only Fletch and I who were underdone due to injuries. Our final practice match had been good and we were looking forward to the new era. We came up against the Kangaroos in Round 1, and we hadn't beaten them for a few years at that stage.

Our leg speed and ability to move the ball was terrific, which makes any forward's eyes light up. But North started well and led by twenty-seven points in the second quarter. After that, though, we ran over the top of them. We were fit and we had belief. I kicked six, which was even a surprise to me considering that I'd had such a limited preseason. In the rooms after the game I started to think that things might have turned around for us.

We met Geelong the next week and were in for a rude awakening. We were a team on the rise but we came up against the reigning Premiers. They gave us no time or space and our new game plan just didn't work. We had been encouraged to run in numbers, but that meant that when the ball was turned over we offered little resistance back the other way.

We were eight goals down at half time, and the Cats players were mouthing off at us – a bit like Essendon had done in 2000. Milburn, Scarlett and Mackie were giving it to us, while Selwood, Ablett and Bartel taught our midfield a lesson on hard-bodied football. Although we fought hard, they dismantled us by ninety-nine points, which showed how far off the pace we were and brought us back to reality.

I learned a lot about our coaches during those two weeks. After Round 1, the club was a great place – everyone was happy and laughing and looking to the future. After Round 2, it was all negative and the contrast was there for all to see.

While Sheeds had always been positive – he'd put an arm around me and say, 'You'll get your goals next week' – Knighta was very much the opposite. After his post-match address in Round 2, Knighta had his head in his hands. He didn't individualise, but I sensed he was bitterly disappointed with the senior players in particular.

That was a sign of things to come, and it became a large factor in why I didn't enjoy my last couple of years of footy. After a game – especially a loss – I had no idea what Knighta thought of me or my performance. It wasn't until Tuesday that I felt he'd calmed down after a match. His highs were high but his lows were very low, and there was no happy medium.

In really good teams, and especially under experienced coaches like Mick Malthouse, there's usually a belief that the feeling and the behaviour around the club should not differ, regardless of whether they've won or lost. Our environment was pretty much the opposite. If we won there'd be a spring in our step, while if we lost we wouldn't want to walk past the coach's office.

Each Monday, we'd sit in the auditorium wondering what was going to happen. After the general meeting, the leadership group would meet. In 2008 that included me, Mark McVeigh, Andrew Welsh, David Hille, Jobe Watson and Adam McPhee. The senior coach also attended the meeting, along with a couple of others. Leigh Russell was the careers manager at the club, and she would facilitate our meetings and take notes.

Another task on Mondays was to review your own video package of your last game, as well as the team edits. These consisted of both good and bad points. When we lost a game, the Monday match-review meeting was the toughest hour of the week to sit through. Sometimes the packages made things look worse than they were, but sometimes you'd know what was coming and just be squirming in your chair. Nine times out of ten, after a loss the package would be totally negative, and if you'd played a stinker in a win you felt protected even though you knew you should have faced more scrutiny. We all had our own mentor coaches, so we'd watch our packages with them and then meet as a bigger group.

Seeing the bad stuff was important – you needed to know what you did wrong so you wouldn't do it again – but it was the way it was handled that was an issue. The players were given the opportunity to critique each other's games, which led to some pretty interesting discussions. It isn't easy to critique your teammates. Apparently, Hawthorn did in 2008, as did Geelong through their dominant era, but we really struggled with it and we were too soft on each other.

The Monday after the big loss to Geelong was a harrowing one. More than anything, we wanted to bounce back with a win. We came up against Carlton, who weren't travelling too well at the time, and we beat them twenty-three goals to twenty-one. I kicked four, which was good after being held goalless by Matthew Scarlett the previous week.

A free-flowing game against a team with a poor defence suited our game plan. We actually enjoyed playing teams we felt we could challenge in a shootout. Teams like Geelong and St Kilda, though, who didn't allow you to score and had a good balance of attack and defence, were always going to hurt us.

I had kicked all my goals against Carlton in the second half, which alleviated a bit of my tension; I'd gone six quarters without kicking one. I couldn't get away from my opponent, Michael Jamison, who was developing into a tight-checking defender. He was bigger and stronger than when I'd first come up against him, and he was a very good spoiler too.

I woke up the next day with a sore calf, though, and could barely walk. I missed a whole week of training and our match against the Bulldogs the next weekend. We lost but we played okay, and I did my best to be ready for our game against St Kilda. They played a fairly similar game to Geelong – they had a rigid defence with no real holes and were able to hurt you on the rebound – but we felt confident heading into the game.

Matthew Knights had a rule where you had to train both sessions during the week to play on the weekend, and I hobbled my way through some drills on the Tuesday night just so I could play. I lined up on Max Hudghton and went goalless. I tackled hard but I just couldn't win the footy. We kicked six in the third quarter to mount a bit of a comeback after a slow start, but even then I was out of it.

I spent the night awake, going over every minute of the game and trying to work out what I could have done differently. Was I fit enough? Max was a top player, but he had dominated me so completely that I felt humiliated.

After our Saturday morning recovery session, as I said in the opening to this book, I was emotionally and physically drained. I was very worried about my leg speed and had lost all my confidence. I wasn't enjoying my footy, and as I told Lisa that morning, I thought I was gone and would struggle to see out that season.

Lisa reminded me that I had started the season with six goals and said she thought I might be over-reacting. In hindsight, she was right. But we were only five rounds into the season and I was concerned about how much longer I wanted to keep playing. I had a contract for the rest of that year and the next.

The change across the competition to a more defensive game style was affecting me greatly. I could no longer just make a lead and have the ball fired at me; instead, I had blokes zoning in front of me. Against the Saints, I'd had Max on my tail and Sam Fisher dropping into the hole in front of me, and neither I nor the team had an answer for that.

The next week we had a humiliating loss to Collingwood in our Anzac Day clash, I think it was the biggest margin ever in one of those games, and it was played in front of 90,000 people. It was such a bad performance that people started to question if we deserved to play in the most important home-and-away match of the year.

I had kicked three goals but I felt I'd played an average game. I did an interview afterwards with Dermott Brereton. 'You kicked a goal and you smiled when you're seventy points down,' he said. 'Is that just you in survival mode, happy that you're going okay even though your team isn't?'

I told him the truth. 'Derm, I had spoken to young Jason Winderlich a minute before that goal and said to him, "Wakelin's zoning off me thinking you'll go long – I'll go back towards goal and I'll come back at you and hit me short." And he did exactly what I asked him for, and I was smiling to say, "Jason, well done." It was just great seeing a young kid think through a situation, and that's what I was smiling about.'

He finished by saying, 'Oh well, I wouldn't have been smiling in that situation.'

I was the captain of the club and I was under siege. So was the team, and it was only Round 6. We were two and four at that stage.

As I said, Knighta reacted pretty savagely to losses and he started to make some big changes at this time. Jason Johnson and Damian Peverill were two players who had already been told their games would be limited that year and they were like lost souls around the club as you would imagine, particularly being so early in the season. The next few weeks were tough, and players were coming in and out of the side. We were all starting to look over our shoulders. Getting through those Monday match reviews was hard, and we ended up losing the next five to make it an eight-game losing streak.

We were scoring okay but we couldn't stop the rebound and the flood of goals. Instead of running in ones and twos, we had three blokes running in a wave, which meant that if there was a turnover we'd be exposed on the rebound. Our skill level simply wasn't good enough.

In the week after the Collingwood match, I met Father Justin through Lisa's sister, Tania, and her husband, Greg. He offered to help me out, if I wanted someone independent to talk to. With a bit of encouragement from Lisa, I had my first proper meeting with him leading into our Round 7 match against Port. We talked through some of my issues and I poured my heart out to him. It got pretty emotional, actually. One key question he had for me was, 'Are you enjoying the game?'

'No,' I said. That was partly to do with the pressure I was putting on myself and how I was playing, but it was also about the team. We weren't playing well and the mood was unpleasant. I was starting to think a bit about Sheeds, whose strengths were becoming more obvious to me through all of this. The way that he and Mark Harvey would get the team up after a loss – but without letting us off the hook – was brilliant and had a huge effect on the way I rebounded from a poor performance. In that, I was no different to a twenty-year-old kid. Everyone needs help at times, and giving it was one of Sheeds' great strengths.

Now, instead of thinking about what I needed to do to improve, I was starting to stress about getting dropped. I *was* in survival mode. The communication at the club started to fall away, even though we were still having our meetings every Monday.

I marked the ball pretty well against Port Adelaide the next week and kicked five straight, and it felt good to contribute in a game again. I played on Alipate Carlile, who was normally pretty good with his body, but I was using mine really well. We lost, but as we were walking off, Scotty Lucas said to me, 'Well done, mate, you can hold your head up high.' That was great for my confidence – I was grasping on to any little bit of positivity I could find.

In reality, though, that was just a bit of personal respite. I could walk around for a week not watching my back, and maybe the Monday meeting would be positive for me. It was not a good way to be thinking. I hadn't personalised the game like that since early in my career.

The next week against Sydney our losing margin was back to more than fifteen goals. In all except the first round, which we'd won, we had scores of more than 100 points against us, and two were up over 150. Against Sydney we'd lost 143 to fifty-four, and Sydney wasn't generally a heavy-scoring team. I had Craig Bolton that day; I kicked one goal and he had more disposals than me.

Sydney played with us. Early in the first quarter, Nick Malceski danced around me when I should have hit him with a big hip-and-shoulder or a bone-crunching tackle. That symbolised my own and the team's performance that day. I copped a serve from Knighta at the Monday meeting for that one. I was my own harshest critic but this stung me. I could see the anger in his eyes towards me. I remember the incident like it was yesterday. Knighta was absolutely right – I should have hit him hard and set the scene for the side early in the match – but my mind and body was all at sea, due to the lack of confidence and enjoyment I was playing my footy with.

Knighta wasn't going to deviate from his game plan, even though it was obvious we were struggling with it. As a playing group, we often spoke about things we could try, but at the end of the day you have to stick to what your coach wants. His philosophy was to get our attack right and then worry about the defensive side later, whereas most coaches start the other way around. The players, including myself, were performing poorly, though, and we understood that.

We were doing a lot of tackling work during the week because Knighta felt we weren't doing that well. But there had to be more to it than that. From where I stood on the ground, I could see that we had to get some numbers back in defence, but instead we had all our numbers running forwards. The balance was out.

Our losses were humiliating, and the media in Melbourne had jumped onto us as a big story. We were a big club and there had been high hopes for us after we started the season with a good win. Even Richmond smashed us with a 38-point win, and they weren't travelling that well either.

It was the Dreamtime at the 'G match so there was a big crowd, and we let through seven goals in the first quarter and didn't score one. Knighta was savage at quarter time. With the last quarter of the Sydney match and now this first quarter, we'd conceded twenty goals without scoring one ourselves. I put through our first about three-quarters of the way through the second quarter and copped Bronx cheers off the Richmond fans who wanted us to remain goalless. It was a relief to have a goal on the board, although we were down by fifty points at half time and facing another mauling.

The spray and the eyeballing from Matthew Knights was memorable. When he wasn't happy, he just glared at you. He was very critical of me at half time for losing my feet in the contest, which was a real pet hate of his. I deserved a blast, and in the third quarter I performed far better, as did the team, and he gave me a massive embrace at three-quarter time for the way that I was now holding my feet and standing tall.

I wanted more of that from him. There were so many times when I was eyeballed and felt small, but this time I gained a bit of self-confidence from him. I always craved positive feedback from my coach, and this was a rare positive moment we shared around this time.

Although the scoreboard looked respectable in the end, really it was another flogging. We'd now had six losses in a row and our season was done.

Against Adelaide the next week, we stayed with them all night. Knighta had finally changed tactics and called for man-on-man contests all over the ground. That stopped our goal flow but we only let nine through, which was our best effort for the year. The Crows kicked inaccurately due to our pressure, and we lost by less than a goal.

All that our fans wanted at that stage of the season was for us to have a go and be competitive, and against Adelaide we were. In some ways it felt like we had won the game. The mood was improved in the change rooms after the game and Knighta was happy. It all came down to our tackling pressure, he said. We had done what he'd asked of us and we'd done it well.

The next week, we were back to our worst as Buddy took us apart again. Paddy Ryder had the job on Franklin and was sitting in the rooms after the match with his head in his hands crying. Buddy had kicked 9.5 and had a lot of the footy. I'd kicked a couple in the first quarter but then Croady held me for the rest of the game. He was at his peak and the Hawks went on to win the Premiership, but it still wasn't good. It was another embarrassing performance from us.

I turned on SEN on my way home and listened to *Finey's Final Siren on SEN*. The first caller I heard said, 'What an insipid performance from Matthew Lloyd yet again. He's meant to be the captain and that was insipid . . . ' I quickly turned it off. It wasn't the smartest move by me to turn the radio on that night.

My stomach was churning and I started going over the match again in my head. I couldn't get near the ball, the team couldn't do anything right, and I really just wanted the season to be over. I was looking for an out and we'd hit rock bottom. It couldn't get any worse than this – eight losses in a row, and I was in a dark place and struggling.

The heat was being turned up on me by the journalists, too. Mike Sheahan wrote an article in the *Herald Sun* saying my time was up, and plenty of others agreed with him. My stats were being analysed and my personal performance was under as much scrutiny as the team's. I was doing it tough.

28

Finding My Feet . . . Again

'In 2008 I wrote an article saying he was finished, which was probably a pretty popular view at the time. After that, he started to play really well again. He had a really solid game against West Coast Eagles which was when Knights moved him out of full-forward on to half-forward flank, and that was the turning point. Then he took that big screamer against Melbourne. He was back.'

Mike Sheahan

AFTER THE HAWTHORN GAME I also copped it from Knighta, who was getting quite savage by this stage. That was understandable – he was a young coach and he felt his message wasn't getting through.

At one stage Campbell Brown had burst out of defence and sidestepped me, and I'd done nothing. Knighta turned to me in the Monday meeting after playing that vision and said, 'You're meant to be the captain! What sort of example was that?'

His statement hit me hard and I thought to myself, 'How can I ask anything of the rest of my team when I'm playing like that?' The vision was indefensible but I felt like I was playing with chains around my ankles. I was at my lowest ebb.

Knighta called me in to see him on the Tuesday. 'I've had a think about things...' he said, and my heart was in my mouth. It had been eleven years since I'd played reserves footy. 'From a leg-speed perspective, I think maybe Jay Neagle would be better suited to playing full-forward. You're a good endurance athlete and I don't feel we're using that enough. Also, from a leadership perspective, it might help you get into the game. So I'm going to play you on the half-forward flank.'

He was positive in this meeting. He spoke about me getting some touches earlier in the match by playing further up the ground and getting my hands on the footy more than I was at full-forward. I was fine with that.

Our next game was against West Coast at Telstra Dome. They were struggling too – we both sat on two wins out of eleven games and they were just in front of us on percentage. Only Fremantle and Melbourne had fewer wins. We went into the match to win, but if that was to happen, each of us had to beat our own man. We tackled and harassed like we hadn't since Round 1.

Knighta was right – playing on the flank did bring me into the game. Darren Glass still came to pick me up but being upfield took him out of his comfort zone and I was able to run him around. I had eight disposals in the first quarter and was tackling and bumping as though I'd never had a form slump. I didn't hit the scoreboard that hard, but I was in the contest and making a difference. It was tough and hard-fought right up until the last quarter. I took a big hanger and kicked an important goal and I felt that my confidence was back. We ended up winning by twenty-two points and I had around twenty-five disposals and kicked a couple of goals.

After the game, I refused an interview on the field with Rick Olarenshaw for Channel Seven. He was a good mate of mine, so I felt bad later on, but at the time I was thinking, 'Stuff you all – you've been giving me hell for weeks, and now you want me?'

The win meant the world to us. It felt as important as a final – we had needed a win and we'd got it. I went to breakfast in Port Melbourne the next morning with Welshy, McVeigh and Fletch, and suddenly we were happy to flick through the papers, which we hadn't done for a few weeks.

We finished breakfast at about midday and I tuned in to 3AW in the car. Dennis Cometti, Nathan Buckley and Mike Sheahan were on, and for the first time in weeks their comments were all positive. Bucks, who had questioned my ability to continue playing after our match against the Crows two weeks earlier, said, 'Matthew Lloyd has proven me wrong.' Mike added, 'Yeah, Bucks, I know it's only one game but he looked a different man last night.'

It was just one game, but I knew things had changed. I could feel it. I'd been in the Eagles game in a way I hadn't been for a long time. The move to the flank had been a positive one and Knighta got a bit of praise for that. To me, though, it wasn't as simple as a positional switch. I was the club captain, so it wouldn't have been easy to drop me. I thought it was actually a 'sink or swim' move: we'll move you out to half-forward and see what happens. I had to reinvent myself mid-season to make the move a success.

Playing at full-forward, I had been too curtailed by the game plan. I was thinking too much about the plan and not relying on my instincts or those of my teammates. At half-forward it was different – the only real instruction to the midfield group was 'hit up the half-forward', and that was exactly what I needed. I presented myself and I got some easy touches, which lifted my confidence. I felt alive again, and I could give instructions to the younger players because I was finally getting a kick myself.

For weeks I had felt worthless and disengaged. Now I was into it and I started to believe I could play footy again. At the Monday meeting, Gary O'Donnell showed my tackle on Dean Cox early in the match and said, 'The captain set the tone – look at this tackle.' I was craving some positive feedback and I got it during and after that game. It was only one game, but to me it felt like much more than that.

Our mood as a team was better too; the pressure valve had lifted. Our next match was against Carlton, who had just crept into the eight with a win over the Pies. We had a leadership dinner with the board that week, and even they were feeling we were about to turn our fortunes around. Ray Horsbrough, our chairman, turned to me during the dinner and said, 'You know that we'll beat Carlton this week, don't you?' That was a big call, but I was feeling the same. It is funny – you win one and the previous eight losses are forgotten. The mood of the whole club had changed.

Against Carlton, I kicked a goal in the first minute and

we could really feel the surge happening. We went on to win by thirty-five points in a great team performance. I finished with four goals on Michael Jamison, and again I felt good about my game.

The next week, against Freo in Perth, I didn't hit the scoreboard as hard, but I did take eight marks and slot through a goal from the forward flank. I was getting plenty of the ball and laying tackles. We won a tight game, and it felt even better because it was on the road. We now had three in a row and sat only two wins outside the eight. Somehow, our finals chances were still alive.

We were scoring heavily and finding a way to stem the flow in the other direction. Against Brisbane the next week, we kicked twenty-four goals to eighteen to record a strong win. My stats continued to be good: seventeen disposals, nine marks and four goals. Since the Eagles game, I hadn't dropped below fifteen possessions or eight marks, and I was making a difference to the team. What was looking like a wasted season was now turning around, and positives were emerging everywhere. David Hille, for instance, was becoming the most dominant ruckmen in the competition.

The next week was no different, although we lost by less than a kick to Richmond. I had seventeen disposals again, but this time I slotted 2.2 rather than 4.0. In any close loss, you wonder what you could have done differently. What if I had converted those two behinds into goals? It was also the game Joel Bowden kept rushing through behinds, which forced the league to change the rules.

We beat Collingwood the next week and I had a really good day with ten marks and four goals. Our younger players such as Kyle Reimers were starting to play very good football, and that was what I really wanted to see at our football club. Beating Collingwood was a huge thrill, especially after they had destroyed us on Anzac Day. We had definitely improved since then.

Against Melbourne in the next round, I had to return to the full-forward line because Lucas and Neagle were both out. I had enjoyed my time up the ground and had strung together six really good games. My role up the ground had caused big problems for opposition sides: they could no longer play the monster full-back on me because I was too mobile, but I was too big for the traditional half back-flanker. Against Brisbane, for instance, the ruckman Mitch Clark came to pick me up, and Melbourne tried the same approach with Stefan Martin. I kicked two goals in the first five minutes of the Melbourne game and felt that I was in for a big one.

My role that day wasn't quite as a traditional full-forward, as Knighta asked me to play about thirty metres out from goal. If we started well as a forward line, he wouldn't make too many changes, and that really helped us. I wasn't the best defensive forward, but I was holding my feet now and scoring heavily.

Martin was taken off me after my two goals in the first quarter; Matthew Warnock was given the job but it didn't make much difference. I was crumbing balls off the packs and taking strong marks, and everything I touched was turning to gold. I was even getting lucky with the bounce of the ball. It was one of those rare games where I got all the luck, which wasn't happening during our eight-game losing streak.

And I had my mouth back, too. After crumbing the ball at the front of a pack and running into an open goal in the third quarter, I turned to Warnock and said, 'You can't just walk into a milk bar and buy experience!' I was entertaining the young blokes like Monfries and Lovett, and we were all having a good laugh.

Later in the third quarter, Peverill got the ball and kicked it to the goal square. I lost Warnock at the back of the pack that was forming, and I launched myself on top of Brad Green and Sam Lonergan to take a screamer, with Warnock scrambling behind me. It was the best mark I'd ever taken in AFL football.

All I was focused on was the footy. I had my eyes on it all the way, and once I had it in my hands I wasn't going to let go. As I took the ball in my hands I could hear the roar of the crowd; sometimes you're in such a zone that you can't hear them at all, but at other times they're so loud they break through.

Lovett and Monfries, who were at the front of the pack, couldn't wipe the smiles off their faces. Jason Laycock had his arms in the air like we were in the schoolyard. I kicked my sixth goal, everyone was jumping on top of me and the crowd started a 'Lloydy' chant. I looked at it on the big screen to see the mark again, and I turned to Warnock and said, 'You've probably always dreamt of being on a footy card – now you will be.'

Warnock turned to everyone in our vicinity and said, 'Listen to this cockhead and some of the dribble he's talking.' But this was one of those rare times, like my Sydney thirteen-goal day, where I felt unstoppable; I didn't care what he thought of me.

I had proved to myself – and my doubters – that I could still play. I was also pleased for the people who had helped me through my rough patch. My mentor, Justin, along with Lisa and her family, as well as my family, particularly my parents – they were the rocks for me when I was doing it tough.

Gary O'Donnell came up to me after the game and said, 'If you weren't playing today, I reckon we might have dropped this one.' I was kicking beautifully from fifty metres, and I had kicked two crucial goals late to help us win the game. I finished with an eight-goal haul.

After this match, I thought it was time I started speaking to the media again. I talked about the team and how exciting it was, and how much better we were playing. On the ground after the game, I looked around the MCG and just took a moment to soak it all up, which I had rarely done in my thirteen-year career.

I had turned down Mike Sheahan for an interview several weeks earlier. He had written a column in the middle of the year saying I was finished, and he had asked a couple of times to do a follow-up with me. After the Melbourne game, we went to Perth to play the Eagles – we lost a close one – but Mike was on the phone again and I agreed to meet with him.

We spent an hour or two talking at my house. He told me he'd got it wrong and written me off too early. I understood that he had just been doing his job, and that he'd made a call he thought was right at the time. I really respected Mike and I was sure he hadn't written a column of that magnitude without giving it serious thought.

After our talk, Mike wrote a follow-up column that

spoke of my turnaround, which I was quite chuffed about. The effort I'd made to improve had taken so much out of me physically and mentally, but I was starting to feel like it was all worth it. Apart from leaving the house for training, I had become a recluse during that eight-week period when we were losing and I wasn't touching it, but now I felt a strong sense of pride in myself and my teammates.

It was my 250th game the next week against Adelaide. It was a pretty big week, and I was happy to celebrate getting to the 250-game milestone. Like they did for all milestone matches, Essendon did a great job to make it special for me. Everyone who mattered to me was at the game.

Two of my best mates, Scott Lucas and Mark McVeigh, spoke about me before the game, even though they were both out injured. One of the things they both said was how much they had wanted to run out onto the field that day to play in my milestone match, and how much character I had shown to fight back from the form slump I was in. They spoke about where I stood in the history of the Essendon Football Club.

Scott is a very intelligent person – in fact, I think he's capable of being a senior coach or a senior football administrator one day if he wants to. He is currently the general manager of a sports management company called Phoenix. He's a very good communicator and reads the game so well. Spike is as loyal a friend as you could hope for, and he is so passionate about the Essendon Football Club. It was fitting that those two guys spoke on my big day. It was lucky the lights were off in the meeting room before the game because the tears started flowing. It wasn't reaching 250 games that got to me, but rather what I had been through that year and the way that Scotty and Spike spoke about me.

We were so undermanned at this point in the season that we just couldn't match Adelaide. We dropped the match and were really struggling again, but this time it wasn't because of poor form. The Bulldogs cleaned us up the next week, and then in the final round we could barely get the numbers up for a team.

Round 22 was one of the worst experiences of my playing career. The Saints were highly motivated for the match: they needed to win by at least 100 points to get the double-chance in the finals. Essendon, on the other hand, had just twenty-four players to choose its twenty-two from.

Earlier in the year, after we'd lost to Geelong, Knighta had told Damien Peverill and Jason Johnson that they were pretty much only going to play if there were injuries. That was the case here and so they lined up for one last match with us. They were pretty gutted by the way they'd been treated, but they continued to carry themselves well in what was the toughest year of their lives.

So they lined up for their last match with us that day, along with Mal Michael and Adam Ramanauskas. Rama, who had come back from a lot of surgery to remove cancerous tumours in his neck, was a pretty confident person. Even during his chemotherapy and his recovery, he would always say to me, 'I reckon I could still beat you in a 100-metre sprint.' But the surgery had taken its toll on his body, and he had come back with limited movement in his neck and shoulder. Even though he would have loved to have played on, he was limited in what he could do physically, and beating cancer had taken its toll on him mentally too. Rama was so strong in what must have been such a scary time for him and his family. He's one of the most inspirational people I have ever met.

Rama's skills were elite from the moment he played in our Premiership win at the age of nineteen. He was cat-like when the ball hit the deck – he reminded me of Peter Matera. He was such a balanced player and was one of the blokes I really enjoyed leading to.

I did my hamstring in the first quarter of that match. I played out the game because it was our last and I had plenty of time to get over it, but I was pretty ineffective. The Saints were treating us like it was a training drill and the ball rarely came my way anyway. We only kicked five goals for the game and had two goalless quarters, and we finished with a 108-point loss. Even with the diminished team we had, we should have put up a better show than that, especially after the second half of our season had been so positive.

After that game, Mark McVeigh asked if he could speak to the players. We formed a circle and locked arms, and with tears in his eyes he said, 'Never ever walk off this ground having played like that again, because that was nothing short of embarrassing. It was a disgrace.' He was spot on.

We had finished the season with three losses. After getting over my initial disappointment, I recognised that they had been to the teams that finished third, fourth and fifth on the ladder, so really there was no shame in that.

It was tough year for me personally and for the team, but we'd fought our way out of a real hole. As a team, we won some footy matches and started to believe that if we did the right things consistently, we could compete well. Injuries destroyed us at the end, but it was a better year than it could have been.

I came second in our best-and-fairest award, which was a great result considering my first half of the season was so bad. The Essendon best-and-fairest is the one award I would have loved to have won but never did.

Our end-of-season review was far more positive than it could have been. But after the emotional roller-coaster I had been on, and all the effort I had put in, as I contemplated the year ahead I thought to myself, 'I've got to do all this over again.'

> 'A lot of times you wouldn't know whether Matthew Lloyd had a great day or a bad day on the footy field. I thought his demeanour stayed the same.'
>
> *Andrew Neophitou*

29

Confidence Lost

> 'I don't think he said anything that would have embarrassed himself during that Knights saga. I don't remember an occasion where I thought he's let himself down or he said more than he should have.'
>
> *Mike Sheahan*

WE HAD PLAYED SOME good footy in the second half of 2008, and, aside from our injuries, we felt like we finished the year positively. It had taken us a while to get on top of Knighta's game plan, but it felt like we were moving in the right direction. We were playing better contested footy and, with the evolution of our game, we genuinely felt we should be finals contenders in 2009.

I was in my thirties now, but I had rediscovered my form and confidence. I attacked the preseason like I always had. We had a couple of new arrivals in Michael Hurley and David Zaharakis, who both looked like pretty good prospects.

We won out first two NAB Cup games by slim margins – to the Bulldogs by a point and then to Brisbane by two points – but we lost our third to Collingwood by a huge margin. To be blunt, they taught us a football lesson and my own form was pretty ordinary. Scott Lucas, Jay Neagle and I all played, but we were all getting in each other's way.

Jay was still not fit enough to rotate further up the ground when needed, while Scotty was battling a knee injury that meant he could only play a deeper role. So I was chasing kicks up around the wings, which wasn't ideal. The three of us lacked authority in the NAB Cup, and I felt that one of us would be a casualty sooner or later. Jay was Knighta's preferred option, so it was always going to be either Scotty or me.

Our final practice match before the main season was against North Melbourne in Bendigo. I needed to find some touch so I could go to Adelaide for our opening match against Port with some confidence. I played half-forward with Scott McMahon as my opponent. He was giving away a fair bit of height to me and I kicked three early goals in the first quarter. I was marking well and finishing off, and Alan Richardson, our new forwards' coach, was pretty pleased, as were my teammates.

Then I started to play with more intent, flying for everything. Those early goals were exactly what I needed and I was attacking the ball with confidence. I was on the half-forward flank and Neagle was full-forward, but he hadn't really touched the footy. A message came out to me: 'You're on Jay's bootlaces – give him more space.'

I didn't agree that I was getting in his way but I thought, 'Okay, the coach isn't happy so I'll push further up the ground.' A few minutes later I went for a ball around the fifty-metre line and was dragged.

As I came off, Alan Richardson was waiting for me. 'Knighta wants you as a half-forward working up the ground,' he said.

'No worries,' I replied, and I went back on and tried to do as I was asked. But it mustn't have been right as I was dragged a couple more times in the next fifteen minutes. Alan was sent down on each occasion to tell me what I was doing wrong, although he looked quite uncomfortable about it.

In the third quarter I worked really hard along the boundary line to give Jay his space and then I went in behind him to go for a ball in the goal square. I flew for the mark but dropped it, and the ball went through for a behind. Knighta sent out another message: 'Stay out of the forward fifty – I don't want to see you in there.'

He may as well have sent me straight to the showers, because after receiving that message I ran around like a headless chook for the rest of the afternoon. I got plenty of touches but had no effect on the game. Knighta might have lost his cool with the way I was playing that day, but I lost a lot of faith in my coach. It seemed to me that he would rather not have me in his side; he was making football harder for me than it had ever been.

I went up to Knighta immediately after the game in the change rooms and said, 'Can I talk to you about what went on today?'

'No – I'll talk to you about it later,' he replied.

We then went into our after-match team meeting, where he gave me a serve in front of the whole team. 'How are you meant to expect this young bloke to do anything when you're continually standing on his bootlaces?' he demanded.

I was furious. It was a good thing that we had the following weekend off before Round 1, as I was becoming very disenchanted with Knighta, and that was a real concern for me, considering we were just a week out from the start of a new season.

On the Monday night after the game I got a phone call from a staff member at the club, who said how embarrassed Alan was about the treatment that I had received during and after the game, which he didn't think was fair. I never spoke to Alan about it, but I believe he felt it was out of line and over the top. At the end of the preseason I was as confused as I had ever been about my position at the club. A pleasant distraction was that Lisa was three-months pregnant, and I was able to share some positive news with family and friends around that time.

Our fitness coach, John Quinn, had left the club and been replaced by Stuart Cormack, who had been with the West Coast Eagles during their Premiership era. Stuey's approach during the preseason had been quite a change. Quinny had been a real motivator who would flog us over sand-dunes during the summer. He'd have us running hills for hours, and boxing was also a prominent part of our training. Stuey had a more basic approach; he reasoned that there were no sand-dunes on a football field so there was no point training on them. None of the players were complaining about that!

Stuey put a lot of faith in the players, particularly those who were injured, to complete their required sessions to the letter. There could be up to ten players in the rehab group at times, each doing a different program, so you were generally left to your own devices. That wasn't an issue if you had an experienced group of players, but we didn't, and some players took advantage of the latitude they were given under the new regime.

Kyle Reimers, who was one of our up-and-comers, had barely played any of our preseason matches because he kept tearing his quad at training. Yet he would be seen kicking a soccer ball around the clubrooms, which simply isn't the way to get over a quad strain. Other injured players also felt he wasn't working as hard in rehab as he should have.

Jay Neagle was another player struggling with poor fitness levels; his skinfold results were in the nineties. For any AFL player they should be at around fifty; midfielders are often in the forties.

During the week leading into Round 1, we had our regular leadership meeting. We discussed Kyle and Jay and agreed that they needed to be given a rocket. Knighta listened and seemed to agree. As a senior playing group, we decided to have a quiet chat with both of them; we needed them to approach their training in a more professional manner. Jay had to get fitter and Kyle had to be more disciplined in his training and his attitude. Both Jay and Kyle took the discussions well.

We went to AAMI Stadium to play Port Adelaide for our first match of the year, but the game was an absolute shocker. We were terrible. I was very ordinary and, as a result, spent the final ten or fifteen minutes of the match on the bench.

Knighta was bitterly disappointed with my output, which was fair enough. During our Monday meeting after the loss, I felt he spent the whole session aiming everything he was saying about the loss at me. What floored me, though, were comments he made about our confidential leadership meeting the week before.

'You want to put Jay Neagle and Kyle Reimers up like they're elephants in the room,' he said, 'but at least they stick to the game plan. At least they don't lose their feet continually.' Anyone who wasn't in the leadership group would have been wondering what this was about, because we'd agreed to deal with our concerns about Jay and Kyle with them privately.

I waited for the team meeting to end, intending to clear the air in our regular leadership meeting afterwards. The leadership group was pretty much the same as in it had been in 2008 – McVeigh, Welsh, McPhee, Hille, Watson and myself. When the meeting got underway, there was a bit of small talk about the game before Knighta said, 'Anything else to discuss?'

I said, 'I'm really disappointed with the way you handled the match review meeting today. We had a private conversation last week about Jay and Kyle, and because some of us here had a poor game it was all thrown back in our faces. Everyone's going to have bad days – does that mean that things from the leadership group can be thrown at any one of us? If I have a bad game, does that mean that, as captain of the club, I can't pull up another player?'

Knighta was just sitting there rubbing his nose, which was a sign he was getting quite fired up. 'You finished?' he asked.

'Yeah, I am,' I replied.

'Well, I'm sick of how poorly you chase out of the forward line. I'm sick of the way you lose your feet.' Then he turned to Jobe Watson and said, 'How are our young players meant to kick properly when you continually kick around corners?' He went around the leadership group and said what we each weren't doing right.

I thought Knighta had lost control of his emotions at this point. I was constantly looking at Leigh Russell, our welfare officer who facilitated the meeting, waiting for her to take some control over the meeting. But she had a blank look on her face and was as white as a ghost. I could tell she was stunned by what was happening and what was being said.

Knighta had one more thing to say. 'And you know what? The younger players have got no respect for you guys as a leadership group.'

Naturally, that's the last thing we wanted to hear, and the comment sparked up Mark McVeigh. 'I don't agree with that,' he said. 'What makes you say that?'

'They've told me,' Knighta said.

'Well, we're fucked then,' said Spike. 'This is Round 1 and we are fucked as a club.'

Adam McPhee chipped in, 'I agree, we're in big trouble if the younger players are thinking like that. What have we done to these younger players that's not right?' McPhee then said he didn't even believe what Knighta was saying.

Jobe Watson settled things down by saying, 'I agree with Knighta – we've got to lift our act and we've got to improve.'

Maybe Jobe was looking to take the heat out of the situation, but I was in no mood to let Knighta feel that what he had said and how he was acting was right. We knew we hadn't done a lot of things right that weekend, but the confidence of the leadership team had been breached. We had to be able to discuss club issues behind closed doors knowing that they would stay confidential. I was very disappointed with Knighta that day.

The way Knighta had responded in that meeting left me thinking we were in for a very long year. It was only Round 1 and I was over the way things were handled when we were facing adversity, and I could tell that mood had spread throughout the club. When we were doing our rehab after the Port Adelaide game, Scott Lucas came past me and whispered in my ear, 'Only twenty-one rounds to go.' Our spirit had been crushed, which was gut-wrenching.

The problem was the way we were being treated. Some might say we were being soft, but I thought it was a really poor way to manage the first week of an AFL season. I'm the first to admit that I didn't perform – I had played poorly and hadn't led the side well that day either. But that had nothing to do with what we had discussed about Reimers and Neagle.

I tried to work out if the younger players really had an issue with the leadership group. I knew for a fact that Michael Hurley, David Zaharakis, Brent Stanton and Jason Winderlich thought the world of the leadership group – as friends, mentors and players. Maybe there were a couple of guys we should have communicated with better, but there is no way it was as big an issue as Knighta was making out. I didn't believe there was much to what he had said; I decided he was just angry when he was challenged and had lashed out.

The mood around the club was at an all-time low. Those in the leadership group tried hard not to let how we were feeling affect the other players, but it was pretty obvious we were all very disappointed. The wounds at Essendon were deeper than just one loss.

30

Lost Love

'I thought he was a genuine champion. I never actually thought about 300 games or 1000 goals, and perhaps without a couple of those injuries he might have done that – he wasn't too far away. But you also have to recognise the changing game to look at what he achieved, and that is what makes it impressive.'

Merv Keane

Despite our falling confidence, we were just lucky to be playing Fremantle at Etihad Stadium that week. I couldn't remember ever losing to Fremantle – we had, of course, but we had certainly never lost to them at our home ground. Even though we were grumpy with our coach, that wasn't going to hold back our effort.

We stuck to Knighta's game plan as well as we could. We still wanted to do our best and we absolutely hated the feeling of a loss and the fallout from a poor performance. We began the game well, kicking five goals to one in the first quarter, and we finished with a thirty-eight-point win. Because we'd reacted in a positive way to Knighta's criticism after Round 1, you might have thought his outburst had worked. But I didn't think he'd gone into that Monday meeting with the intent of giving us a rev-up; rather, he'd lost it in the heat of the moment. To my mind, the fact that we won the next game said more about us than the coach.

I felt like my intensity and pressure around the ball against Freo had been okay, but I was still without a goal in the season. I was on 891 career goals at the time, so a big milestone was approaching too. My preseason and my first two rounds had been a long way off where I wanted to be. I was a little worried but not like I had been twelve months prior. As captain, I was thinking about more than just my own form.

Our next Monday team meeting was fine, but the leadership meeting afterwards wasn't as productive as it should have been, and I felt it never would be again. Our leaders were now giving the bare minimum; no one wanted to have anything thrown back at them afterwards, as had happened after Round 1. There was no trust.

I had a dominant game in Round 3 against Carlton, which was exactly what I needed at the time. I was in the game all night and kicked 5.1. After we won the match, I belted out the club song and was nearly in tears. It was only then that I realised how heavily the situation at the club was weighing down on me.

I was so proud of our effort against Carlton. We'd been twenty points down during the first quarter, but we'd hit back. I was playing on Bret Thornton, who didn't enjoy body contact, so I was jumping into him. I was marking everything, although often well out of range because I was playing up the ground.

We fought our way back from the slow start, and I slotted two goals in a couple of minutes in the third quarter to virtually draw us level. Alwyn Davey and Paddy Ryder slotted two more in quick time to give us the lead at three-quarter time, and we held on for a memorable win. It was always great to beat Carlton, especially in front of 80,000 people.

The win was as emotional as I could ever remember. It had been a big couple of weeks, but what made it even sweeter was that Carlton had been flying and not many people had given us a chance. They got within a point in the final quarter, but our guys were brilliant and we held on for a four-point win under enormous pressure.

Round 4 was a disappointing game for us. I started the game well, although I was wasteful in front of goal. Knighta and Alan Richardson felt like I was staying too close to goal, and this time they were right. Scott Thompson spoiled me a few times in the first half, but in the third quarter I was really starting to play well and mark everything.

I was lining up for my fourth goal of the game – and my 899th career goal – when we were penalised for an interchange infringement and the ball was handed over to the Kangaroos. Then I was taken off as part of our rotations system, and I sat out the next eight minutes of the game. I thought that was crazy, given the influence I had been having.

At three-quarter time, I walked up to Alan Richardson and asked, 'Is there something wrong? Have I done something wrong?'

'No, no, not that I know of,' he replied.

'Well, why was I sitting there for so long with the game at such a critical stage?'

I never found out what was behind it. I don't know if Knighta forgot about me and got caught up in the match, but it killed the momentum of my game at a time when I felt I could have got us over the line. I later managed to kick my fourth goal, leaving me on 899 goals at the end of the match but we wasted so many opportunities and lost in a low-scoring affair.

Anzac Day was next up. It was a game I always longed to be a part of. Its intensity was like that of a big final, and pretty much every year was a sell-out. Not many people rated us a chance to win it in 2009, but we did.

The match was an absolute thriller. We started slowly but the scores were level at half time. I copped a corkie early in the match, so after that I just stood with the goal umpire to take Simon Prestigiacomo out of the game. I went goalless for the day, kicking just three behinds, so my 900th goal had to wait another week.

We traded the lead a few times during the match, and when Paddy Ryder goaled at the eight-minute mark of the final quarter we thought we could go on with it. Instead, we stopped and didn't score for another eighteen minutes. In that time, the Pies scored 2.5 and lead by fourteen points.

Then Leroy Jetta kicked a goal just after the twenty-five-minute mark and we trailed by eight points. A minute or so later, Ricky Dyson put one through from the boundary and the margin was two points. A rushed behind left the margin at one point and Collingwood began to try to eat up the remaining time.

By then it was raining heavily. Jason Winderlich took the ball off the back of the pack from the kick-in and passed it off to Heath Hocking, who then got it over to Nathan Lovett-Murray. He ran on and kicked it to David Zaharakis – one of our first-year players – who turned and, off two steps, launched a long bomb from fifty that I watched sail over my head and through for a goal. The noise at the ground was electrifying.

With the rain, our lightning-speed game plan came into its own and our leg speed left the Collingwood players watching. That was only David Zaharakis's fourth AFL game and his fourth ever goal, but it is one that will live with him forever.

A few seconds after the bounce, the siren sounded for one of the best wins in my time at Essendon. We were gone for all money but we hadn't laid down; the win showed great spirit. Paddy Ryder won the Anzac Day Medal after David Hille had suffered a knee injury earlier in the game. Paddy laid fourteen tackles in what was the most influential game I've seen him play.

We travelled to Brisbane to play the Lions the next week, and I missed a shot early in the first quarter and got nothing in the second. I had now gone for eight quarters without kicking one, so clearly the idea of 900 career goals was having some sort of impact on me, even if I didn't recognise it. 'Remember, it's just another number,' I told myself.

In the third quarter, Leroy Jetta steamed out of the centre and I got the sit on Daniel Merrett's back to take the mark twenty metres out, directly in front. It was a huge thrill to slot that one through, and even though we played poorly and dropped the game, bringing up my 900th goal was a great honour.

Getting past that barrier allowed me to concentrate on winning matches. The next week I played on Campbell Brown of the Hawks – Trent Croad was out injured – and I ran him off his legs. They also tried Tom Murphy and then Robbie Campbell on me, but I was in the zone, as was the team. I took a career-high fifteen marks, and I probably should have kicked at least five, but I kicked poorly and scored only 3.2. The main thing, though, was that we broke our losing streak against the Hawks.

My endurance levels were pretty good. Since Lisa and I had lived in Southbank from 2002–2006, I'd spent a lot of time in the preseason running the Tan – three times a week, in fact. That endurance work paid off for me when I was playing up on the forward flank, even though I still felt my best position was to play a lot deeper.

In modern footy, you can't just have someone sit at full-forward, but Knighta and I disagreed on what my best position was. I felt that if the time was right, I should move to full-forward; if it wasn't, I should play centre half-forward. But he had it in his head that I was a half-forward and that was it. I wanted a bit more flexibility, and I thought that, as players, we should be able to move ourselves around, depending on what was happening. That was what we had done it in the past.

Jay Neagle had the worst fitness at the footy club and couldn't play anywhere other than full-forward, and that had an impact on the team when he was there. Scotty Lucas still had a bung knee that was holding him back, so as a forward group we had lost the ability to rotate our positions during a game, not only to suit us but also to isolate an opposition defender who might not like a certain position in defence.

We were inconsistent after that Hawks win, though. Against St Kilda in Round 8, we started slowly but got on a bit of a run. I was going all right on Sam Fisher and then Zac Dawson moved onto me. Dawson and I had a one-on-one marking contest, which I won, but the umpire paid a dubious free kick against me for holding. If I had goaled, we'd have been within striking distance, but in the end we went down by nineteen points.

In Round 9 we had the Dreamtime Game at the 'G match against Richmond – another of Sheeds' innovations. The occasion celebrated the Indigenous heritage of both clubs. It was always a big night, and this time we won convincingly. We ran out the match well. The scores had been level during time-on in the third quarter but we ran out forty-point winners.

Before I was done as captain at Essendon, I would have to handle some more public speculation about coaches, but I'm glad I never had to go through what Chris Newman did at Richmond in 2009. As a first-year captain, he had been embroiled in the media discussion about the future of coach Terry Wallace, and I could see it was taking a toll on him. After this match, he was looking like a lost soul. As we stood on the ground for the presentations, I went over and had a chat to him. I spoke to him about hanging in there and being strong for his team.

In 1997, when there had been public speculation over Sheeds' position, all the Essendon players were called into a meeting with the club management. We were told quite clearly to stay out of the discussion. 'You play football and let us take care of that side of things,' they said. I had delivered that same message when there was more speculation about Sheeds in 2006 and 2007.

We were fourth on the ladder at this point, and we felt like we were in the hunt, but the fragility of the environment at the club left me feeling we were always at risk. I hated the mood around the club when we lost, and I didn't like what was happening to some players' careers. If we lost, the axe was swung, which meant some guys weren't getting consistent opportunities. The players felt unsettled as a group; I think we made more changes than any other team through that season.

I had started the season not knowing if I wanted to play on in 2010. As the season was unfolding, this uncertainty continued to play on my mind. My doubts weren't caused by the games we'd lost; the Essendon Football Club just wasn't a great place to be and I had never wanted to overstay my welcome as a player. I always thought that I'd rather leave a year early than a year too late.

Geelong mauled us in the next round and we dropped out of the eight. The Cats were unbeaten on top of the ladder at the time and were flying, so it was no disgrace to drop that one. Down my end of the ground, they had Matty Scarlett, Darren Milburn and Andrew Mackie, and they hunted in packs and set up a lot of goals from defence. It was the new model of football, and we clearly hadn't adapted to it.

Mackie, in particular, was very lippy that day. 'You must only be playing for your pay packet – why aren't you retired by now?' I hadn't copped much personal sledging in my time; I'd copped a physical barrage early in my career, but never really a mental attack like this. It reminded me of what

I had said to Glenn Manton in 2000. I'd certainly said plenty during my time, so I just copped it this day and hoped I'd get the chance to play against him again.

I went goalless the next week and we dropped our second in a row. Again our defensive play was poor: we kicked eighteen goals at Etihad Stadium against the Crows, but we let through twenty-one.

Against Melbourne in Round 12 we had a big win, but we knew Melbourne was a young and inexperienced side. If we had any intention to play finals, we had to win that one. I played deeper in this match and kicked three goals in the first quarter but was well held by James Frawley for the remainder of the night.

Even after a win, though, I wasn't feeling the buzz. I felt like I was irrelevant to the side because of the role I had been given. Against Geelong and Adelaide I was being picked up by quality players like Matthew Scarlett and Nathan Bock, but they would have been laughing to themselves when they saw the game I was being asked to play. If I went up to the wing, they were zoning back and cutting off the leads of Jay Neagle and Scott Lucas. The difference to the year before was that we'd had a far more flexible forward line in 2008 and the midfielders had been hitting up the half-forwards far more often. That wasn't happening any more. Suddenly, I wasn't winning any ball up the ground and I was paranoid about staying out of Scotty's and Jay's way because of what had happened earlier in the year. My love of the game was waning, and I was wondering whether I needed it anymore.

I was contracted until the end of the year, and I knew that if things kept going the way they were, there was little chance

I wanted another one. The club wanted to start contract discussions around the time of the Melbourne game, but my manager, Neo, and I put those meetings on hold.

We thumped Carlton next up, again with a strong finish, and we were back in the finals mix. The Carlton fans and the cheer squad absolutely gave it to me in the first half, even though I kicked a couple. Over my career, I had found that of all the Melbourne-based teams, Carlton's supporters were probably the most abusive. When I kicked a goal late in the game I turned around to look at the stands to give them a bit back and they had all gone home. That was a nice feeling, even though I wanted to give it back to them after their sledging in the first quarter.

On the Monday after the match, Mark McVeigh missed training. I went to see Matthew Knights and said, 'Mark's not here because he's had a big night out. Under our standards, I don't think he should play this week.'

That wasn't easy for me, as Mark and I are close mates. In fact, I was about to be in his wedding party. 'Before anything happens,' I said to Knighta, 'let me go around to his house and I'll have a talk to him and get the facts.'

When I got to his place, he looked pale. He was really upset and said, 'I know I've let you down. Hit me with it – what's the penalty?'

'You won't be playing this week,' I said.

'Fair enough,' Mark said. 'The one concern I've got is how it's going to be looked on.'

'I'll talk to people about what we go with publicly,' I said.

The club felt we had to be up-front about the incident. Jobe Watson, in particular, was quite strong about it. 'You can't lie about these things,' he said. 'They get out, so we've got to be honest.'

Mark wasn't too happy but he understood that he'd done the wrong thing.

Collingwood smashed us in Round 14, and then we had a great win in Sydney. That was probably the last game of football I enjoyed. I played on Craig Bolton, who I really rated, and I worked hard across the half-forward line and had a lot of touches. I wasted some opportunities, but Scotty and I kicked three each and were left to play our roles. I think that was the reason I enjoyed it so much – days like that were few and far between at that stage, because neither Scotty nor I were really enjoying our footy.

Lisa and I had decided to stay in Sydney after the game, and we were standing in the SCG car park trying to find a taxi. I was making eye contact with everyone I saw in a car, hoping someone would offer us a lift as the taxi queue was huge. The first person I locked eyes with was Craig Bolton, and he wound his window down and offered us a lift. I'd never been given a lift home by an opposition player I've just been into battle with, so it was quite a unique experience and showed a lot about him as a person. He's a terrific fellow.

I had started to think seriously about life after football and I was keen on a role in the media. Mark Stevens from the *Herald Sun* interviewed me about concepts of leadership after the Swans game; the article was to be a positive one about my captaincy and the legacy I was looking to leave.

Stevens also asked a couple of questions about Mark McVeigh's suspension, and I told him how I'd gone to Mark's house to let him know that he wouldn't be playing the following week. The back page lead a few days later, on the day we were about to play the Bulldogs, read 'Lloyd led the McVeigh sacking'.

Inside was the captaincy article, in which I answered about twenty questions, but the back page quoted my couple of comments on Spike. I nearly choked on my breakfast that morning, and my heart sank when I read it. Spike is a great mate of mine, as loyal a friend as they come. He'd mucked up and was trying to get over it, but now it was on the back page of the *Herald Sun* on the morning of our big Friday night game against the Doggies.

I rang Spike straightaway but he let the phone ring out. I sent him a long text saying, 'I don't know if this means anything to you, but I'm so sorry. It was two innocuous answers just explaining the situation – I didn't think there was going to be any big focus on it but they've used it as a back-page lead.'

He sent me back a text later saying, 'Don't worry. I'm upset but don't worry.'

My opponent that night was Brian Lake, and he was in stunning form. He was marking everything and running off me. To make matters worse, I dislocated a finger in the second quarter and copped a barrage from the coach about the way I was playing, which was fair enough this day.

Knighta felt I wasn't playing to his instructions, which was becoming a common theme, but he was right this time. Lake was in such good form that he was intimidating to play on. I was chasing kicks and uncontested marks up on the wings when I should have tried to keep him occupied closer to goal. I kicked a couple of goals late in that game; little did I realise that the second of them would be my final goal in the AFL.

We lost the game that night, and we went into the rooms afterwards expecting to get a few points on what we'd done wrong. But all that was written on the whiteboard was 'the vault'. Knighta then talked about keeping things in-house and not discussing internal issues with the media. He never said my name specifically but everyone knew full well who he was talking about. I was annoyed that Knighta hadn't talked to me about it to find out my side of the story, but that wasn't his style.

It was a good lesson for me to learn. The last person I ever wanted to hurt was Spike. We got past it, but if I had my time again I wouldn't have answered those questions.

Essendon's football manager, Paul Hamilton, got in touch with Neo around this time to discuss the idea of a one-year contract. But I couldn't even begin to think about negotiating a new contract at that stage, or even talking about one. After Neo put Paul off, Knighta asked me to go out for an orange juice – I guess he knew I didn't drink coffee.

We went to a cafe down the road from Windy Hill. I wanted to get an indication of what he was thinking about my future at the club in 2010. I had no idea whether he wanted me to play on or not. After we talked for a while, he said, 'If you want to play, I'll support you.'

'How do you see the forward line set-up for next year?' I asked.

'I'm planning on playing Laycock, Hille, Hurley, Gumbleton, and Neagle forward next year,' he said. That showed me there were no guarantees about my position. If I played on, I knew it would all come down to my performance, which was fair enough, but I didn't want to finish my career at the Bendigo Bombers.

The next week, against Richmond, I went up for a mark early in the second quarter and landed awkwardly, hurting my heel. The doctors tried strapping it up in all sorts of ways but nothing helped. I played until ten minutes in the third quarter, but I couldn't run so I didn't see out the match.

I could barely walk the next day because of the bleeding to my heel. The club doctors estimated it was a five-week injury, and there were only five rounds left. We lost to the Tigers by less than a kick and only just held on to our spot in the eight. Our prospects for the finals were shaky and so I understood that I might have just played my final game of AFL football.

31

Killing Bambi

> 'Don't think you're killing Bambi here – if you don't want me to play on, just tell me.'
>
> *Matthew Lloyd*

IN THE MONTH THAT I was out with the heel injury, we lost to West Coast in Perth, drew with Brisbane at the MCG, gave the Saints their first loss of the season and then got smashed by Freo in Perth. The reality was that even though we were hanging on to eighth spot, we weren't playing well enough to deserve it, but we were pretty desperate to play a final and all the other contenders were struggling too.

There was no effort made to rush me back into the team, but our medical staff thought I would be fit enough to play in Round 22. We were in the eight going into the round, but either Port or Hawthorn could overtake us and we were playing the Hawks. If we won, we were in the finals, and if Hawthorn beat us, they were in, unless Port had a massive win. So it was a huge weekend and a big game to come back for.

I went into the game still in a fair amount of pain. I reckon I was seventy per cent fit, but the finals were on the line and

I wanted to help my team get there. I also wanted to lead Essendon one more time in a big game at the MCG. I had never captained a team into the finals. We were in the eight and I wanted to make sure we stayed there.

Buddy Franklin had been suspended the week before for a contentious shirtfront on Ben Cousins, so he wasn't there. Jarryd Roughead had gone in for surgery that week, which left Beau Dowler as the Hawks' key forward. I felt that, on paper, we had a really good shot at the game.

Early in the match, I knew I couldn't make any second or third efforts because I had a sharp pain in my heel every time I went for the footy. After four weeks out, I had lost a fair bit of match fitness too. It was such a frustrating injury but I tried my best to make an impact. At half time we were down by four goals and playing insipid football.

In the rooms, instead of doing our usual cool-down, Knighta got us together in front of our lockers. He was angry, and so he should have been as we were terrible. He didn't individualise but he went pretty hard at us as a team, saying, 'With so much at stake, what a poor performance.' I copped a bit of a stare, as did a lot of other blokes.

As we walked up the race to get back into it after half time, we were trying to pump ourselves up. Nathan Lovett-Murray, who loved it hard on the footy field, looked at me and said, 'I know you're struggling a bit here, but I reckon you've got to show more physical presence. Do something strong as the captain of this team.'

I was heavily restricted by my heel injury but I wanted to inspire the team. Sam Mitchell is a great clearance player who often gets the ball out the back of a stoppage, so I thought

I'd try to run off the line at the bounce and lay a big bone-crunching tackle on him. At the bounce, I headed straight for Mitchell but the ball went in the other direction. Spike won the clearance and dribbled the ball forwards towards me.

Brad Sewell was running to collect the ball, which was right in between us. I charged towards the ball but saw that he was going to get to it first, and I realised I had a split-second decision to make. Should I bump or tackle him? He hadn't taken possession of the ball at that stage, so I decided that I would try to hit him down the middle of the body with a hip-and-shoulder.

I braced myself for a bump, getting down as low as I could as I wanted to take him out fairly. I understood the rules, and I knew what had happened with Buddy the week before. But I couldn't get down low enough – Sewell had his knees bent and was bending down over the ball. My shoulder connected with the side of his face and the rest of me hit him down the front. He reeled back and Paddy Ryder gave him a bit of a slam tackle to the ground as he fell.

I knew straightaway I'd got the execution horribly wrong. His fingers were stiff and tight as he was falling to the ground, like they were reaching to the sky, and I realised it was going to be on for young and old between the two sides before he'd even hit the ground. Mitchell was the first to get to me, and he was in my face shouting, 'That's not on! It's just not on! I can't believe you've just done that!' I'd never heard a crowd react like they did, even at the 'line in the sand' game years earlier. The Essendon supporters loved it, while the Hawks supporters had another reason to hate me.

Campbell Brown, Michael Osborne and Luke Hodge were all on their way towards me too, but a few other scuffles started around me and they never got through. When I saw a replay afterwards, I reckon Fletch saved me, as his big Inspector Gadget arms seemed to knock everyone over around me when he was coming to my assistance. I think Campbell Brown bumped heads with Nathan Lovett-Murray, and so he went off the ground with blood running down his face. He was turning around and pointing at me, and I knew there would be a fiery end to the afternoon.

When the Essendon team finally got together in a huddle as they were carrying Sewell off, Spike said, 'That was fucking unbelievable!' Lovett-Murray said, 'That was inspirational!' Everyone was geeing each other up now – 'Come on! Let's get into this, they're one short!'

I was in another world, though. 'What have I just done?' I thought. 'What's the day going to hold for me now?' My season was over, as I knew I'd get rubbed out for the hit for sure. I also knew I didn't really want to play for Essendon anymore, and so I figured I had two quarters left of my Essendon career – and, more than likely, my AFL career.

Just as we were about to go out to our positions, I made a promise to myself. 'Whatever happens here, I'm putting my head over the footy. I won't pull out of any contest or be intimidated by anyone.' As it turned out, I won a couple of free kicks just by playing the ball, as the Hawks were certainly hitting me hard. Chance Bateman actually knocked me out at one stage with a bit of a round-arm and he copped a one-week suspension for it.

We got a run on when we resumed. The Sewell incident

seemed to inspire my teammates as we kicked the next six goals unanswered, but I had no further influence on the game. When it became clear we were going to win, I started to wonder if I'd be better off on the bench – I wasn't sure what Luke Hodge or Jordan Lewis or Campbell Brown might be capable of. But I decided there was no way I would walk away from a challenge.

When the siren rang, we had won by seventeen points and we were in the finals. I ran over to Brad Sewell on the bench. I wanted to see that he was okay, but as soon as I saw him I knew he wasn't – he had black eyes and his face was swollen. He was great, though, and he said, 'That's fine, mate – that's footy.'

When I went back over to my team, the boys were all pretty happy, knowing they'd be playing a final. I was still a bit rattled, though.

After every win, we would give mini footballs to young fans in the crowd. Making a silly mistake, I picked out a Bombers fan who was sitting near the race, right next to the Hawthorn rooms. After giving him the footy, I turned around and saw the whole Hawthorn team and officials heading in my direction.

'I'll look at them in the face at least once,' I thought to myself, 'and then I'll look away.' I locked eyes with Alastair Clarkson and lip-read 'You weak dog!' or something like that. 'You'd better come back and play next year, because we'll get you.'

Clarkson started heading towards me, and there's no doubt he was looking to get physical. He was pretty fired up and very emotional. Mark Evans, Hawthorn's footy manager, was holding him back.

I just wanted to get into the rooms – I didn't feel safe out there. The crowd was still fired up and I felt very uneasy. Once we got there, the boys were still pumped up – it was like we'd actually won a final. Everyone in the room was talking about my hit on Sewell.

When I was getting ready to leave the rooms, David Calthorpe and Stuart Cormack, our team manager and fitness coach, came to me and said, 'We think you need to be escorted to your car. There are a lot of people out there who are pretty upset by what happened.' They took me to my car but there were no dramas.

Even though there was no sun, I had the sunshade down and my sunglasses on for the drive home. I didn't want any Hawthorn supporter trying to run me off the road. When I'd got far enough away from the ground, I relaxed and turned the radio on to see what the media was saying about the match.

The first thing I heard was Hamish McLachlan on Triple M saying, 'What a day it's been of footy! What a spiteful day! Let's recap, and let's listen to Campbell Brown's comments from an interview he's done with us only moments ago.' I then heard Brown saying I was a 'sniper', that I had always been one, and that he hoped I played on the next year. The Triple M boys loved it, of course.

What Campbell said didn't really bother me. He was a bit of a hothead and wouldn't have been thinking that much at the time. I mean, what is a 'sniper' anyway? I took it to mean someone who whacks someone from behind and I thought it was a ridiculous comment, but I could understand the emotions of the Hawthorn people towards me. Campbell and I had a long-running stoush, so I wasn't surprised he was so angry.

It was such a draining day. I knew we'd made the finals but I also knew I wouldn't be the man leading the team out the following week, regardless of how many weeks I got at the tribunal. I left my phone off for three or four hours after the game, but when I turned it on I found some significant voice messages left that meant a lot to me. James Hird had called; he said 'That's what leadership's about – you stood tall when the team needed you to stand tall.'

That was how I viewed it too; I didn't believe it was the crude, callous act some were making it out to be. I didn't mean to hit Sewell in the head but I was trying to hurt him. Why bump someone if you don't want him to feel it? I had been smashed plenty of times before. I didn't feel ashamed of myself at all, but I hated seeing him hurt the way he was.

While the aftermath was very taxing, I was proud that I put myself on the line and changed the course of the match. We'd gone from being a lifeless team to one that found a spark and won its way into a finals series.

I finally made it home, and as I walked in the front door and went to hug Jaeda, she kicked me in the leg and said, 'Go away, Dad!' My emotions finally came out and I said, 'Go to your room! You do not talk to your dad like that!'

It had been a tough day and I was emotionally wrecked. There was the incident itself, my injury, Campbell Brown's comments, and the fact that I was going to miss the finals. My career at Essendon was over and possibly my whole career too. I had feared for my safety and it was all over the news. Everyone was judging me and my actions.

Luckily, I had a few pleasant distractions. Lisa was due any day with our second child, and my brother Brad and his wife, Yvette, had a baby girl, Mila, early the next week, and that provided me with a smile. I still wasn't answering phone calls, but on my way in to visit them I answered one; to my surprise, it was Dermott Brereton. I didn't know what sort of reaction I was going to get from Derm, but he said, 'For what it's worth, Matthew,' he said, 'I know it was a big hit and you're going to do some time, but I just thought that was inspirational. That was a player standing up for a team that was on the brink of its season ending.'

Hearing that gave me a massive boost, and suddenly I felt okay about the whole thing.

Just as I was saying hello to Yvette in the hospital, my phone rang again. This time it was David Calthorpe. 'Lloydy,' he said, 'the tribunal findings have come in. It's six weeks.' My emotions swung totally the other way.

'Six weeks?' I couldn't believe it.

'Yeah, if you take an early plea it's down to four, but as it stands it's six. The club wants to meet with you before training first thing tomorrow to talk about an appeal.'

I went back into the hospital room and was pretty upset, as were the others when I told them the news. We all knew I'd been in trouble, but we hadn't realised it would be that big. Six weeks! Only Lisa knew I was planning on retiring anyway, but everyone was shocked.

Lisa had agreed with me that my time at Essendon looked like it was up, but her view was that I needed to change clubs to get my love for the game back.

So the next day I went in to the club and met with Peter

Jackson, Matthew Knights, Gary O'Donnell, Paul Hamilton, Dominic Cato and a lawyer. We went through the incident on video. As I watched it, I was thinking how bad it looked, but everyone else said, 'So, we're all agreed that we should appeal.'

'What are we appealing?' I asked.

'You've got to try to beat the charge. There's no point accepting it and taking four weeks – you'll either get six or nothing. That's how it'll be.'

'After what happened with Franklin last week, there is no way the AFL will let me play this week,' I said. 'I don't want six weeks on my record.'

Knighta saw I was getting quite worked up and said, 'Okay – everyone leave the room.'

After they did, he asked, 'How are you feeling?'

I just burst out crying. 'This could be it for me,' I said.

Knighta was probably the last bloke I thought I'd pour out my soul to, but he was actually very good. He was very warm and he understood the situation in which I had found myself.

'I don't think I could cope with six weeks,' I said. 'If I play on, there's no way I want to be missing the first five rounds of a season if the boys lose this week. I don't even know if I want to play next year.'

'I don't want anyone seeing you like this,' Knighta said. 'I'll send everyone out for training; you pack your bag and go home for the afternoon.'

When I went to my locker to get my things, Michael Hurley was sitting nearby. He could see I was emotional and said, 'Are you alright, mate?'

'I don't want to talk about it,' I said.

I left Windy Hill and drove straight to Neo's office. 'Two

issues,' I said. 'One, they want me to appeal, and two, I want to talk to you about my future.'

Neo and I talked about the pros and cons of an appeal. Then I rang my brother Brad, whose opinion I really value, particularly in these situations. He gave me the clarity I needed by saying, 'There's no way in the world I'd be appealing that.' That was exactly my thoughts.

I left a message on Paul Hamilton's phone, saying, 'I wanted to take the early plea.' Then I sat with Neo at the Squire's Steakhouse on Queen Street, and as we had lunch we spoke about my future. I felt like I definitely wanted to end my playing career but Neo said, 'Have another two or three weeks to think about it.'

Our Elimination Final was against the Crows in Adelaide. I didn't go to watch it as Lisa was heavily pregnant with our second child. I sat at home and watched the game on TV, which wasn't a great experience. We didn't take any ruckmen over and Nathan Lovett-Murray was in the ruck. The move backfired and we went down by ninety-six points.

As we watched the game, Lisa was squeezing my hand, but it had nothing to do with the state of the match. We watched it all the way through and then went to bed, only for Lisa to wake me at three am and say, 'You've got to get me to the hospital!' At seven am our second daughter, Kira, was born, and if I had gone to Adelaide I would have missed it. So it turned out to be one of the best decisions I ever made to stay in Melbourne with Lisa. Kira was a healthy nine pounds ten.

On the Tuesday or Wednesday after the Adelaide final, I met with Neo, Paul Hamilton, Matthew Knights and Kevin Egan, one of our board members, to discuss my future.

I had previously told Paul all the reasons why I hadn't signed at that stage, and there were a few. Importantly, I felt there was not enough buy-in from the players to Knighta's game style. Also, there wasn't enough flexibility within the forward line – we needed to be able to play to our strengths rather than being robots who were continually being dictated to by opposing defenders. And then there were the communication breakdowns. Paul said, 'Okay, that's fine, but you've got to talk those things through with the coach.'

On the morning of the meeting, however, Paul called me and said, 'I don't think you can talk to Matthew about the game style. I just don't reckon it will go down well.'

'Well, what's the point of this meeting, Paul?' I asked. 'That's the problem around here. If you can't be honest and tell people what you think, what's the point?'

In the meeting, we spoke about the forward line and what we might do in 2010, and I tried to see if there was any chance whatsoever that it was worth me playing. After working through the range of points I had, Neo said, 'I think the question Lloydy's trying to get at is: do you want him to play next year?'

Knighta's response was, 'I'm not into semantics. I don't need to tell Dustin Fletcher I want him to play next year – he just turns up and trains hard.'

'But Paddy Ryder, for example,' I replied, 'I'm sure you want him to play next year?' He said yes, so I continued, 'I just want to know whether you want me here as well. Don't feel like you're killing Bambi here – if you don't want me to play on, just tell me.' He said he would tell me if that was the case, but he never told me he wanted me to play on either. I couldn't get a clear answer from him, so I turned to Neo and said, 'You see what I'm dealing with?'

After the meeting I sat with Neo in his car and we discussed what had just happened. He said, 'Go and do your feedback session with the club to review the year and we'll sort it out later.' The contract Essendon was offering me wasn't as good as my previous one, but it was still a fair amount of income. But I wasn't thinking about the money. I'd done very well out of football and my decision was going to be purely based on my prospects on the field and my enjoyment for the game.

So I went to the end-of-season review, and a few other players were also saying that communication was an issue. I had been starting to think it was partly just me, but now I realised that there were a lot of other players with the same issue. There were also concerns about the game plan. The midfielders said they didn't have enough licence to be bold; the defenders were too scared to leave their men. There was a feeling among the players that things had become very robotic, and that the coach wasn't listening to their needs.

It was good to hear others had the same feelings as me, but I would rather have been at a million other places than there. I'd switched off; I'd already conceded that I couldn't put up with things at the club anymore, and I wanted out.

In mid-September I was at Mark McVeigh's buck's weekend on the Gold Coast, and I told some of the boys on that trip that if there was any possibility of me playing in 2010, it would be with a team other than Essendon. It was still highly unlikely, I added.

A couple of days later, Jake Niall from *The Age* wrote a column that was pretty much spot-on with how I was thinking – that my time with the Bombers was over, but not necessarily my time in football. Neo rang me and said Mark Robinson was running a piece in the *Herald Sun* linking me with Collingwood, and there was a picture of me in a Collingwood jumper on the back page of the newspaper the next day. Eddie McGuire rang me and said, 'Geez, you look good in black and white!'

I told Eddie I looked better in red and black, and that probably went to the heart of my feelings. It was a big risk to go to another club if I didn't have the passion to play, and I couldn't guarantee that a change of club would reignite that flame.

On the Monday of Grand Final week I took Lisa out to lunch at The Pantry in Brighton, where I told her my thoughts. 'I've lost my enjoyment,' I said, 'and I don't want to do this anymore – I'm retiring.'

Lisa burst out crying. Later on we joked that the cafe staff probably thought I was breaking off our marriage or something. Then I rang my Mum and Dad and told them over the phone what I was about to do.

When I told Neo, he urged me to explore other options but I had made my decision and wanted to announce it and move on. We agreed that I should tell Essendon as soon as possible, so the club could start planning its playing list without me.

I rang Sue, the club's receptionist, and said, 'I'm on my way into the club. Can you get Paul Hamilton and Knighta ready to meet me?'

Sue was a nice lady and she asked, 'You're not leaving us, are you, Matthew?'

'You'll find out shortly,' I said.

When I got there, I just said to both Matthew and Paul, 'I've come to the decision to retire,' and I shook hands with both of them. I could see that that Paul was a bit emotional. He had worked pretty hard to keep me on board, and I felt for him.

But I was tired. I was thirty-one years old and I'd been playing top-level footy since I was fifteen at the Western Jets. I needed a break. I wanted to get off the roller-coaster that had been AFL football and find another passion. I also wanted to spend more quality time with my family, rather than be highly strung like I always was. I knew it was time to retire when even games against Carlton and Collingwood weren't exciting me anymore. I'd been to the well one too many times and I'd had enough. I also believed at the time that we'd struggle to have success in the near future and that unless a premiership was a possibility, it wasn't worth me hanging around.

We called a media conference for the Wednesday of Grand Final week. It was a very emotional experience for me. I asked Peter Jackson to sit with me rather than Matthew Knights, because I felt that Peter had had a bigger influence on my career. He'd started at the club in the same year as me and was also set to leave at the same time as me. I had prepared a list of people to thank – all the people whose help and advice had made an impact on me during my career.

Having made my decision and announced it, I felt calm. I was no longer a part of the Essendon Football Club, a place I'd spent half of my life, and I was no longer a professional footballer.

In my mind, it was all over.

'I certainly remember the commotion of the aftermath, but I don't remember anything about the hit itself. From my perspective it was just a case of the wrong spot at the wrong time. There's no hard feelings from my end. I enjoy those hard-at-the-ball contests and I know the crowd does too; it is one of the things that makes our game so special. As for Clarko and Brownie, their outbursts may not have been the smartest thing on a few levels, but I want to play with people that have that passion. It is one of the things that makes Clarko such a great coach – he is the sort of guy we all want to play for.'

Brad Sewell

32

My New Game Plan

'I think he is an absolute champion. He's Essendon's greatest goalkicker and one of Essendon's greatest players and, in his era, right up there with the top players who have ever played. I think everyone who played with Lloydy feels privileged that they played with him and I think Essendon supporters would feel privileged to have seen him play. A lot of opposition supporters hated him, and I reckon that is a good thing.'

James Hird

NOT EVERYONE AGREED WITH my decision to retire. A lot of my teammates felt I had more to give and didn't want to see me end my career. Lisa felt I had more to give as well – she still does. Even the media seemed hell-bent on keeping my career alive after burying me in the middle of 2008.

But I was spent. I couldn't see any way I could get myself up mentally for another season. I'd lost the enjoyment of the game, and I wanted to do other things, especially spend more time with my young family. I never did anything half-heartedly, and if I'd committed to another year at Essendon it would have been just that.

Having invested in property on Sheeds' advice, I had security for my family. We had a nice home in Brighton and no mortgage, so we would manage okay while Neo started investigating my post-footy career options. I was interested in working in the media and also in a coaching role with the AFL.

Neo began talking to the TV networks, the radio stations and *The Age* newspaper, who I already had an arrangement with. That was the order of priority, too. We knew a radio role would eventuate as there was strong interest in me, but TV was going to be more problematic. Those jobs don't come easy.

I had first tried my hand at radio work in 2006, after I ripped my hamstring off the bone in Round 3. When a serious injury like that comes along, you start thinking of life after football. I did some special-comments work on radio for 3AW and the ABC, and I really enjoyed it.

I had also done some work for Channel Ten in 2009, with Essendon's approval. I talked with Knighta about it first, explaining how I wanted to pursue a media role after footy, and told him I'd been offered a role on *One Week at a Time* on One HD. I'd also been offered the chance to do special comments on their footy coverage for four matches. 'Are you comfortable with me doing that?' I asked.

'As long as it doesn't affect us as a club and your form,' Knighta replied, and he followed up with a joke. 'I may need a job in the media myself one day.'

I'd thoroughly enjoyed the experience of *One Week at a Time* and the commentating role, and now I was keen to explore whether I could do it permanently.

I knew I would get some work on radio, at least, although I hadn't decided which station I would sign with. I was leaning towards 3AW, but I met with every station, just to make sure. The ABC's Gerard Whateley told me he wanted me to work with him there. 'I want you to be my main man,' he said. 'I'll be the caller, you'll be the special-comments man, and we can do this together for the next twenty years.'

As it turned out, I didn't get a good feeling from my meeting with 3AW. Shane Healy was very respectful but had doubts about what I could do for them, and as an organisation they didn't have a clear idea of what my role would be. Just like on a football team, I needed clarity.

I knew Anthony Hudson and Andy Maher from the stint I'd done at Channel Ten, and both of them also worked on radio at SEN. Huddo gave me a call. 'There's a few spots open with us,' he said, 'and we'd love you to think about them. I know you're set on other stations, but would you at least listen to what we've got to say if we arrange a meeting?'

So I went in to see them and they blew me away with their presentation. The opportunities they were putting in front of me were great, and they had it all worked out. 'We want you on our primetime shows – *Friday Night Footy*, *Crunch Time* and *Morning Glory*,' they told me. I knew SEN didn't rate like 3AW, but they were a growing station and Huddo was someone I'd forged a good relationship with.

In the end, then, it was a pretty easy decision for me to sign with SEN. Neo had also negotiated with *The Age* to renew my contract to write for them, and I signed on as an assistant coach with the Australian Institute of Sport's AFL Academy.

The only drawback, though, was that no opportunities in

television had emerged. Neo and I met with Channel Ten's boss of football, Dave Barham, but he told us they were signing Tom Harley and there were no other opportunities.

I was bitterly disappointed, but I understood that I needed to improve greatly if I was to create a chance for myself. I was a rookie again, learning a new trade.

Over the next few weeks, with help from Channel Ten, I put together a DVD package of myself to send to Channel Seven. To my surprise, Neo called me soon after to say the landscape had changed – Tom Harley had decided to take a *Friday Night Football* role with Seven. That opened up the door for me at Ten, and I signed a two-year deal.

As I began exploring my future in the media, I reflected on my time as a footballer, which is something I had rarely done when I was playing. I felt pretty proud of what I had achieved in the game. When I was selected for my first game, I never would have thought I would win the three Coleman Medals and kick more than 900 goals. I played in a Premiership and I captained my club, and those were my greatest thrills.

Perhaps the only thing which I craved but never achieved – apart from a second or third Premiership – was a club best-and-fairest award. Wayne Carey won a couple, Jack Riewoldt won his in 2010, and even Richo picked up one near the end of his career. Although I'd come second or third a couple of times, I was never a genuine chance.

I think 2001 was the year that I played well enough to win one, but Jason Johnson's season was phenomenal and he thoroughly deserved the award. In 2000, when I kicked 109 goals, Dustin Fletcher was unstoppable at fullback; he probably stopped 200 goals, I reckon. And when I thought about it, I realised that being in a strong side with good depth was better than winning a best-and-fairest in a lowly team. Playing in the finals is what footy's about, and the friendships and life experiences you gain are priceless.

I think I gave all I could for the Essendon Football Club during the many years I was there. I wanted to be someone that a parent would like their kids to follow as a role model. I hoped my teammates and our fans would remember me as a player who never let his team or his supporters or his family down by anything bar the odd suspension. I think I got the most out of the ability that I was given.

I had my eccentricities, like my goalkicking routine. Pull up my socks, tuck in my jumper and then throw a pinch of grass up in the air. It was intended to relax me as I took the shot at goal, but I was also superstitious. I wore the same jocks as I had the week before if I had gone well, and I never wanted to touch the banner as we ran through. That changed as I got older and I relaxed a little more, but it was all about doing what made me feel comfortable so that I could perform at my best.

I didn't always deal well with scrutiny. I hadn't coped with it as a kid, and that probably got worse as I got older. It's never nice being splashed on the back page of the newspaper for the wrong reasons. I never liked being called 'Pretty Boy Lloyd', which I think Sam Newman came up with on *The Footy Show* one time. That was an image I really didn't want – I wanted to be respected for being a footballer who was hard at the contest. I may have been reading too much into it, but I felt it was a label that wasn't me. 'The Velvet Sledgehammer' was a better nickname from Eddie

McGuire and Sam Newman, as it insinuated I had the look of a nice guy but hit very hard.

Fairytales are rare in footy. When the Hawks won the Premiership in 2008 I watched Shane Crawford dance around the MCG hugging his mates. That was a fairytale I would have liked for my last game of AFL football. But for every Shane Crawford or James Hird who finishes his career by making a lap of honour, there are plenty of others who see their careers ended by crippling injuries or a delisting. Football can be a cruel game at times.

My final game landed me a six-game suspension. Some might find that tough to swallow, but I don't. It's a fine line when you try to play your football hard and within the rules. I crossed the line that day, but I'd rather have bowed out that way than by losing limply to Hawthorn. If we'd done that, I would have been far more gutted.

So I've got no regrets about my hip-and-shoulder on Brad Sewell that day. I never wanted to see someone badly hurt but I can't take back what happened. It's a hard and physical game, after all.

I was uncomfortable with what went on after the game, though, with Campbell Brown and Alastair Clarkson, but I know that was in the heat of battle. It's a very emotional game too. I ran into Clarko on *Before the Game* during Grand Final week. I walked past him thinking he wouldn't want a bar of me, but he followed me out of the studio. 'I just want to explain myself,' he said. 'Seeing Max Bailey do another knee, and then seeing Brad with his face caved in, on top of the loss, I just lost my way. I want to apologise for how I behaved after the game.' I accepted his apology and we both moved on.

That incident is still a topic of conversation among the fans, especially Hawthorn people, but it has subsided over time. Not long after we lost our Elimination Final in 2009 we were at a pub in Albert Park and the Hawthorn boys walked in. Luke Hodge came straight up to me and I thought, 'There could be some trouble here . . . ' But it was the opposite. 'We were beaten fair and square,' he said, 'and what happened on the field should have stayed there.' Hodgey is an old-fashioned footballer who plays hard on the field but is great to talk to off it. Quite a few Hawthorn blokes have admitted to me that they didn't react well on the day. I don't hold grudges and I hope they don't hold any against me. I deserved the six weeks' suspension I got, and that should be that.

So the 2010 season got underway and I settled into my new role as a commentator. My media work was paying nowhere near as much as playing football had, but I was just happy to have joined several quality organisations. I was looking forward to embarking on a new career, off the field.

It was critical for my media career that I made a clean break from Essendon, which had been my second home for so long. I still have a lot of great mates there, but it's a different relationship now.

Everywhere I went, though, people came up to me and said I should still be playing. I was confident that another club would have given me an opportunity if I'd wanted to keep going, but I knew I wasn't as committed as I once had been. Apart from that, I valued being a one-club player.

There had been talk that Collingwood and Carlton were interested in me but I never held any discussions with other clubs. Imagine joining the enemy! I don't know how the

Essendon supporters would have reacted to that. It was never going to happen.

Lisa and I had taken a holiday in Noosa just after I had retired, and we'd bumped into Chris Judd there. He asked me if Greg Swann had called from Carlton.

'No,' I said. 'Why?'

'I've been into them to at least ring you, even though you've retired, to see if you'd come to Carlton,' he replied. 'You'd be ideal for us.'

It was flattering to have someone of that ilk wanting me at his club, but my heart wasn't in it. In fact, I've never regretted my decision. Up until the start of the 2010 Finals Series, I didn't miss competing at AFL level at all. What I miss most, though, is not seeing some of my best mates on a daily basis, like I used to.

The first time I really missed playing was when I watched the Collingwood team celebrating their Premiership win. It took me back to our victory in 2000, and I thought how good it would be to relive that moment.

I absolutely love my role with the AFL and the Australian Institute of Sport. I don't want to coach full-time, but I do want to stay actively involved in football in some way, so it is the perfect role for me. My commitment is for forty days a year, assisting the thirty best sixteen- and seventeen-year-old footballers in the country reach their goal of playing in the AFL. I find I can help them not only on the field but also off it, advising them about what they can expect as professional players. Michael O'Loughlin, Brett Kirk and Tom Harley are also involved in the program.

Now, eighteen months after officially retiring, I couldn't

have asked for anything more. Neo and his company, SEL, have been brilliant to me, confirming for me that I made the right decision in going with them all those years ago. Getting deals in television, radio and the press lined up so quickly meant I could move on smoothly from playing footy. I had so much to look forward too.

I loved playing football, but it was over and time to move on. I knew nothing would ever replace the adrenaline rush of playing, though. The rewards of playing well and celebrating with your mates – singing the club song and, if you're lucky enough, holding the Premiership Cup aloft – are the ultimate.

It may be hard to believe, but standing on the boundary line and opening the TV broadcast of a match also gives me a rush, especially when it's a big game and the crowd finds its voice. Feeling that makes me glad I retired when I did. I had a fifteen-year playing career that exceeded my wildest dreams, and I look back now and think, 'I could have played another year, but would these opportunities still have been waiting for me then?'

A big chapter of my life ended with my retirement from Essendon. But I feel blessed that I have been able to move on to a new career and yet remain involved in the game I love. I get out of bed each morning looking forward to what I'm doing.

It all worked out so well. I'm happy in life, which is the main thing. My new career allows me to spend quality time with Lisa and the girls, and I'm even able to take Jaeda to kinder each morning.

'I've known Matty for a few years but obviously not particularly well until the last year or so of his career when he started to do a bit of stuff with Channel Ten. Matty listened, he was keen to improve his performance and he understood that if he was going to be any good he needed to put the effort in, just like he did when playing football.'

Anthony Hudson

33

Friends and Foes

'We saw Mark McVeigh and Andrew Welsh at a party a little while back, and I looked over and Matt was crying with laughter. They said to me later that's one of the things they miss about him not being at the club – they used to love getting him into these fits of laughter.'

Lisa Lloyd

THERE WERE SO MANY great people I played with and against during my career at Essendon. When I arrived at the club it was a team packed with top players. Some, such as Mark Thompson and Mark Harvey, I only played with for a couple of years, while others such as Michael Long went a little longer.

Probably the only thing I really miss about playing footy is my mates. I still see a lot of them, but it's different now. The mateships I've made working in the media are not really the same. As well as I get on with my colleagues, they're not guys I've battled against the odds with, enjoyed highs and lows on the field with, or put my body on the line for – and they haven't done the same for me, of course.

Essendon was the sort of club that demanded nothing but success from its playing group. When I walked into the club as a sixteen-year-old it was full of champions, which was very daunting. The best times for me, and the times I forged life-long friendships, came during the middle part of my career, when my form was good and the club was going well. Before that I felt very young, and after that the club was struggling.

That said, one of my best friendships at the club was forged very early in my career. I had met Scott Lucas at draft camp in 1994 and we had become close mates immediately. He was a magnificent player for Essendon. He won a best-and-fairest playing at centre half-forward and centre half-back, which is something few people can say they've done.

That connection we had on that first day of draft camp is still there today. Scotty is a great bloke and so intelligent with his football that he could probably do anything he wanted. He's one of the most loyal people I've ever met, and there was never any jealousy between us, although we were very competitive. Like many of my best mates, he's also a family man – between us we have five girls, so any dreams of our kids playing together at Essendon are on hold at the moment, although we're getting close to a netball team!

Mark McVeigh arrived a few years after Scotty and me, but we hit it off immediately, even though we weren't really that similar. In fact, we are opposites in many ways. I first met him in 1998 when he was in the All-Australian under-17 squad and I was playing for the All-Australian team which was going to Ireland. We needed a practice match and the under-17s gave us a hit-out. Afterwards, someone said, 'Grab a younger bloke to have a stretch with.' I grabbed this guy with long surfie hair.

When draft day arrived we took the surfie-haired guy at pick nine, but by the time he arrived at the club he'd cut it all off and had a spiky do. John Quinn labelled him 'Spike' and the nickname stuck. I took him under my wing a bit.

Mark's very protective of his mates and very loyal, and he's passionate about his football and Essendon. You'd never know he grew up in Sydney, such is his love of the Bombers. He's been a really good player for the club and now is in the 200-game club. He's the kind of bloke you love having on your team.

Dustin Fletcher is another player I have a huge amount of affection for. He's one of the nicest blokes you would ever meet and an absolute champion player, even if he doesn't think so himself. He was there at Essendon before me and is still there today, and I would guess he has another year or two in him.

It's hard to go past James Hird as the best player I played with, but I think Fletch was the most important player at Essendon in my time. To have a goalkeeper like him on an AFL field was worth many wins to us. Fletch has played on some of the best full-forwards in the game's history – as a schoolboy in 1993 he played on Tony Modra, Jason Dunstall, Tony Lockett, Stephen Kernahan, Peter Sumich and Allen Jakovich!

Fletch is good at tennis, table tennis and can do pretty much anything, so he's definitely not lacking in much. He's occasionally been in trouble at the tribunal, but – a bit like me – I reckon he'd always think, 'Why did I do that?' We'd often have a laugh when one of us was going to the tribunal because we knew we thought alike on the field and always gave our all.

While Fletch is older than me, he still loves playing the game and competing at that high standard, which was the thing I lost in 2009. We were very different characters, and I think that's why he's lasted longer than me. He never let the game get to him and he takes everything in his stride, where I took everything in and sometimes it ate me up. Whether he can beat Michael Tuck's games record is another question – that would probably take him another four seasons, which would be a big ask. But in my view he is the greatest full-back of the modern era, and he is a ripping bloke as well.

I had a great mateship with Hirdy at the footy club, even though I arrived three years behind him. We had a huge respect for each other and he certainly passed on his passion for Essendon to me. When he handed the captaincy of the club to me, it was a massive honour. He was a great captain and a great source of advice, both on and off the field, and I can see why he is developing into such a good coach.

He was one of the few players who could tell me where to lead when he had the ball; most players would wait to see where I was going and then kick. But he used beautifully weighted kicks to move me to where he wanted me to be, and that meant the backmen really had no chance. There were times where he'd just land a kick over our heads and I'd turn around and run into an open goal. He was a genius as a player.

I still have a strong bond with Sean Wellman and Steve Alessio, who were both Premiership teammates in 2000. I really respect what they've done after football. Welly's a podiatrist and assistant coach at Essendon after spending some time with the Bulldogs and Melbourne; he's got very strong morals and ethics and carries himself really well. Ses is doing a great job at the AFL Players' Association.

He was such a character to play with. I took my footy pretty seriously, and I can remember standing under the shower sometimes thinking, 'What a stinker I played today.' Ses might have copped a big spray himself, but he'd bounce in and say, 'How good was I today?' He never took things like that to heart, whereas I digested them over and over. He used to tell jokes during training drills – I remember one session when he had me running in the wrong direction listening to him tell a joke while Sheedy was explaining something!

Dean Rioli's football skills were just amazing. When he got the ball and was heading your way, your eyes would light up. He only played 100 games but I would have loved to play with him more. He knew where I was going to lead even before I did, it seemed. Sometimes, when he was competing for the ball, he'd tap it instead of grabbing it to create a little extra room before he took it in his hands, which was a skill a lot of the Indigenous players have.

Mark Mercuri was also great to lead to. He was more predictable but he and I each knew exactly what the other was going to do. I think I took some of the players I was playing with in my first six years at the club for granted, but as the years rolled on I realised how lucky I had been. In my latter years, we didn't have the silky midfield that we had during the late 1990s and early 2000s.

Angus Monfries still calls me 'Skip', as in 'Skipper'. We hit it off straightaway when he joined the club; I think I saw a lot of myself in him. We loved working together on the forward line – we'd throw blocks for each other, we'd high-five and we always had a laugh. He really made the game fun for me. He was a hard worker but he loves a laugh, and he'll be a lifelong mate, for sure. I think he has the potential to captain the club one day, although with Jobe Watson being so young it may pass him by.

Andrew Welsh is another guy who loves fun, is passionate about Essendon and doesn't take his footy too seriously. He still works hard, but he knows how to leave it on the ground. In Vegas, Welshy and I would end up walking back to our hotel together having a laugh about the silliest things. McVeigh, Monfries and Welsh were all a bit younger than me and they kept me sane because they love a joke. Along with Jobe and Fletch, they are the ones I miss the most.

The hardest thing about retiring is knowing that you won't be playing with your mates any longer. Perhaps that's why some guys hang on longer than they should.

While I was lucky to play alongside some true champions at Essendon, I also took on many great players from the other clubs. My first lesson in senior football was handed to me by Dean Laidley of the Kangaroos, and I never forgot it. They called him 'the Junkyard Dog', and after playing on him I knew why. I'd never had a backman run off me or get really physical with me, and although Dean warned me about hanging on to him, I didn't listen and he dropped his knee straight into my quad, corking me badly. I quickly learned that these blokes were tough, hard footballers, and anything they could get away with was acceptable.

As I started to make my way in the AFL, I became a tricky match-up for opposition coaches. I'm not super-tall nor massive like 'Plugger' Lockett, but I was big enough and strong enough and yet still mobile. So sometimes I'd have a smaller, faster player as my opponent, like Simon Beaumont from Carlton, while other weeks I'd get a bigger player like Mick Martyn, who was about the same height as me but had ten kilograms more bulk.

In my personal rivalries with opponents, Mick was the first genuine mountain for me to climb. He started picking me up in about my third season and he kept me quiet many times. I dreaded coming up against him. I never wanted my teammates or coaches to think that he had the wood on me, but in my early years, he definitely did. He was really strong and actually quite quick off the mark as well.

I began 1998 well with ten goals against Hawthorn in the preseason competition, but we came up against the Roos next. Mick ran straight down to me at the start of the game and said, 'You won't do that on me.' He was all over me – he scragged, he held me, he mouthed off – and he had David King and Glenn Archer helping him out. I loved to take diving marks, but when I did that against Mick he would drop his knees straight into the middle of my back. I went goalless that day.

I wanted to build greater bulk to counter people like Mick, but John Quinn said that I'd lose my acceleration and take on the added risk of soft-tissue injuries. By the time I'd finished growing, I was 192 centimetres tall and weighed around ninety-three kilograms. With that extra weight the bigger opponents became easier for me and I could still usually outrun them.

Eventually, I started to improve against Mick. At first, if I kicked one against him I'd be pretty happy. Then in the next game I'd aim for two. I played on Mick in my fiftieth game and kicked four, which was a real breakthrough for me. A couple of years later, I kicked my 100th goal of the 2000 season on Mick in a Qualifying Final in which I bagged seven. That was the story with a lot of my rivalries. I'd like to think I got the better of them more often than not, and I worked extremely hard to do it.

By the early 2000s the game was changing. The 100-kilogram-plus full-backs were being replaced by more mobile players who could attack with running rebound football. Guys like Matthew Scarlett were becoming the typical full-back.

Steve Kretiuk of the Bulldogs was another tough opponent for me. He was a bit smaller than Mick and a lot angrier. He was a player who understood his own limitations, and he was often coming up against bigger and more talented opponents such Wayne Carey and Jason Dunstall. His tactic was to scrag, to hold and to make life difficult for his man, and he definitely did.

In 1998 Kretiuk made my life hell for four quarters. That was when Dean Wallis and Mark Harvey took me aside after the game and told me I had to learn how to deal with that sort of treatment – in essence, they told me to toughen up. In 2002, my comeback match after rupturing my finger tendon was against the Dogs and Steve was there waiting for me. I kicked three goals in the second quarter and I got an early one at the start of the third. I gave it to him, saying, 'You haven't got it over me anymore.' I was bigger and stronger than him and I decided to let him know that at every opportunity. In 2003 I played my best game on him, kicking eleven goals.

Carlton's Glenn Manton was another rival for many years. He was like an octopus on the field, and actually I found playing on him much harder than on Steve Silvagni. He played pretty fairly but would hold and scrag in one-on-one contests, which I found really frustrating. Playing against Carlton early in the 2001 season, I had had enough and I crashed into his back way off the ball, and I copped some time on the sidelines for it.

The new full-backs were leaner and would look to rebound off me. Full-backs like that worried me, because if you weren't scoring goals they could be so damaging on the rebound. The new breed included guys like Mal Michael, Matthew Scarlett and Max Hudghton. Fletch was like that too, and I'm glad I never had to play on him.

The first couple of times I played on Scarlett, I thought, 'This skinny kid will never make it.' In fact, he played on me in his first and second games, which were spread over the 1998 and 1999 seasons, and both occasions were good days for me. I kicked thirty goals in our first six matches, but that started to slow down as both he and Geelong improved. He's one of the very best backmen I played on, and he loves a bit of a sledge, too.

I used to study video of my opponent before a game, and I would also study someone who had kicked goals on him in recent weeks. I looked at Scarlett a lot on those tapes but I couldn't find too many weaknesses in his game. Perhaps the only one was endurance, so I always tried to run him off his feet. In my early days I hadn't really understood how running my opponent around could help me. If I'd worked that out more quickly, I wouldn't have had such trouble with the bigger and stronger full-backs like Mick Martyn.

Mal Michael was at his peak when his side, Brisbane, was too. He was deceptively quick and built like Tarzan, but the thing I remember most about him is how he'd come over the top of me and belt the ball thirty metres, which was pretty demoralising. He was so strong that I couldn't wrestle him and so I always had to work hard to create space for myself. I didn't mind it when Sheeds recruited him to Essendon – at least I didn't have to play on him again.

I still find it hard to believe that St Kilda didn't take Max Hudghton into the 2009 Grand Final. His passion was so intense that in a big game it could have made a big difference. He never hurt you by foot like Scarlett did, but his pace off the mark was always a worry. Richmond's Darren Gaspar was another full-back I had some massive duels with. He would hold me consistently and wrap me up in marking contests, which was so frustrating. I rated him very highly.

If a full-back didn't scrag and fight hard he wouldn't last too long, so as a full-forward I just had to get used to it. As my career developed, I started working out my opponents both individually and as a collective group. I enjoyed my battles with them even if I did get frustrated at times. In many ways, winning those personal battles gave me as much pleasure and satisfaction as our team success.

34

Other People's Thoughts

Kevin Sheedy, Coach 1995–2007
When Matthew first arrived at Essendon, I thought he'd come to the wrong place. He looked like he should have been in Hollywood. We had a few good-looking blokes at Essendon at the time, and I wondered if the recruiting staff were using that as a strategy to help our marketing. We probably got more women on board with guys like Matthew and James Hird.

There was a bit of Tom Cruise about him, and I thought the marketing department would love that. He was totally the opposite to Gary Moorcroft, who was a little short-haired, freckle-faced, tattooed guy from the north-eastern suburbs ready to kill. It takes many types of players to make a footy club and to entertain, and we certainly had an entertaining club at the time.

Actually, we had worked pretty hard to get both Matthew and Scott Lucas to the club as we wanted them both. We had a couple of guys we traded back to Western Australia, such as Dale Kickett, who we kept on our list as one of the players we could send back to Perth for a chance at Lloyd. We were twelve months ahead of all the others. Brian Donohoe, who was in recruiting after being chairman of selectors, was set the major task of getting both Lloyd and Lucas.

We knew we could get Lloyd because of the deals, and we hoped Lucas would still be there at pick four in the draft, and it worked out well for us. What we didn't yet know was how we were going to use them. Should we run Lucas as centre half-forward or centre half-back? Should we run Lloyd as a mobile centre half-forward or deeper? When players are that young you've got to let them develop and find their groove. Sometimes we pre-empt that and it doesn't work out. For instance, I thought at one stage that Dustin Fletcher was going to be a wonderfully mobile ruckman, but when I put him in the ruck for his first match I saw that it wasn't for him; look what he's become as a full-back. In Lloydy's case, we decided to play it by ear.

Both Lloyd and Lucas were so young when they came to us – they were still in Year 12 at St Bernard's – so we had to make sure we didn't overload them with training. They had talent, and we had to make sure we didn't kill them early.

We played Fremantle in our first practice match in 1995. We took Matthew to see if he could handle flying and playing, but I wasn't sure what we learned. After the team ran out onto the ground, Fremantle got off to a flying start. I was in the box thinking to myself, 'How could they have got a loose man so quickly and easily?'

Then I worked it out. Matthew Lloyd, the young superstar we gave up so much for, had forgotten to go on the ground and play. He'd been listed to start on the ground but had gone straight to the bench. I called up Danny Corcoran, our team manager at the time, who was sitting on the bench, and asked him if he knew where Matthew Lloyd was. Danny said, 'Yes, coach, he's sitting right next to me.' I said, 'I know. Tell him to read the team board next time before the game starts.'

'Hey, Lloydy,' I said to him after the match, 'one thing we learnt today – one of the most important things in football – is: Read the team board. You know that after today, don't you?' He said, 'Yes, coach, yes, coach.' A lot of fun things happen along the way in footy, and that was a very funny moment. I always knew, though, that Matthew listened hard to me. Despite that hiccup, he had an impeccable attitude and was totally professional right from the time he arrived.

I always had a chat with the younger guys about issues off the field, and I believe it's very important that they use the opportunity football gives them to look after themselves. They need to get their finances in order and think about the future, get a house deposit and get into the market. Once you've got your first house half paid off, you're on the road. That's one of the things I say to all of them, get a house and get a beach house so you've actually got something out of your career, even if it gets cut short. Matthew's got a father who played league footy and he understood that it could end as quickly as it started.

On the field, Lloydy did everything I asked of him. When I started him in the backline in the reserves, he went out there and tried to do his best. I wanted to know what he could do. Can he play close? Has he got speed to defend? Can he rebound? Gavin Wanganeen was recruited as a forward and he won a Brownlow in his first year going down back after Round 3. You just don't know where a player's best position is until you put him there. I always liked my players to have flexibility. Even if he was a key forward, there may be times we needed him to go back, even if it was just for a quarter.

We didn't want to rush Matthew into senior football, so we held him back to get some confidence up and then tried to pick the right match to bring him in. It never really worried me how big the game was. I've put first-gamers into Anzac Day matches if I thought it was right – it's about the individual. Matthew had maybe ten games in the reserves when we brought him up for a game or two, and then we dropped him back again.

I liked to test young kids going into the finals to see what they've got. If they look like they've developed okay, then I'd give them a go on the big stage. If they win a final, then they've got the chance to play in another. If you don't play a kid in a final then you'll never know.

Matthew needed to build some bulk if we were going to use him as a key forward, because I knew the full-backs would smash the hell out of him. The better he got, the more he got hit, but he was up to it. Matthew copped a lot of hits but he was also good at handing them out. When they started calling him 'the Velvet Sledgehammer' I thought it was a perfect nickname. Butter wouldn't melt in his mouth but he'd crunch players so hard it made me flinch. His mum and dad might not have been happy with it, but I thought it was quite funny.

He's easily among the best players I've seen. When I look

at my forward line and the players that I've coached – Paul Salmon, Scott Lucas, Paul Van Der Haar, Terry Daniher, Roger Merrett, Simon Madden, Mark Harvey, Alan Ezard, Tim Watson, Darren Bewick – I know that Matthew Lloyd was a standout.

It is always hard to compare players across different eras unless you were involved, but you can't get away from the obvious comparison for Matthew: John Coleman. But what systems do you use to rate them? John Coleman played in an era where there was no flooding; Lloyd, on the other hand, had to play tactically for most if his career, often on two opponents. There are many different things you have to look at when you start analysing whether one player's better than another.

Jason Dunstall had Darren Jarman firing Exocet missiles at him, and Essendon in Matthew's era didn't do too badly either. We had guys like Michael Long and Darren Bewick who were pretty good kicks. Long used to simply hit the ball for Lloyd to run after; they seemed to have a great understanding of each other.

Weather-wise, Matthew didn't play in the rain as often as other players would have because we played so many games at Docklands, but he did kick some big bags elsewhere. It was hard to work out when he was at his peak – his big bags of goals were evenly spread out over his whole career. Kicking 109 and then 105 goals in a season is a pretty good effort. I think we tend to forget that it's very hard to kick a hundred. I reckon Matthew probably peaked around 2000 onwards. Four years either in the hundreds or one good game away is a very good effort. You could bank on at least four goals a game from him at that stage. Over his career, he averaged 3.4, and that's bloody unbelievable.

He spent a lot of his career being held, crashed and smashed, and he did get agitated at times. He got reported a bit in 2001 but most of it was in retaliation. I don't think the umpires always understand what some players go through. Once you've been reported a few times, they seem to keep a special eye on you. At one stage I went to speak to the umpires to discuss the treatment he was getting from others.

He was accused of staging for free kicks, and I think he did a bit. He wasn't getting much protection from the umpires, though, so he was trying to make sure they noticed what was going on. There were some very ordinary acting performances from him too! We've all done it at times; you can look at games today and see some of the biggest names in football throwing their arms out and pulling faces. So I can't bag Matthew for that. He may have scragged a few easy goals out of it, but he missed out on plenty more which he should have got from genuine free kicks.

As much as I loved Matthew, I would still have traded him for Chris Judd when it was obvious he was going to leave West Coast. Even now I think it would have been an intelligent move for the club. Matthew was well into his career but was still worth a bit on the market. He had maybe three or four more years left at his peak, whereas Judd would have been a seven-year player. Essendon would have got something for Matthew; if he'd left for another club at the end of 2009 they might have got nothing.

Not that it was ever a serious discussion point. Matthew would have coped, though. Remember, the year after that was possible, Essendon cleared Kepler Bradley and Adam McPhee for nothing. Imagine if we'd offered Matthew Lloyd, Adam McPhee and Kepler Bradley to West Coast for Chris Judd – would they have taken it? I'd say probably yes. None of those three players are at Essendon anymore, while Judd is still at Carlton and won a Brownlow Medal last year.

In the end, I think Lloyd retired too early, but it didn't need to happen. I would have put him on a seventeen-game contract, like I did with James Hird in his last year.

I loved all my players, although I know I used to annoy them a lot. There were probably three or four occasions when I was going to get sacked because the players were so annoyed with me. But you've got to leave at some stage – whether it was my twenty-fifth or twenty-seventh season didn't really matter. My time was up, and I think Matt and a few of the senior boys probably felt that having another coach looking at them would be helpful. And I understand that.

In the end, I was replaced and I moved on. Matthew Knights came in and did his three years, while I now have the chance to do something really special at Greater Western Sydney. I've been so lucky to be able to coach those young players – they have been an absolutely marvellous bunch.

Because of the way Matthew approached every part of his football career, I'm sure he is doing a really good job with the Australian Institute of Sport. I still use him as an example for my young squad at Greater Western Sydney. I show them old games I've kept of him as a skinny kid and we discuss the career that he had, along with guys like Lucas, Hird, Fletcher and Mercuri, who all started with us at young ages.

Matthew went from being a young kid to becoming a very strong footballer, and there's nothing wrong with being a robust player. His hit on Brad Sewell in his final game was great. He was playing the game hard and it was unfortunate that Sewell's head was where it was, but if you said to me that Matthew Lloyd had intended to break a guy's jaw and cheekbone, I'd reject that. He's just not that type of person.

Australian rules football is a hard game. Unlike a lot of football codes, players have opponents coming at them from 360 degrees, which makes it dangerous. We use a ball that bounces in odd ways, and the game is played at such pace that there isn't much room for error. Opposition players tried to clean up Lloyd a million times, and they got him a few times, but he also cleaned them up too. I didn't have any problems with what happened in his last game; as a matter of fact, I thought it was a great play. I know that's contrary to what the rules say, but I thought it was great.

Matthew Lloyd would be the full-forward in my best-ever team. You wouldn't get a better person either – he's the type of guy you could roll out at any time to promote your club without fear. These days, as a commentator, he's going through the building phase again. He's gone from sixty to eighty out of 100, I reckon, and he's getting better every week. It's a totally different career for him, but I think his honesty will be refreshing for a long time.

Simon Lloyd, brother
Our parents have always given Brad, Kylie, Matt and me unconditional support in everything we have done, but

especially in our sport. As you could imagine, with three boys playing football and Kylie playing netball, we could be playing all over the place, but there was always at least one of them at every one of our games

Football was always a big thing for our family. Us three boys could all play a bit, but you could see from a very early age that Matt had a special ability. Even my mates who were a few years older than him could see it. In fact, it didn't matter what sport we tried – footy, cricket, pool, soccer, rugby union – Matt excelled at all of them. But really, it was the fact that he's fiercely competitive that lifted him to an elite level, and we saw that from an early age.

I'm seven years older than Matt. I still remember how, when he was about ten, he'd walk into the lounge room and say, 'Right, how about you and I go outside on the grass and run at each other and see who's last man standing?' The difference in our physical development was huge, of course, but he hated getting beaten. I'd drop him and he'd get back up and say, 'I'll get you!' I stopped playing that game with him not long after because I knew he'd get me sooner or later.

I had the upper hand in our sporting contests until he was ten or eleven, and then he started to overtake me. Everything was a life-or-death competition, whether it was billiards upstairs at Mum and Dad's place or soccer in the middle of the snow in our backyard in Scotland. But we always had great laughs too.

When we played cricket in the driveway he'd absolutely terrorise me. I was one of the worst cricketers of all time but I'd imagine I was Kepler Wessels or someone. I remember refusing to walk after he'd got me out once. He started giving me lip and I flicked one of my very trendy western-suburbs moccasins at him and it smacked him in the mouth. I've never seen rage like I did on that day. I back-pedalled and tripped over the metal stumps while this eleven-year-old threw haymakers at me that Carl Ditterich would have been proud of. I was probably the first person to meet the Velvet Sledgehammer that day! He didn't have to throw big punches to hurt.

Matt always had a lot of natural talent, but he was meticulous, detailed and fastidious in his preparation. He gets a lot of that from Mum, who's very precise about doing things right. He doesn't believe in half-measures and he holds other people to the same ideals of commitment and honesty. He's a pretty determined individual.

During a football season, I could call Matt at any time during the week and know exactly what he was doing – from his eating, his sleeping, his mental and physical preparation – everything in his life was focused on his performance in the next game. He'd say himself that his life revolved around the two hours he would spend working on the weekend. I've been working with AFL clubs for twelve years now, and I've seen very few players as professional as Matt.

I always knew that he'd leave nothing to chance, and that he'd get the very best out of himself. He stepped up at each level of his career and thrived on each new challenge. He became a Premiership player and a Coleman Medallist, he kicked more than 900 goals and was the captain of his club, but he never let himself get carried away.

Matt says it as it is, and the fact that he doesn't believe in half-measures made him a great captain. He demanded of his teammates what he demanded of himself in commitment and honesty. He's a very proud person and he would be embarrassed if he had played a bad game. He did have a massive fear of failure, and I felt that the amount of pressure he used to place on himself could take away a lot of the pleasure of what he was doing. When I sent him a birthday card or a message for a milestone match, I always used to write 'Enjoy the journey' because he could get caught up in the moment at times. I felt he sometimes needed to step back to enjoy what was going on and what he had achieved.

On the sporting field he coped well with stress, but when he worked with me at Hoyts he wasn't much good. He was fifteen and working in the candy bar, while I was working as a security guard. One night he 'allegedly' turned off the mains power to the fridge full of choctops, which defrosted the lot of them! The girl who was on duty with Matt had won 'Staff Member of the Month' and so we were all pointing the finger at Matt. He resigned not long after, which I saw as an admission of guilt.

I worked as a runner at Hawthorn for a number of years, and Mum warned me once that there'd be consequences if she saw me trying to put Matt off while he was shooting for goal. She knew that if it came down to Matt having a shot to win the game, I'd do everything I could to put him off. I did the running against Matt a number of times. One was a night game out at Waverley where Matt was just destroying Hawthorn. I tried to deliver a message to him at one stage and Dean Wallis punched me in the midriff. I thought I'd keep away from Matt after that.

Over time, I learned that there was no point in trying to put Matt off – the more you tried, the more focused and determined he became. As a sports psychologist, I've studied plenty of sportspeople and he is one out of the box. If you look at personality traits that relate to success, he pretty much has them all – he's attentive to detail, he's meticulous, he's driven to high achievements, he's intuitively motivated, and he's got high resilience.

Now I'm working at Fremantle, and we tried to get him to join us in a support role for the 2010 season. I thought we had a good shot as Brad, Mark Harvey and I were all at the club, but we couldn't get him across the line. But it's not over – it'll never be over until we get him! Matt's knowledge of the game is excellent, and he built his career on having good timing, reading the play and concentrating well. We think he'd be a great teacher of those things.

He's very well suited to a role in the media, though. As a young kid, he'd lie on his bed reading stats and studying the game. A local bloke by the name of Bob Missen, who was President of the Avondale Heights Football Club, nicknamed Matt 'Scoop' at a young age. He would have made a great investigative journalist. If you ever needed to know a fact about the game, you'd always ask Scoop.

Brad Lloyd, brother

Growing up, Matt just loved his sport. He had a real intellect when it came to it. Right from a young age he'd get the *Herald Sun* every morning and study the sports pages. He knew his football and he was also cricket-mad. He loved Mark Waugh and he was just unbelievable with stats. He took a real interest in it.

Matt couldn't see a ball game without wanting to get involved. I remember being in France once on a family holiday and seeing some kids playing soccer. It was almost embarrassing – Matt just kept edging closer and closer to the field until he was virtually standing in the middle of the pitch and they asked him to play. He's one of those blokes who always wanted to be involved.

Because we lived in Scotland when Matt was young, his first ball games were really soccer and rugby. As a junior rugby player, he was pretty dominant. He was strong for his age and athletic, and some of the young skinny Scottish kids who had hardly seen the sun were struggling to hang onto him as he charged through the rucks. He'd run to exhaustion and score try after try.

He was always up for anything and was very courageous. I recall one time when he was three or four when I called him outside to play. I had set up the big rubbish bin on top of a baby's pool, which had about an inch of water in it. I somehow talked him into diving off the rubbish bin head-first into the pool. As he was climbing up the bin, I was thinking, 'I'm in trouble here, if he actually does it.' Sure enough, he dived off and split his head open. He had no fear, and even from a young age it was clear he would never shirk a challenge.

Even though he was a skinny kid, he was built really well. I remember seeing him getting out of a pool once and you could see his frame was just right. He wasn't super-tall, though, and when he was young he played more as an onballer who could go forward. I had never seen someone so desperate to play league footy.

We all played sport, but there was no doubt he was the

most talented footballer. He also had a drive like few people I've known. I was invited to do a preseason at Essendon once, and I remember after doing a drill that seemed pretty straightforward to me, Matt wasn't happy with it. I was waiting to give him a lift home but he said, 'I don't feel like I had those drills spot-on, so I'm just going to speak to the fitness staff about it.' We spent another forty-five minutes correcting the technique of the drill. Matt was only seventeen years old or so, and it struck me then how professional and diligent he was. He had a real thirst to be the best.

Matt's always been a pretty humble and modest sort of guy. Because he was good at sport he was pretty popular at school, although academically he really just did enough to get through. He's an intelligent person, though, and always does well at whatever he puts his mind to. He had to grow up pretty quickly because he was drafted as a sixteen-year-old and had a pretty heavy workload to juggle.

In some situations he might come across as shy, but he's pretty confident and he knows what he wants. He's very strong and direct in his thoughts and opinions. He's the least likely person I know to sit on a fence – if he's got an opinion on something, he'll definitely let you know about it.

I played against him a couple of times, but I didn't get to play a lot of footy with him because of our age difference. I was captain of the St Bernard's First XVIII in Year 12. When we picked the team for our knockout final against Parade College, I pushed pretty hard for Matt to come into the side even though he was a Year 10 student. There were a few doubts about his age, but he had one of the best games I'd ever seen him play and we won.

I played against him a few times in later years. I was on the supplementary list for the Bulldogs in the late 1990s, and I think they were a bit worried about matching up on Matt as he was starting to go okay for Essendon. They thought about playing me on him just to try and put him off his game; I'm glad it didn't eventuate because I wasn't a full-back and I definitely wouldn't have been able to hold Matt down.

I was eventually drafted to Hawthorn. We played an Ansett Cup game against Essendon, and within the first ten minutes or so I copped a big hip-and-shoulder from Damian Hardwick. The first thing I remember is looking up at Matt having a shot for goal. I said to someone, 'Is this Matt's first goal?' They said it was number seven but I'd missed the rest. He ended up kicking ten for the day. It wasn't a great day for me but I was pretty happy seeing Matt kick a bag.

We have all enjoyed the ride with him. I was at the MCG with Simon when Matt was getting near his first century of goals, and I turned to Simon and said, 'Let's get involved!' Simon wasn't too sure about it but we went down to the fence. When the ball left Matt's boot and was going through, we jumped onto the ground with hundreds of others. There was a heap of security coming at us and Simon got caught and was pinned, but I got through and made it out to see him, which was a real buzz. I wouldn't have missed that for the world – it was an unbelievable experience.

I've loved watching Matt's career develop. When he was a junior I knew he had some pretty special qualities, but it was only when I picked up the paper and read about him being linked to Essendon that I realised he was up there as one of the best prospects in the whole country. One of my favourite memories of his career was a match against Adelaide at Princes Park when he was still a teenager. He kicked seven from a half-forward flank and dominated the game. That was when I realised that he was going to become one of the best in the game.

These days, I'm very impressed with the way he's applying himself to his work in the media and at the Australian Institute of Sport. I know he'll have a really good career in both those fields, because he'll never stop improving.

Kylie Lloyd, *sister*

I always saw Matt as my baby brother. Even now, I never call him 'Matt' – I still call him 'Bub'! I'm five years older than him so when he was small I spent my time pushing him around in a pram like he was a doll. I'd actually prayed for a sister, but right from the time he was born I loved him to death.

As Matt started to grow up, sport became the main thing everywhere in our house. When we were young we had a one-storey house with a big hallway, and after dinner the boys would always play kick-to-kick. If I wanted to get to my bedroom I had to scoot through without getting hit by the ball or tackled, and they'd try to hit me too. But we were all equal, boys or girls, so I had to be good with it.

One time, just after I got my driver's licence, I drove past Matt and Brad as they were walking up the massive hill leading up to our home. It was a hot summer day and they had their cricket bags. I gave them a toot and a wave and they immediately smiled, thinking I was going to stop and pick them up, but I kept driving.

After I'd driven off, I thought, 'Gee, maybe I shouldn't have done that...' By the time I got home I was sure they were going to come after me. I can't remember whether I hid behind the curtains or if they pushed me behind there, but they laid into me and I hit the deck. I told Mum and she said, 'You deserved it, Kylie.' And I did.

Matt was always either playing sport or hanging around the home. Half the time you wouldn't know if he was home, he was so quiet. But if I walked past his room I could usually hear 'Love Songs and Dedications' playing on the radio, or maybe the Southern Sons. I always had some dance music going downstairs but he liked all the softer music, which was pretty funny.

In many ways, he was a shy young boy. Because he was such a homebody, it was always him that would answer the phone when my girlfriends rang the house. They'd ask for me and he'd say, 'I'll get her.' That's the most they ever got out of him! Matt was easy to tease when he was young, but I tried not to do it too much because he already spent enough time in his room listening to soppy music.

If I ever asked him about a girl he'd almost cry – he hated to be asked about girls, even when he was eight. It's just as well he met Lisa! She came from out of the blue and their relationship was full-on from the beginning.

By the time Matt got drafted, I had moved out of home and was living near Windy Hill. He had a key to the house, and between training sessions he'd come to my house and lie on the bed or watch TV, but he wouldn't say much to my housemates. Yet Matt's very reliable and loyal. If he ever misses a phone call from me, he calls back straightaway.

These days we can speak for hours and football doesn't even come up.

I was always supportive of my brothers' sport, even though I didn't really like going to football games. It's true that I once fell asleep while watching one of Matt's games at the MCG – if the footy wasn't near him I'd just lose interest. In fact, I don't ever remember watching a full game. I loved it when my brothers had milestone matches because I could make the banner, and I enjoyed working in the tuckshop, but I just wasn't interested in the actual mechanics of the game. I always wanted to be a Blue Bird because I went for Carlton – I would have loved that, but the football itself bored me.

Matt was a brave kid – a little accident-prone, but always brave. It seemed like he was always hurting himself. I think that's why I saw him as my little baby brother – I always felt sorry for him and he seemed so fragile. Half the time I didn't know he'd brought it all on himself. Once, on holiday in Echuca, we were all running around the fire and Matt decided to run through it. He ended up with burns on his feet and had to wear ice bags on them for ages.

In the snow in Scotland, the three boys used to ride their BMXs with blindfolds on. Matt always wanted to do everything that the older boys did, even if there was a chance he was going to get hurt. The closest I got to doing anything risky was lying in the driveway so the boys could jump their BMXs over me and some friends.

But on the other side of the daredevil with no fear is a caring man. Once when Matt found out I was dating someone he didn't think much of, he rang up. 'Do you really think he's the right person for you,' he asked me. 'You're probably scraping the bottom of the barrel.' He'd heard of this bloke and eventually I realised he was right. Matt and Brad had met for a coffee to discuss how he was going to approach it with me. He didn't want to upset me but he was very direct.

Another time, when I lost a lot of weight and all the family were all worried about me, Matt was the one who called me up and said, 'You might think you look good, but you look terrible.' Again, he'd met with my brothers to discuss how they were going to talk to me about it but he was the one who actually came forward and did the job. He was changing from the shy boy who I was always looking after to being a very direct leader.

I've been most proud of Matt when I've read his articles in *The Age*, as that's been when he's shown more of himself. Growing up, I never really knew he could write because he didn't enjoy school, and when he worked at Foxtel I couldn't call him at work because he wouldn't answer the phone in case he had to do some work. To see him growing into his work in the media now makes me very proud of him.

Matt and Lisa have two girls, Jaeda and Kira, and to be honest, I wouldn't mind if football skipped a generation in the Lloyd family! I don't think he would either. Jaeda and Matt are like best mates – she's a real Daddy's girl. I get along really well with Lisa, too, and that's one of the reasons Matt and I are so close now. They are both really good friends.

He's such a good dad. At Jaeda's fourth birthday party she was giving a little speech and Matt started crying, just like he did at his retirement press conference. She's quite similar to Matt. She was a bit nervous about her school concert last year and he said to her, 'You can either be nervous or you can be confident, but you're better being confident.'

As I see it, that is exactly how Matt has conducted his life.

John and Bev Lloyd, parents
We have been married for forty-three years. Funnily enough, we met at a game of football in 1965 – Carlton versus Footscray. Mutual friends introduced us. John was playing for Carlton but was out injured with a broken thumb, while Bev was a keen Footscray supporter.

Matt grew up the youngest of four children. He was very easygoing and well behaved – in fact, the only time he became upset was if he was blamed for something he didn't do. He was willing to accept the consequences of his own actions but not those of his siblings.

He was a daredevil and a bit accident-prone. When he was young he'd be talked into doing things by his brothers, Simon and Brad, and he would often hurt himself. Simon is seven years older and Brad two and a half years older, but Matt always thought he could do what they did. At Bright, where we'd go for summer holidays, the kids would all jump off the cliffs into the Ovens River. They were usually joined by their father, who liked them to be daring.

John coached Braybrook in the Footscray District League, and then Avondale Heights in the Essendon District League. Matt always loved going to the games, and especially going onto the ground to have a kick and into the changing rooms after the game to talk to the players. The Avondale team selection was done at our home on Thursday night, and Matt was always close by listening.

In 1983 our family moved to Balerno in Scotland for three years. John was given an overseas posting to the Australian Consulate in Edinburgh. It was a big move for such a footy family, but Matt was soon playing both rugby and soccer.

When we first arrived, Matt was only six and was told that he had to be seven to play junior rugby. Eventually, the Currie Rugby Club said that if we took full responsibility he would be allowed to play, and he never looked back. Matt and his brothers loved the game. When we were due to leave Scotland, the club held a farewell function for us; we were told we could go home but that we should leave the boys there to continue playing rugby!

Despite learning to love rugby, the whole family missed Australian Rules football. So we were pleased to be able to travel to Ireland to support Australia against Ireland in the Gaelic Series. The games weren't without incident, and the Irish supporters weren't happy with the Australians' fierce tackling, so we thought it would be in our best interests to roll up our Aussie flag, which Simon did without prompting.

Simon and Brad were always big influences on Matt. From a young age, they would kick the ball up to him in the backyard or in the hallway – he was always competing against them and the other older boys in our street when we moved back to Australia. It seemed like there was always a game going on.

Matt looked like being a good footballer from a very young age. He could kick and mark well and was never without a ball in his hands. He started playing with Avondale Heights in the under-9s and won several competition best-and-fairest awards as he moved up through the age groups, before going to the Western Jets under-18 team when he was fifteen. From there he was selected to represent Victoria at the Commonwealth Bank Under-18 Championships in Perth in 1994, where he won a place in the All-Australian Under-18 team.

Carlton had spoken to us about recruiting Matt under the father/son rule when the number of games required was twenty, however by the time he was eligible for the draft, the AFL had increased the requisite number of games by the father to fifty. John played twenty-nine, so that option was ruled out.

The following year, we were delighted when Matt was drafted to Essendon as a sixteen-year-old. He would be close to home and could continue his schooling at St Bernard's College in Essendon.

We helped Matt to choose VCE subjects that he enjoyed – his favourite was English. Essendon was very good about his schooling. Matt played a few senior games in his first year and was able to balance his football training with his school commitments. After school and training, he would disappear up to his room for some quiet time. Having such a busy schedule, he needed that time to himself before joining the family for dinner.

It was at around this time that Matt met Lisa. We loved her from the beginning and immediately saw how well suited they were. We were delighted when they married some years later. Lisa and her mother, Mary, along with her extended family, have been a great support to Matt.

We loved watching Matt play with Essendon and were always very proud of him. We went to the presentation night where he won an award as the club's best first-year player. He walked up to the podium to receive his trophy and made his first speech. We couldn't believe how well he spoke, and he didn't seem to be nervous at all. As it happened, that award was the first of many in his AFL career.

Football has its highs and lows, and Matt has had a number of serious injuries. The most worrying for us was when he ruptured his spleen in the Preliminary Final against the Sydney Swans in 1996. He spent five days in intensive care at St Vincent's Hospital. We were at the game and stayed in Sydney until he could be flown home. Luckily, he didn't lose his spleen as the bleeding stabilised.

Another low point was in his first year as captain of Essendon. Having started the season well, he tore his hamstring from the bone in Round 3 against the Western Bulldogs and missed the rest of the season.

But those low points were the exception and we have had so many proud moments during Matt's football career at Essendon. Firstly, he played 270 games and was captain of the Essendon Football Club. He kicked a goal with his first kick in league football and went on to kick a total of 926 goals, and twice kicked over 100 goals in a season. He played in two Grand Finals and was a member of the winning Premiership team in 2000. He also won three Coleman Medals and was named as an All-Australian five times.

We always believed Matt had the skill and dedication to achieve his ambition to be an AFL footballer. Early in Matt's career, Kevin Sheedy said to us that he would become a

200-game player. Kevin was very good at looking after his young players and was always conscious of their longevity in the game.

More recently, we have enjoyed following Matt's new career in the media. It has given the wider public the opportunity to see the other side of Matt – he can give out as much as he gets and is very good with the one-liners. He has always enjoyed a laugh and has a good sense of humour.

We are proudest, though, when strangers come up to tell us that they have met Matt and what a nice person he is. In this, he has never changed. He's very caring and loves spending time with his family. Matt and Lisa have given us two wonderful granddaughters, Jaeda and Kira, who we love dearly and have lots of fun with.

Epilogue

by Andrew Clarke

It was line and length. Just as Glenn McGrath delivered year after year, just as Matthew Lloyd had admired. The balls were flung down with a remarkable fluency after a stuttering run in. There were a couple of short balls that made the batter duck, but otherwise, consistency. And three wickets.

Earlier he'd pulled in a screamer at first slip. If it was a football match, his confidence would have been sky high after it clunked into his hands. He spoke about it later in the match with the excitement of a ten-year-old kid who'd just pulled in a beauty, not that of a man who routinely marked balls for a living – 1704 times at AFL level, in fact.

Yes, it was only a cricket game for the Bentleigh seconds, and yes, it was a bottom of the ladder fight, but it was Matthew Lloyd's annual cricket fix. It was also Matthew Lloyd in unfamiliar surrounds for me, a cricket nut indulging his passion.

I had watched him on a football field for more than a decade, wishing most of the time he played for my team instead of Essendon. I admired him; I felt at one stage – perhaps controversially – that he was more important to Essendon than James Hird. His ability to bust a game open at full forward was not dissimilar to that of the other great power forwards, but his capacity to run up to the wing to lay a bone-crunching bump or to run down a smaller bloke who should have been able to get away, was way more than a Lockett or Dunstall could deliver. He was big, mobile and talented.

I stood and jeered at his last game. I got caught up in the emotion of the day, just like the rest of the 77,278 who packed the MCG for the twice-yearly Essendon–Hawthorn grudge match. Without being able to view the replay, it seemed clear that he was the villain in a game that was progressively being sanitised. The crunch on Brad Sewell turned the game. Essendon came to life, and an ailing Lloyd – who had limped into the game – had used the velvet sledgehammer one last time, in much the same way that Hawthorn's hero Dermott Brereton would have done a couple of decades earlier. Something had to be done, Lloyd was the captain and decided he'd put his own body on the line to do it. The straight and serious pretty boy was an assassin (and I say that with the utmost admiration and affection, despite knowing how much he hates the 'Pretty Boy Lloyd' tag).

Having co-written this book with Matthew, what I now know is that there is so much more to the man. Apparently emotionless on the field, he is the opposite off. His goal-kicking routine, while annoying, was very effective, but it was just that: a routine. It was a process developed over many years of practice to get ball onto boot and through the goals. That, to me, was Lloyd: efficient and process-driven.

Then he started to appear on TV and radio, and I came to

EPILOGUE

see his frankness as refreshing in the increasingly bland or outrageous world of TV sport. I started to see that there was more to the man, and that was when my desire to write this book germinated. There was more to Matthew Lloyd than I had ever imagined. He loves a laugh, is devoted to his family and, ultimately, is motivated to succeed at whatever he does. And he does so with a system.

He didn't just turn up for his once-a-year cricket match in January; he trained. He doesn't just turn up to give his special comments on a football match; he prepares. And he didn't just do this book off the top of his head; he researched to jog his memory, and that made it all the better for me.

My thanks go to all those who gave me time for this book. Your insights helped me to understand Matthew better, even if we didn't use all the thoughts we captured: Matthew's parents, John and Bev Lloyd; his siblings, Simon, Kylie and Brad; his wife, Lisa; his former coaches Kevin Sheedy and Merv Keane; Essendon people past and present, including Bruce Reid, John Quinn and Mark Harvey; media people, including Mike Sheahan and Anthony Hudson; his manager, Andrew Neophitou; and his former teammates who sat down with me for a chat (James Hird, Scott Lucas, Dustin Fletcher, Mark McVeigh, Angus Monfries, Jobe Watson and Andrew Welsh). Thanks also to The Groove Train in Brighton for the drip-feed of coffee (and banana smoothies for the boy still worried about skin-folds); to Hayley Orr at Orr Solutions, who is a star in her own right; the team at Random House, especially Alison Urquhart, Brandon VanOver and Julian Welch; Champion Data, whose information kept us accurate; and lastly to Jacquie, for guidance on all things Essendon and life.

My thanks especially to Matthew, for your trust and openness. You are indeed a straight shooter and I enjoyed getting to know you as a person.

Acknowledgements

It has been such a pleasurable experience to put this book together, and that is due to the amazing people who have assisted me along the way. Firstly, to Ali Urquhart and everyone at Random House: thank you so much for your friendship, enthusiasm and guidance in the process of putting all the pieces of the puzzle together. To Andrew Clarke: I felt so comfortable with you from the first time I met you back in August last year, and we have gone on this journey together and learnt a lot about each other along the way. Your passion for what you do is infectious, and through all the hard work and countless coffees, we became great mates and had so much fun together. For a Hawthorn man, you're not a bad bloke! Thank you so much for all you have done to make this all come together.

To Scott Lucas: I respect you greatly and I thank you for agreeing to write the foreword. To Kevin Sheedy and the past and current-day players and everyone else involved with the Essendon Football Club who contributed: thank you. We were all part of a wonderful football club. To Andrew Neophitou: you have always given me the knowledge and guidance to achieve what I want in life, and you've assisted me hugely in making the transition to life after football. I am so lucky to call you my manager but also, more importantly, a lifelong friend.

I am so grateful to have the most loving family anybody could ever hope for. Mum and Dad: you have always given – and continue to give – your four children all the tools and guidance to succeed in life. From a young age, I realised how lucky I was to have both parents be so hands on with me at school and on the sporting fields when many other kids were simply dropped off and picked up, and had no one there to share the special moments with. The respect for others and morals you have instilled in us is no doubt what Lisa and I are looking to instil in our children. I have met some pretty special role models in my lifetime, but they don't come close to the regard I hold you in. You inspire me to be the best person and father I can be, and I love nothing more than spending quality time with you both. Jaeda and Kira absolutely adore you, and I thank you for being the most down-to-earth, loving parents that you are. My brothers, Simon and Brad, and sister, Kylie: you have always played a huge part in my success and have supported me 100 per cent.

I often think how I wouldn't have had the career I had if I'd never met Lisa. Yes, I had the talent and the drive before meeting her, but in my weaker moments over the journey of my AFL career, she was the rock behind the scenes that picked up the pieces when I was at my most vulnerable through injuries and form lapses. Lisa continually pushed me to be the best I could possibly be, and from the moment we met I always put my professional career ahead of all else, as she took as much pleasure out of seeing me succeed as I did. The pre-game meals, the sleeping patterns, the bad moods on my part, I could go on forever about all that she has sacrificed for me, but that pales in significance to the joy she has provided me with in the birth of our two daughters, Jaeda and Kira. Our daughters are my world. Lisa is a warm, gentle person with a massive heart and a smile to match, but she does have a harder edge when required. All these attributes have come out in spades in the nurturing of our daughters, with whom I love spending every minute I can. I'll never forget the agony I was in after rupturing my spleen in the 1996 Preliminary Final. I was 18, in a Kings Cross hospital in Sydney and feeling disenchanted with the world, and Lisa walked in after deciding she would make the flight to stay with me for a few hours. Lisa, that is the beautiful person you are, and I am so lucky to have you as my wife and the mother of our children. Thank you for all your love and support from the day we met as teenagers, I can't imagine my life without you.

Finally, thank you to all who have played such a significant role in, not only this book, but in my life to date.

STATISTICS

1978 Born 16 April, Matthew James Lloyd

1983 Moved to Scotland

1986 Returned from Scotland
Cricket for Avondale Heights Cricket Club

1987 **Avondale Heights Under-10s**
Cricket for Avondale Heights Cricket Club

1988 **Avondale Heights Under-10s**
- Club Best & Fairest Winner
- EDFL Best & Fairest Winner

Cricket for Avondale Heights Cricket Club

1989 **Avondale Heights Under-12s**
Cricket for Avondale Heights Cricket Club

1990 **Avondale Heights Under-12s**
- Club Best & Fairest Winner
- EDFL Best & Fairest Winner

Cricket for Avondale Heights Cricket Club

1991 **Avondale Heights Under-14s**
- Club Best & Fairest Winner
- EDFL Best & Fairest Winner

Cricket for Avondale Heights Cricket Club

1992 **Avondale Heights Under-14s**
- Club Best & Fairest Winner

Cricket for Avondale Heights Cricket Club

1993 **Avondale Heights Under-16s**
St Bernard's College First 18
- Played for Victorian Under-15s
- All-Australian Schoolboy Representative

Cricket for Avondale Heights Cricket Club

1994 **St Bernard's College First 18**
Western Jets (TAC Cup), leading goal kicker with 50 goals
- Under-18 Victorian Team in Teal Cup
- Under-18 All-Australian selection

Cricket for Avondale Heights Cricket Club: topped the bowling in the McCabe Shield with 37 wickets at an average of 9.27

1995 **St Bernard's College First 18**
- Best & Fairest Winner

Essendon Football Club
- AFL debut against Adelaide Crows in Round 14
- Best First Year Player
- Played first AFL final in fourth match against West Coast Eagles

1996 **Essendon Football Club**
- AFL Rising Star nomination in Round 13 against Adelaide Crows (30 disposals, 13 marks, 7 goals)
- Ruptured spleen in Preliminary Final against Sydney Swans

1997 **Essendon Football Club**
- Third in EFC Best & Fairest
- First EFC Goal Kicking Award

1998 **Essendon Football Club**
- First All-Australian selection
- Played 50th game against North Melbourne in Round 14
- Represented Australia in International Rules Series against Ireland
- Second EFC Goal Kicking Award

1999 **Essendon Football Club**
- All-Australian

- International Rules Series against Ireland
- Third EFC Goal Kicking Award
- Kicked 13 goals against Sydney Swans in Round 3

2000 Essendon Football Club
- AFL Premiership Player
- All-Australian
- Coleman Medallist
- Ansett Cup Premiership Player
- Kicked 100 goals in a season for the first time
- Played 100th game against Hawthorn in Round 19
- Fourth EFC Goal Kicking Award

2001 Essendon Football Club
- All-Australian
- International Rules Series against Ireland (Jim Stynes Medallist for Best Australian in Series)
- Second in EFC Best & Fairest
- Coleman Medallist
- Kicked 100 goals in a season for the second time
- Fifth EFC Goal Kicking Award

2002 Essendon Football Club
- Ruptured finger tendon in Round 6 against Fremantle
- Ranked twenty-second in EFC's Champions of Essendon Function
- Sixth EFC Goal Kicking Award

Married Lisa in November

2003 Essendon Football Club
- All-Australian
- Coleman Medallist
- Played 150th game against Richmond in Round 7
- Broke Essendon goal-kicking record in Round 19 against Western Bulldogs with 576th career goal
- Seventh EFC Goal Kicking Award

2004 Essendon Football Club
- Eighth EFC Goal Kicking Award

- Missed Coleman Medal by one goal
- Awarded Life Membership at Essendon Football Club

2005 **Essendon Football Club**
- Played 200th game against St Kilda in Round 13
- Ninth EFC Goal Kicking Award

2006 **Essendon Football Club**
- Appointed Captain for the season
- Ruptured hamstring tendon in Round 3 and missed rest of the season

Jaeda born in December

2007 **Essendon Football Club** (Captain)
- Captain for second season
- Tenth EFC Goal Kicking Award
- Goal of the Year Award for a goal against Carlton in Round 20

2008 **Essendon Football Club** (Captain)
- Captain for third season
- Played 250th game against Adelaide in Round 20
- Second in EFC Best & Fairest
- Eleventh EFC Goal Kicking Award
- Mark of the Year Award against Melbourne in Round 18

2009 **Essendon Football Club** (Captain)
- Captain for fourth season
- Twelfth EFC Goal Kicking Award
- Retired from AFL football with 270 games and 926 goals
- Last game against Hawthorn in Round 22 with the Brad Sewell incident

Kira born in September

2010 Media work with Network Ten, SEN Radio and *The Age*
Assistant coach of the AIS-AFL Academy

2011 Media work with Network Ten, SEN Radio and *The Age*
Assistant coach of the AIS-AFL Academy

Matthew Lloyd, Essendon Football Club Career Summary

Year	Games (W-D-L)	Kicks	Marks	Handballs	Disposals	Goals	Behinds	Hit-Outs	Tackles	Frees For	Frees Against	Brownlow Votes
1995	5 (2-1-2)	31	22	17	48	7	6		1	3	2	
1996	11 (7-0-4)	78	46	34	112	18	7	1	11	9	9	3
1997	20 (7-0-13)	212	125	60	272	63	33	3	17	16	17	7
1998	23 (12-0-11)	249	156	77	326	70	38	2	24	17	34	5
1999	22 (18-0-4)	239	142	54	293	87	40		22	19	26	9
2000	25 (24-0-1)	323	186	68	391	109	60	4	21	31	35	14
2001	21 (15-0-6)	244	158	49	293	105	36	2	23	18	24	15
2002	16 (8-1-7)	143	96	40	183	47	29	4	11	17	15	6
2003	22 (13-0-9)	204	140	66	270	93	30		21	18	18	14
2004	24 (13-0-11)	228	134	49	277	96	39	1	35	29	24	10
2005	20 (8-0-12)	181	104	51	232	59	29		23	23	19	3
2006	3 (1-0-2)	34	23	17	51	13	3		1	3	3	3
2007	19 (10-0-9)	214	124	59	273	62	31		33	27	30	
2008	21 (8-0-13)	199	144	83	282	62	16		35	26	20	5
2009	18 (9-0-9)	131	104	88	219	35	27		26	16	16	3
Totals	270 (155-2-113)	2710	1704	812	3522	926	424	17	304	272	292	97
Ave/game		10.0	6.3	3.0	13.0	3.4	1.6	0.1	1.1	1.2	1.2	0.4
Game highs		22	15	12	30	13	7	3	7	5	5	3

Matthew Lloyd Career Summary by Opponent

Opposition	Games (W-D-L)	Kicks	Marks	H.Balls	Disp	Goals	Bhd	Average Goals	H.O.	Tack	FrF	FrA
Adelaide	18 (10-0-8)	172	110	62	234	54	15	3.0		23	15	16
Brisbane Lions	19 (8-0-11)	189	105	50	239	57	28	3.0	1	19	21	15
Carlton	25 (16-0-9)	238	156	79	317	86	50	3.4	2	19	22	26
Collingwood	25 (15-0-10)	249	153	74	323	77	40	3.1	6	28	25	30
Fremantle	17 (12-0-5)	177	117	51	228	61	28	3.6		15	15	15
Geelong	16 (7-0-9)	155	103	42	197	52	26	3.1	1	14	14	20
Hawthorn	13 (9-0-4)	136	84	41	177	46	23	3.5	1	11	15	22
Melbourne	16 (13-0-3)	166	89	41	207	66	26	4.1	1	20	26	16
North Melbourne	15 (8-0-7)	166	106	47	213	58	25	3.9	2	21	14	13
Port Adelaide	13 (5-0-8)	134	76	41	175	41	21	3.2		10	19	15
Richmond	24 (14-1-9)	240	152	69	309	86	41	3.6	2	29	27	19
St Kilda	14 (7-0-7)	124	83	44	168	46	24	3.3		21	13	23
Sydney	17 (10-0-7)	179	113	48	227	69	28	4.1	1	21	18	29
West Coast	20 (12-0-8)	206	128	64	270	59	23	3.0		29	16	18
Western Bulldogs	18 (9-1-8)	179	129	59	238	68	26	3.8		24	12	15

Matthew Lloyd Career Summary by Venues

Venue	Games (W-D-L)	Kicks	Marks	H.Balls	Disp	Goals	Bhd	Average Goals	H.O.	Tack	FrF	FrA
Docklands	76 (48-1-27)	792	544	238	1030	299	120	3.9	1	96	89	74
Football Park	16 (4-0-12)	139	82	44	183	32	15	2.0		16	15	16
Gabba	10 (3-0-7)	101	57	24	125	30	16	3.0		9	15	10
MCG	133 (84-1-48)	1348	815	396	1744	461	231	3.5	15	136	130	153
Princes Park	3 (2-0-1)	33	21	19	52	14	3	4.7		2	1	5
SCG	6 (4-0-2)	54	30	18	72	15	8	2.5	1	10	4	9
Stadium Australia	4 (0-0-4)	29	21	10	39	13	2	3.3		8	2	6
Subiaco	16 (5-0-11)	160	99	51	211	47	16	2.9		20	12	16
Waverley Park	6 (5-0-1)	54	35	12	66	15	13	2.5		7	4	3

Matthew Lloyd Career Summary by Each AFL Match

1995

Game #	Opponent	Rd	R	Kicks	Marks	H.Balls	Disp	Goals	Bhd	H.O.	Tack	FrF	FrA	BM
1	Adelaide	14	W	7	3	5	12	3	2				2	
2	Richmond	15	D			1	1							
3	Carlton	22	L	9	6	5	14	1			1			
4	West Coast	QF	W	8	8	4	12	2	3			1		
5	Richmond	SF	L	7	5	2	9	1	1			2		
	Totals	5		31	22	17	48	7	6		1	3	2	

1996

Game #	Opponent	Rd	R	Kicks	Marks	H.Balls	Disp	Goals	Bhd	H.O.	Tack	FrF	FrA	BM
6	Carlton	2	L	1	1	3	4	1			1	1	1	
7	West Coast	3	W	2		2	4	2				1		
8	Collingwood	5	L	3	1	1	4					1	1	
9	Melbourne	9	W	6	4	2	8	1				1		
10	Adelaide	19	W	18	13	12	30	7	1		1	1	1	3
11	Collingwood	20	W	9	5	3	12	2	2	1	2	1	2	
12	Sydney	21	W	10	6	2	12	3	3			2	4	

Game #	Opponent	Rd	R	Kicks	Marks	H.Balls	Disp	Goals	Bhd	H.O.	Tack	FrF	FrA	BM
13	Footscray	22	W	5	2	2	7	1			3			
14	Brisbane Bears	QF	L	10	6	2	12				3	1		
15	West Coast	SF	W	12	7	3	15	1	1		1			
16	Sydney	PF	L	2	1	2	4							
	Totals	11		78	46	34	112	18	7	1	11	9	9	3

1997

Game #	Opponent	Rd	R	Kicks	Marks	H.Balls	Disp	Goals	Bhd	H.O.	Tack	FrF	FrA	BM
17	North Melbourne	3	W	6	2		6	4	1		1	1		
18	Geelong	4	L	10	3	3	13	3	1			1		1
19	Collingwood	5	L	13	5	2	15	2				2	2	
20	Brisbane Lions	6	W	8	4	4	12	1	1		1	1		
21	Adelaide	7	L	11	8	3	14	5				1		
22	St Kilda	8	L	11	6	3	14	2	4				2	
23	West Coast	9	L	6	3	1	7	2	1			1		
24	Western Bulldogs	10	L	15	10	4	19	6	2		2	1		
25	Hawthorn	11	L	14	8	3	17	5	3	1	1		1	
26	Fremantle	12	L	5	4	5	10	1	1					

Game #	Opponent	Rd	R	Kicks	Marks	H.Balls	Disp	Goals	Bhd	H.O.	Tack	FrF	FrA	BM
27	Richmond	13	W	8	7	6	14	2	2			1		
28	Melbourne	14	W	13	10	1	14	8	1		3	2	3	2
29	Sydney	15	L	14	9	3	17	4	1	1	2			
30	Carlton	16	L	8	4	2	10	2	2	1	1		1	
31	Port Adelaide	17	L	12	5	2	14	1	3			2		
32	North Melbourne	18	L	8	5	4	12	1	1		1		1	
33	Geelong	19	W	8	4	2	10		1		3	1	2	
34	Collingwood	20	L	18	12	3	21	4	3		2	1	1	1
35	Brisbane Lions	21	W	13	10	5	18	5	3			1	3	3
36	Adelaide	22	W	11	6	4	15	5	2				1	
	Totals	20		212	125	60	272	63	33	3	17	16	17	7

1998

Game #	Opponent	Rd	R	Kicks	Marks	H.Balls	Disp	Goals	Bhd	H.O.	Tack	FrF	FrA	BM
37	Richmond	1	L	8	5	2	10	4	1				1	
38	St Kilda	2	W	10	3	2	12	5	1			1	4	
39	Carlton	3	W	11	5	2	13	1	5			3		
40	Fremantle	4	L	11	6	1	12		4		1	1		

Game #	Opponent	Rd	R	Kicks	Marks	H.Balls	Disp	Goals	Bhd	H.O.	Tack	FrF	FrA	BM
41	Collingwood	5	L	13	10	5	18	4					1	
42	Western Bulldogs	6	L	4	2	3	7	2			1		3	
43	Geelong	7	L	10	7	3	13	2	1		1	1	5	
44	Brisbane Lions	8	W	11	3	4	15		1		1	1		
45	Melbourne	9	W	6	4	5	11	3	2		2	1		
46	Hawthorn	10	W	13	7	2	15	2	2		2			
47	Sydney	11	W	16	11	1	17	5	4		1	1	3	1
48	Adelaide	12	L	8	5	2	10	1	1		1	2		
49	West Coast	13	L	14	10	11	25		1		1		1	
50	North Melbourne	14	L	14	9	2	16	4	4		3	1		
51	Port Adelaide	15	W	10	9	5	15	3	2				2	
52	Richmond	16	W	12	8	2	14	3	3			1	1	
53	St Kilda	17	W	9	7	1	10	4			2		1	
54	Carlton	18	W	11	9	5	16	6				1	3	2
55	Fremantle	19	W	15	9	5	20	5			1	1	1	1
56	Collingwood	20	W	9	8	4	13	3	2	1	3		2	
57	Western Bulldogs	21	L	12	7	2	14	6	2		1		3	1

Game #	Opponent	Rd	R	Kicks	Marks	H.Balls	Disp	Goals	Bhd	H.O.	Tack	FrF	FrA	BM
58	Geelong	22	L	12	7	4	16	6	1				2	
59	North Melbourne	QF	L	10	5	4	14	1	1	1	3	2	1	
	Totals	23		249	156	77	326	70	38	2	24	17	34	5

1999

Game #	Opponent	Rd	R	Kicks	Marks	H.Balls	Disp	Goals	Bhd	H.O.	Tack	FrF	FrA	BM
60	Carlton	1	W	9	5	2	11	3	1			1	1	
61	Kangaroos	2	W	9	8	4	13	3			1		2	
62	Sydney	3	W	22	14	4	26	13	4					3
63	West Coast	4	L	10	3	3	13	1			1		2	
64	Collingwood	5	W	15	9	1	16	6	4		1	1	1	1
65	Richmond	6	W	15	10	2	17	3	5		1		1	
66	Melbourne	7	L	9	3		9	7				1		1
67	St Kilda	8	L	9	5	4	13	1	2			1	3	
68	Hawthorn	9	W	11	7	2	13	5	4		2	1	2	
69	Adelaide	10	W	9	5	3	12	1			1	2	1	
70	Geelong	11	W	11	11	2	13	5	3		2			1
71	Brisbane Lions	12	W	9	3	1	10	3	1		3	2		

Game #	Opponent	Rd	R	Kicks	Marks	H.Balls	Disp	Goals	Bhd	H.O.	Tack	FrF	FrA	BM
72	Western Bulldogs	13	W		1	2	2							
73	Carlton	16	W	11	5	2	13	4	1		1	1		
74	Kangaroos	17	W	15	7	2	17	7	2			2		1
75	Sydney	18	W	4	3	2	6	1			2	1	3	
76	West Coast	19	W	12	5	3	15	2	1		2	1	2	
77	Collingwood	20	W	8	5	1	9	3	1		1		4	
78	Richmond	21	W	15	11	3	18	6	3		1	1	2	2
79	Melbourne	22	W	13	8	6	19	3	3		1	2		
80	Sydney	QF	W	12	11	5	17	5	2			1	2	
81	Carlton	PF	L	11	3		11	5	3		2	1		
	Totals	22		239	142	54	293	87	40		22	19	26	9

2000

Game #	Opponent	Rd	R	Kicks	Marks	H.Balls	Disp	Goals	Bhd	H.O.	Tack	FrF	FrA	BM
82	Port Adelaide	1	W	11	6		11	7	2		2	5	1	2
83	Richmond	2	W	15	8	7	22	7			1	2		1
84	Fremantle	3	W	14	10	3	17	4	3		1		2	
85	Hawthorn	4	W	11	6	3	14	4	1				2	

Game #	Opponent	Rd	R	Kicks	Marks	H.Balls	Disp	Goals	Bhd	H.O.	Tack	FrF	FrA	BM
86	Carlton	5	W	9	5	5	14	3	2		2		1	
87	Western Bulldogs	6	W	11	6	3	14	3	4		3	2	1	
88	Collingwood	7	W	13	7	2	15	5	3	1	1	2		
89	Brisbane Lions	8	W	16	4	1	17	5	2			4	2	1
90	Melbourne	9	W	12	7	1	13	6	2		1	3	3	2
91	Adelaide	10	W	8	5	1	9	1						
92	Geelong	11	W	15	10	2	17	7	2	1	2	1	3	
93	St Kilda	12	W	18	13	6	24	6	5				2	3
94	Kangaroos	13	W	8	7	4	12	1	4		1	1	1	
95	Sydney	14	W	14	4	2	16	4	3		1	2	3	
96	West Coast	15	W	14	7		14	3	2				2	
97	Port Adelaide	16	W	16	11	2	18	3	4			1	1	
98	Richmond	17	W	12	5	2	14	4	2			2		
99	Fremantle	18	W	18	12	6	24	9	2		1			3
100	Hawthorn	19	W	13	9	2	15	5	2		1	2	5	2
101	Carlton	20	W	10	6	6	16	1	1			1		
102	Western Bulldogs	21	L	12	7		12	2	2		2		1	
103	Collingwood	22	W	12	8	2	14	4	5			1		

Game #	Opponent	Rd	R	Kicks	Marks	H.Balls	Disp	Goals	Bhd	H.O.	Tack	FrF	FrA	BM
104	Kangaroos	QF	W	16	9	4	20	7	3	1	1		1	
105	Carlton	PF	W	11	9	2	13	4	3			1	1	
106	Melbourne	GF	W	14	5	2	16	4	1	1	1	1	3	
	Totals			323	186	68	391	109	60	4	21	31	35	14

2001

Game #	Opponent	Rd	R	Kicks	Marks	H.Balls	Disp	Goals	Bhd	H.O.	Tack	FrF	FrA	BM
107	Kangaroos	1	W	11	3	1	12	4	2		2	1	2	
108	Port Adelaide	2	W	10	5	2	12	4	2		1	1	1	
109	Carlton	3	L	10	9	2	12	5	1				2	
110	Collingwood	5	W	11	3	3	14	1	1		2		2	
111	West Coast	6	W	17	13	3	20	10	4			2		3
112	Richmond	7	W	11	5	4	15	4	2		2	1	2	
113	Melbourne	8	W	12	7	2	14	3	3		1	1	1	
114	Hawthorn	9	W	10	6	4	14	8				2	1	3
115	Brisbane Lions	10	L	10	7	1	11	3	1			2	1	
116	St Kilda	11	W	13	7	2	15	2	5		2	1	1	
117	Adelaide	12	W	16	9		16	6	2			1	1	3

2002

Game #	Opponent	Rd	R	Kicks	Marks	H.Balls	Disp	Goals	Bhd	H.O.	Tack	FrF	FrA	BM
118	Fremantle	13	W	10	8		10	5	1				2	1
119	Western Bulldogs	14	W	12	12	3	15	5			1		2	
120	Geelong	15	W	10	9		10	6	2				1	
121	Kangaroos	16	W	10	11	6	16	9						2
122	Port Adelaide	17	L	14	8	5	19	4	2		3	3		
123	Carlton	18	L	11	6	4	15	4	2				2	
124	West Coast	21	W	12	10	3	15	7	1		2	2	1	2
125	Richmond	22	L	8	8		8	6	1	1	2			1
126	Richmond	QF	W	15	6	3	18	4	2		2			
127	Brisbane Lions	GF	L	11	6	1	12	5	2	1	3	1	1	
	Totals	21		244	158	49	293	105	36	2	23	18	24	15

Game #	Opponent	Rd	R	Kicks	Marks	H.Balls	Disp	Goals	Bhd	H.O.	Tack	FrF	FrA	BM
128	Geelong	1	W	12	9	2	14	6	1			1	1	1
129	Richmond	2	W	13	8	4	17	3	3			1	1	
130	Brisbane Lions	3	L	7	6	1	8	3	2			1	3	
131	Adelaide	4	W	10	9	2	12	6	1		3	1	1	1

Game #	Opponent	Rd	R	Kicks	Marks	H.Balls	Disp	Goals	Bhd	H.O.	Tack	FrF	FrA	BM
132	Collingwood	5	L	7	5	2	9	2	2		1	1	2	
133	Fremantle	6	L	4	4	3	7	1					1	
134	Western Bulldogs	14	D	12	8	5	17	5	2			3	1	
135	West Coast	15	L	10	5	3	13	1	3		1		1	
136	Geelong	16	L	8	4	2	10	2	3		2	2		
137	Richmond	17	W	10	6	3	13	2	2		1	2		
138	Brisbane Lions	18	L	3	3	3	6	1						
139	Adelaide	19	L	5	2		5	1			2			
140	Collingwood	20	W	15	11	4	19	5	1	3		1	1	2
141	Fremantle	21	W	15	6	2	17	4	5		1	4	2	
142	Carlton	22	W	12	10	3	15	5	4	1			1	2
143	West Coast	EF	W			1	1							
	Totals	16		143	96	40	183	47	29	4	11	17	15	6

2003

Game #	Opponent	Rd	R	Kicks	Marks	H.Balls	Disp	Goals	Bhd	H.O.	Tack	FrF	FrA	BM
144	Brisbane Lions	1	L	6	3	3	9	4	1		1	1		
145	Melbourne	2	W	10	8	6	16	3	1		1	2	1	

Game #	Opponent	Rd	R	Kicks	Marks	H.Balls	Disp	Goals	Bhd	H.O.	Tack	FrF	FrA	BM
146	Carlton	3	L	8	5	2	10	2	3			1	2	
147	Western Bulldogs	4	W	15	8	2	17	5	3		1	1		2
148	Collingwood	5	W	12	9	5	17	6			1			
149	Fremantle	6	L	11	9	5	16	5			1	1		
150	Richmond	7	L	6	6	2	8	1			1	1	2	
151	West Coast	10	W	13	11	4	17	6	1		3	1		3
152	Sydney	11	L	13	9	2	15	5					1	
153	Kangaroos	12	L	9	5	3	12	5	1		2	1		
154	Geelong	13	W	7	8	4	11	1	1		2			
155	St Kilda	14	W	10	9	3	13	8	2				2	3
156	Adelaide	15	L	7	4	3	10	1	1		2	1	2	
157	Brisbane Lions	16	W	10	6	2	12	5	2		1			
158	Melbourne	17	W	11	2	1	12	3	1		3	3	3	
159	Carlton	18	W	5	5	3	8	2	2		1	1	1	
160	Western Bulldogs	19	W	12	10	2	14	11	1		1	1		3
161	Richmond	20	W	11	8	5	16	6	3					2
162	Fremantle	21	W	11	9	2	13	6	3				3	1
163	Collingwood	22	L	8	2	4	12	2	2			1	2	

Game #	Opponent	Rd	R	Kicks	Marks	H.Balls	Disp	Goals	Bhd	H.O.	Tack	FrF	FrA	BM
164	Fremantle	EF	W	6	3	1	7	5	1			2		
165	Port Adelaide	SF	L	3	1	2	5	1	1				2	
	Totals			204	140	66	270	93	30		21	18	18	14

2004

Game #	Opponent	Rd	R	Kicks	Marks	H.Balls	Disp	Goals	Bhd	H.O.	Tack	FrF	FrA	BM
166	Port Adelaide	1	L	10	6	4	14	4			1	2		
167	St Kilda	2	L	4	4	4	8	1			2	1	2	
168	West Coast	3	W	9	7	1	10	8			5	3	3	3
169	Carlton	4	W	11	7	4	15	2	7		3	3	1	
170	Collingwood	5	W	6	6	4	10	3	1			1	1	
171	Sydney	6	W	5	2	1	6	3	1		1	1	2	
172	Western Bulldogs	7	W	10	7	1	11	5	2		1	1	1	2
173	Adelaide	8	W	8	7		8	4						
174	Geelong	9	L	10	4	2	12	2	4			3	1	
175	Fremantle	10	W	9	8	1	10	5				1	2	
176	Hawthorn	11	W	13	7	4	17	7	2			2		1
177	Brisbane Lions	12	L	10	8	2	12	5	2		1		2	

2005

Game #	Opponent	Rd	R	Kicks	Marks	H.Balls	Disp	Goals	Bhd	H.O.	Tack	FrF	FrA	BM
178	Melbourne	13	L	11	3	2	13	5	2		1			
179	Kangaroos	14	L	8	4	2	10	1	1		2		1	
180	Richmond	15	W	15	8	2	17	9	1	1	5	3	1	1
181	West Coast	16	L	9	5	2	11	2	2		2			
182	St Kilda	17	L	9	6	2	11	6	1		3	2		
183	Port Adelaide	18	W	17	8	2	19	7	1		2	1	3	2
184	Carlton	19	L	4	2	1	5		1		1		1	
185	Collingwood	20	W	9	1	2	11	1	2		1	2		
186	Sydney	21	L	5	3		5	3	1		2			
187	Western Bulldogs	22	W	12	9	4	16	6	3				1	1
188	Melbourne	EF	W	15	7	1	16	4	5		1	2		
189	Geelong	SF	L	9	5	1	10	3			1	1	2	
	Totals	24		228	134	49	277	96	39	1	35	29	24	10

Game #	Opponent	Rd	R	Kicks	Marks	H.Balls	Disp	Goals	Bhd	H.O.	Tack	FrF	FrA	BM
190	Hawthorn	3	W	9	5	1	10		3		1	1	2	
191	Geelong	4	L	8	4	2	10	5	2			1		

Game #	Opponent	Rd	R	Kicks	Marks	H.Balls	Disp	Goals	Bhd	H.O.	Tack	FrF	FrA	BM
192	Collingwood	5	W	6	3	1	7	1	2			1		
193	Brisbane Lions	6	L	9	2	1	10	2	2		1	1	1	
194	Sydney	7	L	8	7	2	10	4	1		4	1	2	
195	Fremantle	8	W	6	5	3	9	1	2				1	
196	Port Adelaide	9	L	10	4	6	16	1	3			1	1	
197	Western Bulldogs	10	W	8	7	5	13	3	1					
198	Adelaide	11	L	7	3	2	9	2	2		1	1	3	
199	West Coast	12	L	12	3	5	17	3			2	2	2	
200	St Kilda	13	W	9	8	3	12	4			2	1	1	
201	Kangaroos	14	L	17	12	1	18	2	2		1	2		
202	Richmond	15	L	5	4		5	4			7		1	
203	Collingwood	16	W	11	6	2	13	8	1		1	3	1	2
204	Brisbane Lions	17	L	9	4	1	10	1	3			1	1	
205	Geelong	18	W	12	7	5	17	3	1					
206	Sydney	19	L	12	8		12	4	2		1	4	1	
207	Hawthorn	20	L	8	3	4	12	3				1	1	
208	Carlton	21	W	11	8	5	16	7	2			1		1

2006

Game #	Opponent	Rd	R	Kicks	Marks	H.Balls	Disp	Goals	Bhd	H.O.	Tack	FrF	FrA	BM
209	Melbourne	22	L	4	1	2	6	1			2	1	1	
	Totals	20		181	104	51	232	59	29		23	23	19	3

Game #	Opponent	Rd	R	Kicks	Marks	H.Balls	Disp	Goals	Bhd	H.O.	Tack	FrF	FrA	BM
210	Sydney	1	W	19	10	7	26	8	2			3	2	3
211	Brisbane Lions	2	L	10	8	4	14	4			1			
212	Western Bulldogs	3	L	5	5	6	11	1	1				1	
	Totals	3		34	23	17	51	13	3		1	3	3	3

2007

Game #	Opponent	Rd	R	Kicks	Marks	H.Balls	Disp	Goals	Bhd	H.O.	Tack	FrF	FrA	BM
213	Adelaide	1	W	14	8	3	17	2	1		3			
214	Fremantle	2	W	11	5	2	13	4			1	1	1	
215	Carlton	3	L	12	7	6	18	5	3		1	1	1	
216	St Kilda	4	W	9	5	5	14	3			4	3	2	
217	Collingwood	5	L	7	2	5	12	3	2		1	2	2	

Game #	Opponent	Rd	R	Kicks	Marks	H.Balls	Disp	Goals	Bhd	H.O.	Tack	FrF	FrA	BM
218	Brisbane Lions	8	W	16	7	2	18	4	2		2	2	1	
219	Richmond	9	W	7	8	2	9	3	3		1	1	2	
220	Sydney	10	W	10	5	4	14	3	2		3	1	3	
221	West Coast	11	W	9	6	3	12	3	1		1			
222	Port Adelaide	12	L	9	5		9	1	1			1	2	
223	Melbourne	13	W	13	10	3	16	4	2		2	4	1	
224	Western Bulldogs	15	L	11	8	8	19	1	2		4	1		
225	Collingwood	16	L	13	7	3	16	3	1				2	
226	Adelaide	17	W	13	8	4	17	5	1		2	3	1	
227	Hawthorn	18	L	12	5	1	13	2	2		3	3	3	
228	Fremantle	19	L	14	7		14	5	1		2	2	2	
229	Carlton	20	W	12	11	3	15	6	2		1		4	
230	Richmond	21	L	11	4	2	13	4	4			3	1	
231	West Coast	22	L	11	6	3	14	1	1		2		2	
	Totals	19		214	124	59	273	62	31		33	27	30	

2008

Game #	Opponent	Rd	R	Kicks	Marks	H.Balls	Disp	Goals	Bhd	H.O.	Tack	FrF	FrA	BM
232	North Melbourne	1	W	13	11	5	18	6	1		2	2	2	1
233	Geelong	2	L	11	8	3	14		3		1	1	2	
234	Carlton	3	W	10	5		10	4	2		1	2		
235	St Kilda	5	L	2	1	5	7		1		4	1	2	
236	Collingwood	6	L	6	6	3	9	3			2			
237	Port Adelaide	7	L	9	5	5	14	5			1	2		
238	Sydney	8	L	3	2	6	9	1			2	1	3	
239	Richmond	9	L	8	6	4	12	4	1		2	1	1	
240	Adelaide	10	L	5	2	3	8	1			2		1	
241	Hawthorn	11	L	7	5	2	9	2			1	1	1	
242	West Coast	12	W	14	9	7	21	2			4	2		1
243	Carlton	13	W	11	8	4	15	4	1		2	1	1	
244	Fremantle	14	W	9	8	7	16	1	1		3	1		
245	Brisbane Lions	15	W	10	9	7	17	4						
246	Richmond	16	L	15	8	2	17	2	2			3	2	

Game #	Opponent	Rd	R	Kicks	Marks	H.Balls	Disp	Goals	Bhd	H.O.	Tack	FrF	FrA	BM
247	Collingwood	17	W	14	10	3	17	4	1		3	3	1	
248	Melbourne	18	W	11	8	4	15	8	1		1	1		3
249	West Coast	19	L	12	10	2	14	3	1		2		2	
250	Adelaide	20	L	10	9	6	16	3			1	1	1	
251	Western Bulldogs	21	L	15	11	3	18	4			1	2	1	
252	St Kilda	22	L	4	3	2	6	1	1			1		
	Totals	21		199	144	83	282	62	16		35	26	20	5

2009

Game #	Opponent	Rd	R	Kicks	Marks	H.Balls	Disp	Goals	Bhd	H.O.	Tack	FrF	FrA	BM
253	Port Adelaide	1	L	3	3	6	9						2	
254	Fremantle	2	W	8	4	5	13		3		3	2	1	
255	Carlton	3	W	10	10	6	16	5	1		1	1	1	1
256	North Melbourne	4	L	12	8	5	17	3	2		1	1	1	
257	Collingwood	5	W	4	3	3	7		3		3	1	1	
258	Brisbane Lions	6	L	11	6	5	16	2	3		2	2		
259	Hawthorn	7	W	11	15	8	19	3	2			1	2	1
260	St Kilda	8	L	7	6	2	9	3	2		2	1	1	

Game #	Opponent	Rd	R	Kicks	Marks	H.Balls	Disp	Goals	Bhd	H.O.	Tack	FrF	FrA	BM
261	Richmond	9	W	10	7	2	12	4			1	1	1	
262	Geelong	10	L	2	3	5	7	1				1	1	
263	Adelaide	11	L	5	4	9	14		2		4	1		
264	Melbourne	12	W	6	2	3	9	3	2			1		
265	Carlton	13	W	10	5	2	12	4	1			1	1	
266	Collingwood	14	L	7	9	6	13	2	1		3		2	
267	Sydney	15	W	10	8	5	15	3	2		2			1
268	Western Bulldogs	16	L	8	9	4	12	2	1		2			
269	Richmond	17	L	3	1	7	10				2	1		
270	Hawthorn	22	W	4	1	5	9		2			1	2	
	Totals	18		131	104	88	219	35	27		26	16	16	3